RECONSTRUCTION OF RELIGIOUS THOUGHTS IN ISLAM

RECONSTRUCTION OF RELIGIOUS THOUGHTS IN ISLAM

Dr Y A Sabba

MD PUBLICATIONS PVT LTD
NEW DELHI
www.mdppl.com

Published by :

MD Publications Pvt Ltd
"MD House", 11, Darya Ganj,
New Delhi - 110 002
Phone : +91-11-41563325 (Customer Service)
+91-11-41562846 (Editorial)
E-mail (orders): order@mdppl.com
Website: www.mdppl.com

ISBN: 978-81-7533-238-6

Published and Printed by Mr. Pranav Gupta on behalf of **MD Publications Pvt Ltd** at Mohit Enterprises, New Delhi.

Preface

Religious pluralism and tolerance is one of the basic foundations of a civil society. It is the belief that no religion, singularly, has a monopoly of the truth or of the life that leads to salvation. Religious pluralism establishes the possibility of tolerance and co-existence of followers of different religions and cultures.

Islam, one of the main religions of the world, is often labeled exclusivist and accordingly intolerant. It is important to examine what is the real attitude of Islam towards pluralism and tolerance? Is there a pluralistic interpretation of Islam? Muslim scholars have different views on this subject. Among the three main intellectual movements in Islamic world, fundamentalists reject religious pluralism and tolerance, and consider it as an aspect of the ideological war of the western world but both traditionalists and modernists accept it, though traditionalists generally do not emphasize and specify pluralism and prefer to accept solely the religious tolerance. Traditionalists mainly rely on Islamic transcripts and Sufism, but modernists use modern western philosophical theories such as Kant's noman-phenomena theory and John Hick's religious pluralism theory.

Contemporary Muslim scholars hold different positions on religious pluralism and tolerance; some (so-called 'fundamentalists') are exclusivist and regard Islam as the only true religion and reject the religious pluralism and tolerance, others (so-called 'traditionalists' and 'modernists') believe that religious pluralism and tolerance are acceptable in Islam.

The Quran is a book which emphasizes 'deed' rather than 'idea'. There are, however, men to whom it is not possible organically to assimilate an alien universe by re-living, as a vital process that special type of inner experience on which religious faith ultimately rests. Moreover, the modern man, by developing habits of concrete thought - habits which Islam itself fostered at least in the earlier stages of its cultural career - has rendered himself less capable of that experience which he further suspects because of its liability to illusion. The more genuine schools of Sufism have, no doubt, done good work in shaping and directing the evolution of religious experience in Islam; but their latter-day representatives, owing to their ignorance of the modern mind, have become absolutely incapable of receiving any fresh inspiration from modern thought and experience.

Thinkers and philosophers both Islamic and others have tried to identify Islamic thought and philosophy since long. This book highlights the Islamic philosophy and thought in detail, probably this is the most relevant and useful book in this area, ever written. According to the Holy Book revealed to Muhammad (peace and blessings of God be on him), this is the only true religion professed by all Prophets from Adam, to Muhammad, the Last Prophet.

I am very grateful to Mr. Pranav Gupta, Director of MD Publications Pvt Ltd, New Delhi, for his kind cooperation and support for this book.

Dr Y A Sabba

Contents

1

Reconstruction of Religious Thoughts in Islam

An Introduction

The Spirit of Muslim Culture

'Muhammad of Arabia ascended the highest Heaven and returned. I swear by God that if I had reached that point, I should never have returned.' These are the words of a great Muslim saint, 'AbdulQuddës of Gangoh. In the whole range of Sufi literature it will be probably difficult to find words which, in a single sentence, disclose such an acute perception of the psychological difference between the prophetic and the mystic types of consciousness. The mystic does not wish to return from the repose of 'unitary experience'; and even when he does return, as he must, his return does not mean much for mankind at large. The prophet's return is creative. He returns to insert himself into the sweep of time with a view to control the forces of history, and thereby to create a fresh world of ideals. For the mystic the repose of 'unitary experience' is something final; for the prophet it is the awakening, within him, of world-shaking psychological forces, calculated to completely transform the human world.

The desire to see his religious experience transformed into a living world-force is supreme in the prophet. Thus his return amounts to a kind of pragmatic test of the value of his religious experience. In its creative act the prophet's will judges both itself and the world of concrete fact in which it endeavours to objectify itself. In penetrating the impervious material before him the prophet discovers himself for himself, and unveils himself to the eye of history. Another way of judging the value of a prophet's religious experience, therefore, would be to examine the type of manhood that he has created, and the cultural world that has sprung out of the spirit of his message. In this lecture I want to confine myself to the latter alone. The idea is not to give you a description of the achievements of Islam in the domain of knowledge. I want rather to fix your gaze on some of the ruling concepts of the culture of Islam in order to gain an insight into the process of ideation that underlies them, and thus to catch a glimpse of the soul that found expression through them. Before, however, I proceed to do so it is necessary to understand the cultural value of a great idea in Islam - I mean the finality of the institution of prophethood.

A prophet may be defined as a type of mystic consciousness in which 'unitary experience' tends to overflow its boundaries, and seeks opportunities of redirecting or refashioning the forces of collective life. In his personality the finite centre of life sinks into his own infinite depths only to spring up again, with fresh vigour, to destroy the old, and to disclose the new directions of life. This contact with the root of his own being is by no means peculiar to man. Indeed the way in which the word WaÁâ (inspiration) is used in the Qur'an shows that the Qur'an regards it as a universal property of life; though its nature and character are different at different stages of the evolution of life. The plant growing freely in space, the animal developing a new organ to suit a new environment, and a human being receiving light from the inner depths of life, are all cases of inspiration varying in character according to the needs of the recipient, or the needs of the species to which the recipient belongs. Now during the minority of mankind psychic energy develops what I call prophetic consciousness - a mode of economizing individual thought and choice by providing ready-made judgements, choices, and ways of action.

With the birth of reason and critical faculty, however, life, in its own interest, inhibits the formation and growth of non-rational modes of consciousness through which psychic energy flowed at an earlier stage of human evolution. Man is primarily governed by passion and instinct. Inductive reason, which alone makes man master of his environment, is an achievement; and when once born it must be reinforced by inhibiting the growth of other modes of knowledge. There is no doubt that the ancient world produced some great systems of philosophy at a time when man was comparatively primitive and governed more or less by suggestion. But we must not forget that this system-building in the ancient world was the work of abstract thought which cannot go beyond the system-atization of vague religious beliefs and traditions, and gives us no hold on the concrete situations of life.

Looking at the matter from this point of view, then, the Prophet of Islam seems to stand between the ancient and the modern world. In so far as the source of his revelation is concerned he belongs to the ancient world; in so far as the spirit of his revelation is concerned he belongs to the modern world. In him life discovers other sources of knowledge suitable to its new direction. The birth of Islam, as I hope to be able presently to prove to your satisfaction, is the birth of inductive intellect. In Islam prophecy reaches its perfection in discovering the need of its own abolition. This involves the keen perception that life cannot for ever be kept in leading strings; that, in order to achieve full self-consciousness, man must finally be thrown back on his own resources. The abolition of priesthood and hereditary kingship in Islam, the constant appeal to reason and experience in the Qur'an, and the emphasis that it lays on Nature and History as sources of human knowledge, are all different aspects of the same idea of finality.

The idea, however, does not mean that mystic experience, which qualitatively does not differ from the experience of the prophet, has now ceased to exist as a vital fact. Indeed the Qur'an regards both Anfus (self) and ÿfq (world) as sources of knowledge. God reveals His signs in inner as well as outer experience, and it is the duty of man to judge the knowledge-yielding capacity of all aspects of experience.

The idea of finality, therefore, should not be taken to suggest that the ultimate fate of life is complete displacement of emotion by reason. Such a thing is neither possible nor desirable. The intellectual value of the idea is that it tends to create an independent critical attitude towards mystic experience by generating the belief that all personal authority, claiming a supernatural origin, has come to an end in the history of man. This kind of belief is a psychological force which inhibits the growth of such authority. The function of the idea is to open up fresh vistas of knowledge in the domain of man's inner experience. Just as the first half of the formula of Islam has created and fostered the spirit of a critical observation of man's outer experience by divesting the forces of nature of that Divine character with which earlier cultures had clothed them.

Mystic experience, then, however unusual and abnormal, must now be regarded by a Muslim as a perfectly natural experience, open to critical scrutiny like other aspects of human experience. This is clear from the Prophet's own attitude towards Ibn Âayyd's psychic experiences. The function of Sufism in Islam has been to systematize mystic experience; though it must be admitted that Ibn Khaldën was the only Muslim who approached it in a thoroughly scientific spirit. But inner experience is only one source of human knowledge. According to the Qur'an, there are two other sources of knowledge - Nature and History; and it is in tapping these sources of knowledge that the spirit of Islam is seen at its best. The Qur'an sees signs of the Ultimate Reality in the 'sun', the 'moon', 'the lengthening out of shadows', 'the alternation of day and night', 'the variety of human colours and tongues',10 'the alternation of the days of success and reverse among peoples' - in fact in the whole of Nature as revealed to the sense-perception of man.

And the Muslim's duty is to reflect on these signs and not to pass by them 'as if he is dead and blind', for he 'who does not see these signs in this life will remain blind to the realities of the life to come'. This appeal to the concrete combined with the slow realization that, according to the teachings of the Qur'an, the universe is dynamic in its origin, finite and capable of increase, eventually brought Muslim thinkers into conflict with Greek thought which, in the beginning of their intellectual career, they had studied with so much enthusiasm. Not realizing that the spirit of the Qur'an was essentially anti-classical, and putting full confidence in Greek thinkers, their first impulse was to understand the Qur'an in the light of Greek philosophy. In view of the concrete spirit of the Qur'an, and the speculative nature of Greek philosophy which enjoyed theory and was neglectful of fact, this attempt was foredoomed to failure. And it is what follows their failure that brings out the real spirit of the culture of Islam, and lays the foundation of modern culture in some of its most important aspects.

This intellectual revolt against Greek philosophy manifests itself in all departments of thought. I am afraid I am not competent enough to deal with it as it discloses itself in Mathematics, Astronomy, and Medicine. It is clearly visible in the metaphysical thought of the Ash'arite, but appears as a most well-defined phenomenon in the Muslim criticism of Greek Logic. This was only natural; for dissatisfaction with purely speculative philosophy means the search for a surer method of knowledge. It was, I think, Naïï m who first formulated the principle of 'doubt' as the beginning of all knowledge. Ghazzlâ further amplified it in his 'Revivification of the Sciences of Religion', and prepared the way for 'Descartes' Method'. But Ghazzlâ remained on the whole a follower of Aristotle in Logic. In his Qists he puts some of the Qur'anic arguments in the form of Aristotelian figures, but forgets the Qur'anic Sërah known as Shu'ar' where the proposition that retribution follows the gainsaying of prophets is established by the method of simple enumeration of historical instances.

It was Ishrqâand Ibn Taimâyyah who undertook a systematic refutation of Greek Logic. Abë Bakr Rzâ was perhaps the first to criticize Aristotle's first figure, and in our own times his objection, conceived in a thoroughly inductive spirit, has been reformulated by John Stuart Mill. Ibn Àazm, in his 'Scope of Logic', emphasizes sense-perception as a source of knowledge; and Ibn Taimâyyah in his 'Refutation of Logic', shows that induction is the only form of reliable argument. Thus arose the method of observation and experiment. It was not a merely theoretical affair. Al-Bârënâ's discovery of what we call reaction-time and al-Kindâ's discovery that sensation is proportionate to the stimulus are instances of its application in psychology. It is a mistake to suppose that the experimental method is a European discovery. Dü hring tells us that Roger Bacon's conceptions of science are more just and clear than those of his celebrated namesake. And where did Roger Bacon receive his scientific training? - In the Muslim unlversities of Spain.

Indeed Part V of his Opus Majus which is devoted to 'Perspective' is practically a copy of Ibn Haitham's Optics. Nor is the book, as a whole, lacking in evidences of Ibn Hazm's influence on its author. Europe has been rather slow to recognize the Islamic origin of her scientific method. But full recognition of the fact has at last come. Let me quote one or two passages from Briffault's Making of Humanity,

'. . . it was under their successors at that Oxford school

that Roger Bacon learned Arabic and Arabic science. Neither Roger Bacon nor his later namesake has any title to be credited with having introduced the experimental method. Roger Bacon was no more than one of the apostles of Muslim science and method to Christian Europe; and he never wearied of declaring that knowledge of Arabic and Arabian science was for his contemporaries the only way to true knowledge. Discussions as to who was the originator of the experimental method . . . are part of the colossal misrepresentation of the origins of European civilization. The experimental method of the Arabs was by Bacon's time widespread and eagerly cultivated throughout Europe'.. .

'Science is the most momentous contribution of Arab civilization to the modern world, but its fruits were slow in ripening. Not until long after Moorish culture had sunk back into darkness did the giant to which it had given birth rise in his might. It was not science which brought Europe back to life. Other and manifold influences from the civilization of Islam communicated its first glow to European life'.

'For although there is not a single aspect of European growth in which the decisive influence of Islamic culture is not traceable, nowhere is it so clear and momentous as in the genesis of that power which constitutes the paramount distinctive force of the modern world, and the supreme source of its victory - natural science and the scientific spirit'.

'The debt of our science to that of the Arabs does not consist in startling discoveries or revolutionary theories; science owes a great deal more to Arab culture, it owes its existence. The ancient world was, as we saw, pre-scientific. The astronomy and mathematics of the Greek were a foreign importation never thoroughly acclimatized in Greek culture. The Greeks systematized, generalized, and theorized, but the patient ways of investigation, the accumulation of positive knowledge, the minute methods of science, detailed and prolonged observation, experimental inquiry, were altogether alien to the Greek temperament. Only in Hellenistic Alexandria was any approach to scientific work conducted in the ancient classical world. What we call science arose in Europe as a result of a new spirit of inquiry, of new methods of investigation, of the method of experiment, observation, measurement, of the development of mathematics in a form unknown to the Greeks. That spirit and those methods were introduced into the European world by the Arabs'.

The first important point to note about the spirit of Muslim culture then is that, for purposes of knowledge, it fixes its gaze on the concrete, the finite. It is further clear that the birth of the method of observation and experiment in Islam was due not to a compromise with Greek thought but to a prolonged intellectual warfare with it. In fact, the influence of the Greeks who, as Briffault says, were interested chiefly in theory, not in fact, tended rather to obscure the Muslims' vision of the Qur'an, and for at least two centuries kept the practical Arab temperament from asserting itself and coming to its own. I want, therefore, definitely to eradicate the misunderstanding that Greek thought, in any way, determined the character of Muslim culture. Part of my argument you have seen; part you will see presently.

Knowledge must begin with the concrete. It is the intellectual capture of and power over the concrete that makes it possible for the intellect of man to pass beyond the concrete. As the Qur'an says:

'O company of djinn and men, if you can overpass the bounds of the heaven and the earth, then overpass them. But by power alone shall ye overpass them' (55:33).

But the universe, as a collection of finite things, presents itself as a kind of island situated in a pure vacuity to which time, regarded as a series of mutually exclusive moments, is nothing and does nothing. Such a vision of the universe leads the reflecting mind nowhere. The thought of a limit to perceptual space and time staggers the mind. The finite, as such, is an idol obstructing the movement of the mind; or, in order to overpass its bounds, the mind must overcome serial time and the pure vacuity of perceptual space. 'And verily towards thy God is the limit', says the Qur'an. This verse embodies one of the deepest thoughts in the Qur'an; for it definitely suggests that the ultimate limit is to be sought not in the direction of stars, but in an infinite cosmic life and spirituality. Now the intellectual journey towards this ultimate limit is long and arduous; and in this effort, too, the thought of Islam appears to have moved in a direction entirely different to the Greeks. The ideal of the Greeks, as Spengler tells us, was proportion, not infinity.

The physical present ness of the finite with its well-defined limits alone absorbed the mind of the Greeks. In the history of Muslim culture, on the other hand, we find that both in the realms of pure intellect and religious psychology, by which term I mean higher Sufism, the ideal revealed is the possession and enjoyment of the Infinite. In a culture, with such an attitude, the problem of space and time becomes a question of life and death. In one of these lectures I have already given you some idea of the way in which the problem of time and space presented itself to Muslim thinkers, especially the Ash'arite. One reason why the atomism of Democritus never became popular in the world of Islam is that it involves the assumption of an absolute space. The Ash'arite were, therefore, driven to develop a different kind of atomism, and tried to overcome the difficulties of perceptual space in a manner similar to modern atomism.

On the side of Mathematics it must be remembered that since the days of Ptolemy (A.D. 87-165) till the time of Naâr ñësâ (A.D. 120-74) nobody gave serious thought to the difficulties of demonstrating the certitude of Euclid's parallel postulate on the basis of perceptual space. It was ñësâ who first disturbed the calm which had prevailed in the world of Mathematics for a thousand years; and in his effort to improve the postulate realized the necessity of abandoning perceptual space. He thus furnished a basis, however slight, for the hyperspace movement of our time. It was, however, al-Bârënâ who, in his approach to the modern mathematical idea of function saw, from a purely scientific point of view, the insufficiency of a static view of the universe. This again is a clear departure from the Greek view. The function-idea introduces the element of time in our world-picture. It turns the fixed into the variable, and sees the universe not as being but as becoming. Spengler thinks that the mathematical idea of function is the symbol of the West of which 'no other culture gives even a hint'.

In view of al-Bârënâ, generalizing Newton's formula of interpolation from trignometrical functions to any function whatever. Spengler's claim has no foundation in fact. The transformation of the Greek concept of number from pure magnitude to pure relation really began with Khwarizmâs movement from Arithmetic to Algebra. al-Bârënâ took a definite step forward towards what Spengler describes as chronological number which signifies the mind's passage from being to becoming. Indeed, more recent developments in European mathematics tend rather to deprive time of its living historical character, and to reduce it to a mere representation of space. That is why Whitehead's view of Relativity is likely to appeal to Muslim students more than that of Einstein in whose theory time loses its character of passage and mysteriously translates itself into utter space.

Side by side with the progress of mathematical thought in Islam we find the idea of evolution gradually shaping itself. It was Ja'hiz who was the first to note the changes in bird-life caused by migrations. Later Ibn Maskawaih who was a contemporary of al-Bârënâ gave it the shape of a more definite theory, and adopted it in his theological work - al-Fauz al-Asghar. I reproduce here the substance of his evolutionary hypothesis, not because of its scientific value, but because of the light which it throws on the direction in which Muslim thought was moving. According to Ibn Maskawaih plant-life at the lowest stage of evolution does not need any seed for its birth and growth. Nor does it perpetuate its species by means of the seed. This kind of plant-life differs from minerals only in some little power of movement which grows in higher forms, and reveals itself further in that the plant spreads out its branches, and perpetuates its species by means of the seed.

The power of movement gradually grows farther until we reach trees which possess a trunk, leaves, and fruit. At a higher stage of evolution stand forms of plant-life which need better soil and climate for their growth. The last stage of development is reached in vine and date-palm which stand, as it were, on the threshold of animal life. In the date-palm a clear sex-distinction appears. Besides roots and fibres it develops something which functions like the animal brain, on the integrity of which depends the life of the date-palm. This is the highest stage in the development of plant-life, and a prelude to animal life. The first forward step towards animal life is freedom from earth-rootedness which is the germ of conscious movement. This is the initial state of animality in which the sense of touch is the first, and the sense of sight is the last to appear. With the development of the senses of animal acquires freedom of movement, as in the case of worms, reptiles, ants, and bees.

Animality reaches its perfection in the horse among quadrupeds and the falcon among birds, and finally arrives at the frontier of humanity in the ape which is just a degree below man in the scale of evolution. Further evolution brings physiological changes with a growing power of discrimination and spirituality until humanity passes from barbarism to civilization. But it is really religious psychology, as in 'Iraqâand Khwajah Muhammad Parsa, which brings us much nearer to our modern ways of looking at the problem of space and time. 'Iraqâ's view of time-stratifications I have given you before. I will now give you the substance of his view of space.

According to 'Iraqâ the existence of some kind of space in relation to God is clear from the following verses of the Qur'an:

'Dost thou not see that God knoweth all that is in the heavens and all that is in the earth? Three persons speak not privately together, but He is their fourth; nor five, but He is their sixth; nor fewer nor more, but wherever they be He is with them' (58:7).

'Ye shall not be employed in affairs, nor shall ye read a text out of the Qur'an, nor shall ye do any work, but We will be witness over you when you are engaged therein; and the weight of an atom on earth or in heaven escapeth not thy Lord; nor is there aught that is less than this or greater, but it is in the Perspicuous Book' (10:61).

'We created man, and we know what his soul whispered to him, and we are closer to him than his neck-vein' (50:16).

But we must not forget that the words proximity, contact, and mutual separation which apply to material bodies do not apply to God. Divine life is in touch with the whole universe on the analogy of the soul's contact with the body. The soul is neither inside nor outside the body; neither proximate to nor separate from it. Yet its contact with every atom of the body is real, and it is impossible to conceive this contact except by positing some kind of space which befits the subtleness of the soul. The existence of space in relation to the life of God, therefore, cannot be denied; only we should carefully define the kind of space which may be predicated of the Absoluteness of God. Now, there are three kinds of space - the space of material bodies, the space of immaterial beings, and the space of God. The space of material bodies is further divided into three kinds. First, the space of gross bodies of which we predicate roominess.

In this space movement takes time, bodies occupy their respective places and resist displacement. Secondly, the space of subtle bodies, e.g. air and sound. In this space too bodies resist each other, and their movement is measurable in terms of time which, however, appears to be different to the time of gross bodies. The air in a tube must be displaced before other air can enter into it; and the time of sound-waves is practically nothing compared to the time of gross bodies. Thirdly, we have the space of light. The light of the sun instantly reaches the remotest limits of the earth. Thus in the velocity of light and sound time is reduced almost to zero. It is, therefore, clear that the space of light is different to the space of air and sound. There is, however, a more effective argument than this. The light of a candle spreads in all directions in a room without displacing the air in the room; and this shows that the space of light is more subtle than the space of air which has no entry into the space of light. In view of the close proximity of these spaces, however, it is not possible to distinguish the one from the other except by purely intellectual analysis and spiritual experience.

Again, in the hot water the two opposites - fire and water - which appear to interpenetrate each other cannot, in view of their respective natures, exist in the same space. The fact cannot be explained except on the supposition that the spaces of the two substances, though closely proximate to each other, are nevertheless distinct. But while the element of distance is not entirely absent, there is no possibility of mutual resistance in the space of light. The light of a candle reaches up to a certain point only, and the lights of a hundred candles intermingle in the same room without displacing one another. Having thus described the spaces of physical bodies possessing various degrees of subtleness 'Iraqâ proceeds briefly to describe the main varieties of space operated upon by the various classes of immaterial beings, e.g. angels.

The element of distance is not entirely absent from these spaces; for immaterial beings, while they can easily pass through stone walls, cannot altogether dispense with motion which, according to 'Iraqâ, is evidence of imperfection in spirituality. The highest point in the scale of spatial freedom is reached by the human soul which, in its unique essence, is neither at rest nor in motion. Thus passing through the infinite varieties of space we reach the Divine space which is absolutely free from all dimensions and constitutes the meeting point of all infinities. From this summary of 'Iraqâ's view you will see how a cultured Muslim Sufi` intellectually interpreted his spiritual experience of time and space in an age which had no idea of the theories and concepts of modern Mathematics and Physics. 'Iraqâ is really trying to reach the concept of space as a dynamic appearance. His mind seems to be vaguely struggling with the concept of space as an infinite continuum; yet he was unable to see the full implications of his thought partly because he was not a mathematician and partly because of his natural prejudice in favour of the traditional Aristotelian idea of a fixed universe.

Again, the interpenetration of the super-spatial 'here' and super-eternal 'now' in the Ultimate Reality suggests the modern notion of space-time which Professor Alexander, in his lectures on 'Space, Time, and Deity', regards as the matrix of all things. A keener insight into the nature of time would have led 'Iraqâ to see that time is more fundamental of the two; and that it is not a mere metaphor to say, as Professor Alexander does say, that time is the mind of space. 'Iraqâ conceives God's relation to the universe on the analogy of the relation of the human soul to the body; but, instead of philosophically reaching this position through a criticism of the spatial and temporal aspects of experience; he simply postulates it on the basis of his spiritual experience. It is not sufficient merely to reduce space and time to a vanishing point-instant.

The philosophical path that leads to God as the omni psyche of the universe lies through the discovery of living thought as the ultimate principle of space-time. 'Iraqâ's mind, no doubt, moved in the right direction, but his Aristotelian prejudices, coupled with a lack of psychological analysis, blocked his progress. With his view that Divine Time is utterly devoid of change - a view obviously based on an inadequate analysis of conscious experience - it was not possible for him to discover the relation between Divine Time and serial time, and to reach, through this discovery, the essentially Islamic idea of continuous creation which means a growing universe. Thus all lines of Muslim thought converge on a dynamic conception of the universe. This view is further reinforced by Ibn Maskawaih's theory of life as an evolutionary movement, and Ibn Khaldën's view of history.

History or, in the language of the Qur'an, 'the days of God', is the third source of human knowledge according to the Qur'an. It is one of the most essential teachings of the Qur'an that nations are collectively judged, and suffer for their misdeeds here and now. In order to establish this proposition, the Qur'an constantly cites historical instances, and urges upon the reader to reflect on the past and present experience of mankind.

"Of old did We send Moses with Our signs, and said to him: 'Bring forth thy people from the darkness into the light, and remind them of the days of God." Verily, in this are the signs for every patient, and grateful person' (14:5).

'And among those whom We had created are a people who guide others with truth, and in accordance therewith act justly. But as for those who treat Our signs as lies, We gradually ring them down by means of which they know not; and though I lengthen their days, verily, My stratagem is effectual' (7:181-83).

'Already, before your time, have precedents been made. Traverse the Earth then, and see what hath been the end of those who falsify the signs of God!' (3:137).

'If a wound hath befallen you, a wound like it hath

already befallen others; We alternate the days of successes and reverses among peoples' (3:140).

'Every nation hath its fixed period' (7:34).

The last verse is rather an instance of a more specific historical generalization which, in its epigrammatic formulation, suggests the possibility of a scientific treatment of the life of human societies regarded as organisms. It is, therefore, a gross error to think that the Qur'an has no germs of a historical doctrine. The truth is that the whole spirit of the 'Prolegomena' of Ibn Khaldën appears to have been mainly due to the inspiration which the author must have received from the Qur'an. Even in his judgements of character he is, in no small degree, indebted to the Qur'an. An instance in point is his long paragraph devoted to an estimate of the character of the Arabs as a people. The whole paragraph is a mere amplification of the following verses of the Qur'an:

'The Arabs of the desert are most stout in unbelief and dissimulation; and likelier it is that they should be unaware of the laws which God hath sent down to His Apostle; and God Knows, Wise.

'Of the Arabs of the desert there are some who reckon what they expend in the cause of God as tribute, and wait for some change of fortune to befall you: a change for evil shall befall them! God is the Hearer, the Knower' (9:97-98).

However, the interest of the Qur'an in history, regarded as a source of human knowledge, extends farther than mere indications of historical generalizations. It has given us one of the most fundamental principles of historical criticism: Since accuracy in recording facts which constitute the material of history is an indispensable condition of history as a science, and an accurate knowledge of facts ultimately depends on those who report them, the very first principle of historical criticism is that the reporter's personal character is an important factor in judging his testimony. The Qur'an says:

'O believers! if any bad man comes to you with a report clear it up at once' (49:6).

It is the application of the principle embodied in this verse to the reporters of the Prophet's traditions out of which were gradually evolved the canons of historical criticism. The growth of historical sense in Islam is a fascinating subject. The Qur'anic appeal to experience, the necessity to ascertain the exact sayings of the Prophet, and the desire to furnish permanent sources of inspiration to posterity - all these forces contributed to produce such men as Ibn Ishaq, ñabarâ, and Mas'ëdâ. But history, as an art of firing the reader's imagination, is only a stage in the development of history as a genuine science. The possibility of a scientific treatment of history means a wider experience, a greater maturity of practical reason, and finally a fuller realization of certain basic ideas regarding the nature of life and time. These ideas are in the main two; and both form the foundation of the Qur'anic teaching.

1. The Unity of Human Origin. 'And We have created you all from one breath of life', says the Qur'an. But the perception of life as an organic unity is a slow achievement, and depends for its growth on a people's entry into the main current of world-events. This opportunity was brought to Islam by the rapid development of a vast empire. No doubt, Christianity, long before Islam, brought the message of equality to mankind; but Christian Rome did not rise to the full apprehension of the idea of humanity as a single organism. As Flint rightly says, 'No Christian writer and still less, of course, any other in the Roman Empire, can be credited with having had more than a general and abstract conception of human unity.' And since the days of Rome the idea does not seem to have gained much in depth and root age in Europe. On the other hand, the growth of territorial nationalism, with its emphasis on what is called national characteristics, has

tended rather to kill the broad human element in the art and literature of Europe. It was quite otherwise with Islam. Here the idea was neither a concept of philosophy nor a dream of poetry. As a social movement the aim of Islam was to make the idea a living factor in the Muslim's daily life, and thus silently and imperceptibly to carry it towards fuller fruition.

2. A Keen Sense of the Reality of Time, and the Concept of Life as a Continuous Movement in Time. It is this conception of life and time which is the main point of interest in Ibn Khaldën's view of history, and which justifies Flint's eulogy that 'Plato, Aristotle, and Augustine were not his peers, and all others were unworthy of being even mentioned along with him'. From the remarks that I have made above I do not mean to throw doubt on the originality of Ibn Khaldën. All that I mean to say is that, considering the direction in which the culture of Islam had unfolded itself, only a Muslim could have viewed history as a continuous, collective movement, a real inevitable development in time. The point of interest in this view of history is the way in which Ibn Khaldën conceives the process of change. His conception is of infinite importance because of the implication that history, as a continuous movement in time, is a genuinely creative movement and not a movement whose path is already determined. Ibn Khaldën was not a metaphysician. Indeed he was hostile to Metaphysics. But in view of the nature of his conception of time he may fairly be regarded as a forerunner of Bergson. I have already discussed the intellectual antecedents of this conception in the cultural history of Islam. The Qur'anic view of the 'alternation of day and night' as a symbol of the Ultimate Reality which 'appears in a fresh glory every moment', the tendency in Muslim Metaphysics to regard time as objective, Ibn Maskawaih's view of life as an evolutionary movement, and lastly al-Bârënâ's

definite approach to the conception of Nature as a process of becoming - all this constituted the intellectual inheritance of Ibn Khaldën. His chief merit lies in his acute perception of, and systematic expression to, the spirit of the cultural movement of which he was a most brilliant product. In the work of this genius the anti-classical spirit of the Qur'an scores its final victory over Greek thought; for with the Greeks time was either unreal, as in Plato and Zeno, or moved in a circle, as in Heraclitus and the Stoics. Whatever may be the criterion by which to judge the forward steps of a creative movement, the movement itself, if conceived as cyclic, ceases to be creative. Eternal recurrence is not eternal creation; it is eternal repetition.

We are now in a position to see the true significance of the intellectual revolt of Islam against Greek philosophy. The fact that this revolt originated in a purely theological interest shows that the anti-classical spirit of the Qur'an asserted itself in spite of those who began with a desire to interpret Islam in the light of Greek thought.

It now remains to eradicate a grave misunderstanding created by Spengler's widely read book, The Decline of the West. His two chapters devoted to the problem of Arabian culture constitute a most important contribution to the cultural history of Asia. They are, however, based on a complete misconception of the nature of Islam as a religious movement, and of the cultural activity which it initiated. Spengler's main thesis is that each culture is a specific organism, having no point of contact with cultures that historically precede or follow it. Indeed, according to him, each culture has its own peculiar way of looking at things which is entirely inaccessible to men belonging to a different culture. In his anxiety to prove this thesis he marshals an overwhelming array of facts and interpretations to show that the spirit of European culture is through and through anti-classical. And this anti-classical spirit of European culture is entirely due to the specific genius of Europe, and not to any inspiration she may have received from the culture of Islam which, according to Spengler, is thoroughly 'Magian' in spirit and character. Spengler's view of the spirit of modern culture is, in my opinion, perfectly correct. I have, however, tried to show in these lectures that the anti-classical spirit of the modern world has really arisen out of the revolt of Islam against Greek thought. It is obvious that such a view cannot be acceptable to Spengler; for, if it is possible to show that the anti-classical spirit of modern culture is due to the inspiration which it received from the culture immediately preceding it, the whole argument of Spengler regarding the complete mutual independence of cultural growths would collapse. I am afraid of Spengler's anxiety to establish this thesis has completely perverted his vision of Islam as a cultural movement.

By the expression 'Magian culture' Spengler means the common culture associated with what he calls 'Magian group of religions', i.e. Judaism, ancient Chaldean religion, early Christianity, Zoroastrianism, and Islam. That a Magian crust has grown over Islam, I do not deny. Indeed my main purpose in these lectures has been to secure a vision of the spirit of Islam as emancipated from its Magian overlayings which, in my opinion, have misled Spengler. His ignorance of Muslim thought on the problem of time, as well as of the way, in which the 'I', as a free centre of experience, has found expression in the religious experience of Islam, is simply appalling. Instead of seeking light from the history of Muslim thought and experience, he prefers to base his judgement on vulgar beliefs as to the beginning and end of time. Just imagine a man of overwhelming learning finding support for the supposed fatalism of Islam in such Eastern expressions and proverbs as the 'vault of time', and 'everything has a time!' However, on the origin and growth of the concept of time in Islam, and on the human ego as a free power, I have said enough in these lectures. It is obvious that a full examination of Spengler's view of Islam, and of the culture that grew out of it, will require a whole volume. In addition to what I have said before, I shall offer here one more observation of a general nature.

'The kernel of the prophetic teaching,' says Spengler, 'is already Magian. There is one God - be He called Yahweh, Ahuramazda, or Marduk-Baal - who is the principle of good, and all other deities are either impotent or evil. To this doctrine there attached itself the hope of a Messiah, very clear in Isaiah, but also bursting out everywhere during the next centuries, under pressure of an inner necessity. It is the basic idea of Magian religion, for it contains implicitly the conception of the world-historical struggle between Good and Evil, with the power of Evil prevailing in the middle period, and the Good finally triumphant on the Day of Judgement.'60 If this view of the prophetic teaching is meant to apply to Islam it is obviously a misrepresentation. The point to note is that the Magian admitted the existence of false gods; only they did not turn to worship them. Islam denies the very existence of false gods. In this connection Spengler fails to appreciate the cultural value of the idea of the finality of prophet hood in Islam.

No doubt, one important feature of Magian culture is a perpetual attitude of expectation, a constant looking forward to the coming of Zoroaster's unborn sons, the Messiah, or the Paraclete of the fourth gospel. I have already indicated the direction in which the student of Islam should seek the cultural meaning of the doctrine of finality in Islam. It may further be regarded as a psychological cure for the Magian attitude of constant expectation which tends to give a false view of history. Ibn Khaldën, seeing the spirit of his own view of history, has fully criticized and, I believe, finally demolished the alleged revelational basis in Islam of an idea similar, at least in its psychological effects, to the original Magian idea which had reappeared in Islam under the pressure of Magian thought.

2

The Structure of Islam and its Principle of Movement

As a cultural movement Islam rejects the old static view of the universe, and reaches a dynamic view. As an emotional system of unification it recognizes the worth of the individual as such, and rejects blood-relationship as a basis of human unity. Blood-relationship is earth-rooted ness. The search for a purely psychological foundation of human unity becomes possible only with the perception that all human life is spiritual in its origin. Such a perception is creative of fresh loyalties without any ceremonial to keep them alive, and makes it possible for man to emancipate himself from the earth. Christianity which had originally appeared as a monastic order was tried by Constantine as a system of unification. Its failure to work as such a system drove the Emperor Julian to return to the old gods of Rome on which he attempted to put philosophical interpretations. A modern historian of civilization has thus depicted the state of the civilized world about the time when Islam appeared on the stage of History:

It seemed then that the great civilization that it had taken four thousand years to construct was on the verge of disintegration, and that mankind was likely to return to that condition of barbarism where every tribe and sect was against the next, and law and order were unknown . . . The old tribal sanctions had lost their power. Hence the old imperial methods would no longer operate. The new sanctions created by Christianity were working division and destruction instead of unity and order. It was a time fraught with tragedy. Civilization, like a gigantic tree whose foliage had overarched the world and whose branches had borne the golden fruits of art and science and literature, stood tottering, its trunk no longer alive with the flowing sap of devotion and reverence, but rotted to the core, riven by the storms of war, and held together only by the cords of ancient customs and laws, that might snap at any moment. Was there any emotional culture that could be brought in, to gather mankind once more into unity and to save civilization? This culture must be something of a new type, for the old sanctions and ceremonials were dead, and to build up others of the same kind would be the work of centuries.'

The writer then proceeds to tell us that the world stood in need of a new culture to take the place of the culture of the throne, and the systems of unification which were based on blood-relationship. It is amazing, he adds, that such a culture should have arisen from Arabia just at the time when it was most needed. There is, however, nothing amazing in the phenomenon. The world-life intuitively sees its own needs, and at critical moments defines its own direction. This is what, in the language of religion, we call prophetic revelation. It is only natural that Islam should have flashed across the consciousness of a simple people untouched by any of the ancient cultures, and occupying a geographical position where three continents meet together. The new culture finds the foundation of world-unity in the principle of Tauhâd.' Islam, as a polity, is only a practical means of making this principle a living factor in the intellectual and emotional life of mankind. It demands loyalty to God, not to thrones.

And since God is the ultimate spiritual basis of all life, loyalty to God virtually amounts to man's loyalty to his own ideal nature. The ultimate spiritual basis of all life, as conceived by Islam, is eternal and reveals itself in variety and change. A society based on such a conception of Reality must reconcile, in its life, the categories of permanence and change. It must possess eternal principles to regulate its collective life, for the eternal gives us a foothold in the world of perpetual change. But eternal principles when they are understood to exclude all possibilities of change which, according to the Qur'an , is one of the greatest 'signs' of God, tend to immobilize what is essentially mobile in its nature. The failure of the Europe in political and social sciences illustrates the former principle; the immobility of Islam during the last five hundred years illustrates the latter. What then is the principle of movement in the structure of Islam? This is known as Ijtihad.

The word literally means to exert. In the terminology of Islamic law it means to exert with a view to form an independent judgement on a legal question. The idea, I believe, has its origin in a well-known verse of the Qur'an - 'And to those who exert We show Our path'. We find it more definitely adumbrated in a tradition of the Holy Prophet. When Mu'adh was appointed ruler of Yemen, the Prophet is reported to have asked him as to how he would decide matters coming up before him. 'I will judge matters according to the Book of God,' said Mu'adh. 'But if the Book of God contains nothing to guide you?' 'Then I will act on the precedents of the Prophet of God.' 'But if the precedents fail?' 'Then I will exert to form my own judgement.' The student of the history of Islam, however, is well aware that with the political expansion of Islam systematic legal thought became an absolute necessity, and our early doctors of law, both of Arabian and non-Arabian descent, worked ceaselessly until all the accumulated wealth of legal thought found a final expression in our recognized schools of Law.

These schools of Law recognize three degrees of Ijtihad:

(1) complete authority in legislation which is practically confined to be founders of the schools, (2) relative authority which is to be exercised within the limits of a particular school, and (3) special authority which relates to the determining of the law applicable to a particular case left undetermined by the founders. In this paper I am concerned with the first degree of Ijtihad only, i.e. complete authority in legislation. The theoretical possibility of this degree of Ijtihad is admitted by the Sunni's, but in practice it has always been denied ever since the establishment of the schools, inasmuch as the idea of complete Ijtihad is hedged round by conditions which are well-nigh impossible of realization in a single individual.

Such an attitude seems exceedingly strange in a system of law based mainly on the groundwork provided by the Qur'an which embodies an essentially dynamic outlook on life. It is, therefore, necessary, before we proceed farther, to discover the cause of this intellectual attitude which has reduced the Law of Islam practically to a state of immobility. Some European writers think that the stationary character of the Law of Islam is due to the influence of the Turks. This is an entirely superficial view, for the legal schools of Islam had been finally established long before the Turkish influence began to work in the history of Islam. The real causes are, in my opinion, as follows:

1. We are all familiar with the Rationalist movement which appeared in the church of Islam during the early days of the Abbasids and the bitter controversies which it raised. Take for instance the one important point of controversy between the two camps - the conservative dogma of the eternity of the Qur'an. The Rationalists denied it because they thought that this was only another form of the Christian dogma of the eternity of the word; on the other hand, the conservative thinkers whom the later Abbasids, fearing the political implications of Rationalism, gave their full support,

thought that by denying the eternity of the Qur'an the Rationalists were undermining the very foundations of Muslim society. Naïïam, for instance, practically rejected the traditions, and openly declared Abë Hurairah to be an untrustworthy reporter. Thus, partly owing to a misunderstanding of the ultimate motives of Rationalism, and partly owing to the unrestrained thought of particular Rationalists, conservative thinkers regarded this movement as a force of disintegration, and considered it a danger to the stability of Islam as a social polity. Their main purpose, therefore, was to preserve the social integrity of Islam, and to realize this the only course open to them was to utilize the binding force of Sharâ'ah, and to make the structure of their legal system as rigorous as possible.

2. The rise and growth of ascetic Sufism, which gradually developed under influences of a non-Islamic character, a purely speculative side, is to a large extent responsible for this attitude. On its purely religious side Sufism fostered a kind of revolt against the verbal quibbles of our early doctors. The case of Sufyan Thaurâ is an instance in point. He was one of the acutest legal minds of his time, and was nearly the founder of a school of law, but being also intensely spiritual, the dry-as-dust subtleties of contemporary legists drove him to ascetic Sufism. On its speculative side which developed later, Sufism is a form of free thought and in alliance with Rationalism. The emphasis that it laid on the distinction of ïahir and baÇin (Appearance and Reality) created an attitude of indifference to all that applies to Appearance and not to Reality.

   This spirit of total other-worldliness in later Sufism obscured men's vision of a very important aspect of Islam as a social polity, and, offering the prospect of unrestrained thought on its speculative side, it attracted and finally absorbed the best minds in Islam. The Muslim state was thus left generally in the hands of intellectual mediocrities, and the unthinking masses of Islam, having no personalities of a higher caliber to guide them, found their security only in blindly following the schools.

3. On the top of all this came the destruction of Baghdad - the centre of Muslim intellectual life - in the middle of the thirteenth century. This was indeed a great blow, and all the contemporary historians of the invasion of Tartars describe the havoc of Baghdad with a half-suppressed pessimism about the future of Islam. For fear of further disintegration, which is only natural in such a period of political decay, the conservative thinkers of Islam focused all their efforts on the one point of preserving a uniform social life for the people by a jealous exclusion of all innovations in the law of Sharâ'ah as expounded by the early doctors of Islam. Their leading idea was social order, and there is no doubt that they were partly right, because organization does to a certain extent counteract the forces of decay. But they did not see, and our modern 'Ulema do not see, that the ultimate fate of a people does not depend so much on organization as on the worth and power of individual men. In an over-organized society the individual is altogether crushed out of existence. He gains the whole wealth of social thought around him and loses his own soul. Thus a false reverence for past history and its artificial resurrection constitute no remedy for a people's decay. 'The verdict of history', as a modern writer has happily put it, 'is that worn-out ideas have never risen to power among a people who have worn them out.' The only effective power, therefore, that counteracts the forces of decay in a people is the rearing of self-concentrated individuals. Such individuals alone reveal the depth of life. They disclose new standards in the light of which we begin to see that our environment is not wholly inviolable and requires revision. The tendency to over-organization

by a false reverence of the past, as manifested in the legists of Islam in the thirteenth century and later, was contrary to the inner impulse of Islam, and consequently invoked the powerful reaction of Ibn Taimâyyah, one of the most indefatigable writers and preachers of Islam, who was born in 1263, five years after the destruction of Baghdad.

Ibn Taimâyyah was brought up in Hanbalite tradition. Claiming freedom of Ijtihad for himself he rose in revolt against the finality of the schools, and went back to first principles in order to make a fresh start. Like Ibn Àazm - the founder of Êahirâschool of law - he rejected the Hanafite principle of reasoning by analogy and Ijma' as understood by older legists; for his thought agreement was the basis of all superstition. And there is no doubt that, considering the moral and intellectual decrepitude of his times, he was right in doing so. In the sixteenth century Suyëtâ claimed the same privilege of Ijtihad to which he added the idea of a renovator at the beginning of each century. But the spirit of Ibn Taimâyyah's teaching found a fuller expression in a movement of immense potentialities which arose in the eighteenth century, from the sands of Nejd, described by Macdonald as the 'cleanest spot in the decadent world of Islam'.

It is really the first throb of life in modern Islam. To the inspiration of this movement are traceable, directly or indirectly, nearly all the great modern movements of Muslim Asia and Africa, e.g. the Sanâsâ movement, the Pan-Islamic movement, and the Babâ movement, which is only a Persian reflex of Arabian Protestantism. The great puritan reformer, Muhammad Ibn 'Abd al-Wahhah, who was born in 1700, studied in Medina, travelled in Persia, and finally succeeded in spreading the fire of his restless soul throughout the whole world of Islam. He was similar in spirit to Ghazzalâ's disciple, Muhammad Ibn Tëmart - the Berber puritan reformer of Islam who appeared amidst the decay of Muslim Spain, and gave her a fresh inspiration. We are, however, not concerned with the political career of this movement which was terminated by the armies of Muhammad 'Alâ Pasha. The essential thing to note is the spirit of freedom manifested in it, though inwardly this movement, too, is conservative in its own fashion. While it rises in revolt against the finality of the schools, and vigorously asserts the right of private judgement, its vision of the past is wholly uncritical, and in matters of law it mainly falls back on the traditions of the Prophet.

Passing on to Turkey, we find that the idea of Ijtihad, reinforced and broadened by modern philosophical ideas, has long been working in the religious and political thought of the Turkish nation. This is clear from Àalim Sabit's new theory of Muhammadan Law, grounded on modern sociological concepts. If the renaissance of Islam is a fact, and I believe it is a fact, we too one day, like the Turks, will have to re-evaluate our intellectual inheritance. And if we cannot make any original contribution to the general thought of Islam, we may, by healthy conservative criticism, serve at least as a check on the rapid movement of liberalism in the world of Islam. I now proceed to give you some idea of religio-political thought in Turkey which will indicate to you how the power of Ijtihad is manifested in recent thought and activity in that country. There were a short time ago, two main lines of thought in Turkey represented by the Nationalist Party and the Party of Religious Reform.

The point of supreme interest with the Nationalist Party is above all the State and not Religion. With these thinkers religion as such has no independent function. The state is the essential factor in national life which determines the character and function of all other factors. They, therefore, reject old ideas about the function of State and Religion, and accentuate the separation of Church and State. Now the structure of Islam as a religio-political system, no doubt, does permit such a view, though personally I think it is a mistake to suppose that the idea of state is more dominant and rules all other ideas embodied in the system of Islam.

In Islam the spiritual and the temporal are not two distinct domains, and the nature of an act, however secular in its import, is determined by the attitude of mind with which the agent does it. It is the invisible mental background of the act which ultimately determines its character. An act is temporal or profane if it is done in a spirit of detachment from the infinite complexity of life behind it; it is spiritual if it is inspired by that complexity. In Islam it is the same reality which appears as Church looked at from one point of view and State from another. It is not true to say that Church and State are two sides or facets of the same thing. Islam is a single unanalysable reality which is one or the other as your point of view varies.

The point is extremely far-reaching and a full elucidation of it will involve us in a highly philosophical discussion. Suffice it to say that this ancient mistake arose out of the bifurcation of the unity of man into two distinct and separate realities which somehow have a point of contact, but which are in essence opposed to each other. The truth, however, is that matter is spirit in space-time reference. The unity called man is body when you look at it as acting in regard to what we call the external world; it is mind or soul when you look at it as acting in regard to the ultimate aim and ideal of such acting. The essence of Tauhâd, as a working idea, is equality, solidarity, and freedom. The state, from the Islamic standpoint, is an endeavour to transform these ideal principles into space-time forces, an aspiration to realize them in a definite human organization.

It is in this sense alone that the state in Islam is a theocracy, not in the sense that it is headed by a representative of God on earth who can always screen his despotic will behind his supposed infallibility. The critics of Islam have lost sight of this important consideration. The Ultimate Reality, according to the Qur'an, is spiritual, and its life consists in its temporal activity. The spirit finds its opportunities in the natural, the material, the secular. All that is secular is, therefore, sacred in the roots of its being. The greatest service that modern thought has rendered to Islam, and as a matter of fact to all religion, consists in its criticism of what we call material or natural - a criticism which discloses that the merely material has no substance until we discover it rooted in the spiritual. There is no such thing as a profane world. All this immensity of matter constitutes a scope for the self-realization of spirit. All is holy ground. As the Prophet so beautifully puts it: 'The whole of this earth is a mosque.' The state, according to Islam, is only an effort to realize the spiritual in a human organization. But in this sense all state, not based on mere domination and aiming at the realization of ideal principles, is theocratic.

The truth is that the Turkish Nationalists assimilated the idea of the separation of Church and State from the history of European political ideas. Primitive Christianity was founded, not as a political or civil unit, but as a monastic order in a profane world, having nothing to do with civil affairs, and obeying the Roman authority practically in all matters. The result of this was that when the State became Christian, State and Church confronted each other as distinct powers with interminable boundary disputes between them. Such a thing could never happen in Islam; for Islam was from the very beginning a civil society, having received from the Qur'an a set of simple legal principles which, like the twelve tables of the Romans, carried, as experience subsequently proved, great potentialities of expansion and development by interpretation. The Nationalist theory of state, therefore, is misleading inasmuch as it suggests a dualism which does not exist in Islam.

The Religious Reform Party, on the other hand, led by Sa'âd Àalâm Pasha, insisted on the fundamental fact that Islam is a harmony of idealism and positivism; and, as a unity of the eternal verities of freedom, equality, and solidarity, has no fatherland. 'As there is no English Mathematics, German Astronomy or French Chemistry,' says the Grand Vizier, 'so there is no Turkish, Arabian, Persian or Indian Islam. Just as the universal character of scientific truths engenders varieties of scientific national cultures which in their totality represent human knowledge, much in the same way the universal character of Islamic verities creates varieties of national, moral and social ideals.' Modern culture based as it is on national egoism is, according to this keen-sighted writer, only another form of barbarism. It is the result of an over-developed industrialism through which men satisfy their primitive instincts and inclinations.

He, however, deplores that during the course of history the moral and social ideals of Islam have been gradually deislamized through the influence of local character, and pre-Islamic superstitions of Muslim nations. These ideals today are more Iranian, Turkish, or Arabian than Islamic. The pure brow of the principle of Tauhâd has received more or less an impress of heathenism, and the universal and impersonal character of the ethical ideals of Islam has been lost through a process of localization. The only alternative open to us, then, is to tear off from Islam the hard crust which has immobilized an essentially dynamic outlook on life, and to rediscover the original verities of freedom, equality, and solidarity with a view to rebuild our moral, social, and political ideals out of their original simplicity and universality. Such are the views of the Grand Vizier of Turkey. You will see that following a line of thought more in tune with the spirit of Islam, he reaches practically the same conclusion as the Nationalist Party, that is to say, the freedom of Ijtihad with a view to rebuild the laws of Sharâ'ah in the light of modern thought and experience.

Let us now see how the Grand National Assembly has exercised this power of Ijtihad in regard to the institution of Khilafat. According to Sunni Law, the appointment of an Imam or Khalâfah is absolutely indispensable. The first question that arises in this connection is this - Should the Caliphate be vested in a single person? Turkey's Ijtihad is that according to the spirit of Islam the Caliphate or Imamate can be vested in a body of persons, or an elected Assembly. The religious doctors of Islam in Egypt and India, as far as I know, have not yet expressed themselves on this point. Personally, I believe the Turkish view is perfectly sound. It is hardly necessary to argue this point. The republican form of government is not only thoroughly consistent with the spirit of Islam, but has also become a necessity in view of the new forces that are set free in the world of Islam.

In order to understand the Turkish view let us seek the guidance of Ibn Khaldën - the first philosophical historian of Islam. Ibn Khaldën, in his famous 'Prolegomena', mentions three distinct views of the idea of Universal Caliphate in Islam: (1) That Universal Imamate is a Divine institution, and is consequently indispensable. (2) That it is merely a matter of expediency. (3) That there is no need of such an institution. The last view was taken by the Khawarij. It seems that modern Turkey has shifted from the first to the second view, i.e. to the view of the Mu'tazilah who regarded Universal Imamate as a matter of expediency only. The Turks argue that in our political thinking we must be guided by our past political experience which points unmistakably to the fact that the idea of Universal Imamate has failed in practice.

It was a workable idea when the Empire of Islam was intact. Since the break-up of this Empire independent political units have arisen. The idea has ceased to be operative and cannot work as a living factor in the organization of modern Islam. Far from serving any useful purpose it has really stood in the way of a reunion of independent Muslim States. Persia has stood aloof from the Turks in view of her doctrinal differences regarding the Khilafat; Morocco has always looked askance at them, and Arabia has cherished private ambition. And all these rupture in Islam for the sake of a mere symbol of a power which departed long ago. Why should we not, they can further argue, learn from experience in our political thinking? Did not Qadâ Abë Bakr Baqilanâ drop the condition of Qarshâyat in the Khalâfah in view of the facts of experience, i.e. the political fall of the Quraish and their consequent inability to rule the world of Islam? Centuries ago Ibn Khaldën, who personally believed in the condition of Qarshâyat in the Khali'fah, argued much in the same way.

Since the power of the Quraish, he says, has gone, there is no alternative but to accept the most powerful man as Ima'm in the country where he happens to be powerful. Thus Ibn Khaldën, realizing the hard logic of facts, suggests a view which may be regarded as the first dim vision of an International Islam fairly in sight today. Such is the attitude of the modern Turk, inspired as he is by the realities of experience, and not by the scholastic reasoning of jurists who lived and thought under different conditions of life. To my mind these arguments, if rightly appreciated, indicate the birth of an International ideal which, though forming the very essence of Islam, has been hitherto over-shadowed or rather displaced by Arabian Imperialism of the earlier centuries of Islam. This new ideal is clearly reflected in the work of the great nationalist poet Êiya whose songs, inspired by the philosophy of Auguste Comte, have done a great deal in shaping the present thought of Turkey. I reproduce the substance of one of his poems from Professor Fischer's German translation:

In order to create a really effective political unity of Islam, all Muslim countries must first become independent: and then in their totality they should range themselves under one Caliph. Is such a thing possible at the present moment? If not today, one must wait. In the meantime the Caliph must reduce his own house to order and lay the foundations of a workable modern State.

'In the International world the weak find no sympathy; power alone deserves respect.'

These lines clearly indicate the trend of modern Islam. For the present every Muslim nation must sink into her own deeper self, temporarily focus her vision on herself alone, until all are strong and powerful to form a living family of republics. A true and living unity, according to the nationalist thinkers, is not so easy as to be achieved by a merely symbolical over lordship. It is truly manifested in a multiplicity of free independent units whose racial rivalries are adjusted and harmonized by the unifying bond of a common spiritual aspiration. It seems to me that God is slowly bringing home to us the truth that Islam is neither Nationalism nor Imperialism but a League of Nations which recognizes artificial boundaries and racial distinctions for facility of reference only, and not for restricting the social horizon of its members.

From the same poet the following passage from a poem called 'Religion and Science' will throw some further light on the general religious outlook which is being gradually shaped in the world of Islam today:

"Who were the first spiritual leaders of mankind? Without doubt the prophets and holy men. In every period religion has led philosophy; from it alone morality and art receive light. But then religion grows weak, and loses her original ardour! Holy men disappear, and spiritual leadership becomes, in name, the heritage of the Doctors of Law! The leading star of the Doctors of Law is tradition; They drag religion with force on this track; but philosophy says: 'My leading star is reason: you go right, I go left."

'Both religion and philosophy claim the soul of man and draw it on either side!'

'When this struggle is going on pregnant experience delivers up positive science, and this young leader of thought says, "Tradition is history and Reason is the method of history! Both interpret and desire to reach the same indefinable something!"

'But what is this something?'

'Is it a spiritualized heart?'

'If so, then take my last word - Religion is positive science, the purpose of which is to spiritualize the heart of man!'

It is clear from these lines how beautifully the poet has adopted the Comtian idea of the three stages of man's intellectual development, i.e. theological, metaphysical and scientific - to the religious outlook of Islam. And the view of religion embodied in these lines determines the poet's attitude towards the position of Arabic in the educational system of Turkey. He says:

'The land where the call to prayer resounds in Turkish; where those who pray understand the meaning of their religion; the land where the Qur'an is learnt in Turkish; where every man, big or small, knows full well the command of God; O! Son of Turkey! That land is thy fatherland!'

If the aim of religion is the spiritualization of the heart, then it must penetrate the soul of man, and it can best penetrate the inner man, according to the poet, only if its spiritualizing ideas are clothed in his mother tongue. Most people in India will condemn this displacement of Arabic by Turkish. For reasons which will appear later the poet's Ijtihad is open to grave objections, but it must be admitted that the reform suggested by him is not without a parallel in the past history of Islam. We find that when Muhammad Ibn Tëmart - the Mahdi of Muslim Spain - who was Berber by nationality, came to power, and established the pontifical rule of the Muwaidën, he ordered for the sake of the illiterate Berbers, that the Qur'an should be translated and read in the Berber language; that the call to prayer should be given in Berber; and that all the functionaries of the

Church must know the Berber language.

In another passage the poet gives his ideal of womanhood. In his zeal for the equality of man and woman he wishes to see radical changes in the family law of Islam as it is understood and practised today:

'There is the woman, my mother, my sister, or my daughter; it is she who calls up the most sacred emotions from the depths of my life! There is my beloved, my sun, my moon and my star; it is she who makes me understand the poetry of life! How could the Holy Law of God regard these beautiful creatures as despicable beings? Surely there is an error in the interpretation of the Qur'an by the learned?

'The foundation of the nation and the state is the family!'

'As long as the full worth of the woman is not realized, national life remains incomplete.'

'The upbringing of the family must correspond with justice;'

'Therefore equality is necessary in three things - in divorce, in separation, and in inheritance.'

'As long as the woman is counted half the man as regards inheritance and one-fourth of man in matrimony, neither the family nor the country will be elevated. For other rights we have opened national courts of justice;'

'he family, on the other hand, we have left in the hands of schools.'

I do not know why we have left the woman in the lurch?

Does she not work for the land? Or, will she turn her needle into a sharp bayonet to tear off her rights from our hands through a revolution?

The truth is that among the Muslim nations of today, Turkey alone has shaken off its dogmatic slumber, and attained to self-consciousness. She alone has claimed her right of intellectual freedom; she alone has passed from the ideal to the real - a transition which entails keen intellectual and moral struggle. To her the growing complexities of a mobile and broadening life are sure to bring new situations suggesting new points of view, and necessitating fresh interpretations of principles which are only of an academic interest to a people who have never experienced the joy of spiritual expansion. It is, I think, the English thinker Hobbes who makes this acute observation that to have a succession of identical thoughts and feelings is to have no thoughts and feelings at all. Such is the lot of most Muslim countries today. They are mechanically repeating old values, whereas the Turk is on the way to creating new values. He has passed through great experiences which have revealed his deeper self to him. In him life has begun to move, change, and amplify, giving birth to new desires, bringing new difficulties and suggesting new interpretations.

The question which confronts him today, and which is likely to confront other Muslim countries in the near future is whether the Law of Islam is capable of evolution - a question which will require great intellectual effort, and is sure to be answered in the affirmative, provided the world of Islam approaches it in the spirit of 'Umar - the first critical and independent mind in Islam who, at the last moments of the Prophet, had the moral courage to utter these remarkable words: 'The Book of God is sufficient for us.' We heartily welcome the liberal movement in modern Islam, but it must also be admitted that the appearance of liberal ideas in Islam constitutes also the most critical moment in the history of Islam. Liberalism has a tendency to act as a force of disintegration, and the race-idea which appears to be working in modern Islam with greater force than ever may ultimately wipe off the broad human outlook which Muslim people have imbibed from their religion. Further, our religious and political reformers in their zeal for liberalism may overstep the proper limits of reform in the absence of check on their youthful fervour. We are today passing through a period similar to that of the Protestant revolution in Europe, and the lesson which the rise and outcome of Luther's movement teaches should not be lost on us.

A careful reading of history shows that the Reformation was essentially a political movement, and the net result of it in Europe was a gradual displacement of the universal ethics of Christianity by systems of national ethics. The result of this tendency we have seen with our own eyes in the Great European War which, far from bringing any workable synthesis of the two opposing systems of ethics, has made the European situation still more intolerable. It is the duty of the leaders of the world of Islam today to understand the real meaning of what has happened in Europe, and then to move forward with self-control and a clear insight into the ultimate aims of Islam as a social polity.

I have given you some idea of the history and working of Ijtihad in modern Islam. I now proceed to see whether the history and structure of the Law of Islam indicate the possibility of any fresh interpretation of its principles. In other words, the question that I want to raise is - Is the Law of Islam capable of evolution? Horten, Professor of Semitic Philology at the University of Bonn, raises the same question in connection with the Philosophy and Theology of Islam. Reviewing the work of Muslim thinkers in the sphere of purely religious thought he points out that the history of Islam may aptly be described as a gradual interaction, harmony, and mutual deepening of two distinct forces, i.e. the element of Aryan culture and knowledge on the one hand, and a Semitic religion on the other. The Muslim has always adjusted his religious outlook to the elements of culture which he assimilated from the peoples that surrounded him. From 800 to 1100, says Horten, not less than one hundred systems of theology appeared in Islam, a fact which bears ample testimony to the elasticity of Islamic thought as well as to the ceaseless activity of our early thinkers. Thus, in view of the revelations of a deeper study of Muslim literature and thought, this living European Orientalist has been driven to the following conclusion:

1. The spirit of Islam is so broad that it is practically boundless. With the exception of atheistic ideas alone it has assimilated all the attainable ideas of surrounding peoples, and given them its own peculiar direction of development.'

The assimilative spirit of Islam is even more manifest in the sphere of law. Says Professor Hurgronje - the Dutch critic of Islam:

1. When we read the history of the development of Mohammadan Law we find that, on the one hand, the doctors of every age, on the slightest stimulus, condemn one another to the point of mutual accusations of heresy; and, on the other hand, the very same people, with greater and greater unity of purpose, try to reconcile the similar quarrels of their predecessors.'

These views of modern European critics of Islam make it perfectly clear that, with the return of new life, the inner catholicity of the spirit of Islam is bound to work itself out in spite of the rigorous conservatism of our doctors. And I have no doubt that a deeper study of the enormous legal literature of Islam is sure to rid the modern critic of the superficial opinion that the Law of Islam is stationary and incapable of development. Unfortunately, the conservative Muslim public of this country is not yet quite ready for a critical discussion of Fiqh, which, if undertaken, is likely to displease most people, and raise sectarian controversies; yet I venture to offer a few remarks on the point before us.

1. In the first place, we should bear in mind that from the earliest times practically up to the rise of the Abbasids, there was no written law of Islam apart from the Qur'an.
2. Secondly, it is worthy of note that from about the middle of the first century up to the beginning of the

fourth not less than nineteen schools of law and legal opinion appeared in Islam. This fact alone is sufficient to show how incessantly our early doctors of law worked in order to meet the necessities of a growing civilization. With the expansion of conquest and the consequent widening of the outlook of Islam these early legists had to take a wider view of things, and to study local conditions of life and habits of new peoples that came within the fold of Islam. A careful study of the various schools of legal opinion, in the light of contemporary social and political history, reveals that they gradually passed from the deductive to the inductive attitude in their efforts at interpretation.

3. Thirdly, when we study the four accepted sources of Muhammadan Law and the controversies which they invoked, the supposed rigidity of our recognized schools evaporates and the possibility of a further evolution becomes perfectly clear. Let us briefly discuss these sources.

a. **The Qur'an-**The primary source of the Law of Islam is the Qur'an. The Qur'an, however, is not a legal code. Its main purpose, as I have said before, is to awaken in man the higher consciousness of his relation with God and the universe. No doubt, the Qur'an does lay down a few general principles and rules of a legal nature, especially relating to the family - the ultimate basis of social life. But why are these rules made part of a revelation the ultimate aim of which is man's higher life? The answer to this question is furnished by the history of Christianity which appeared as a powerful reaction against the spirit of legality manifested in Judaism. By setting up an ideal of otherworldliness it no doubt did succeed in spiritualizing life, but its individualism could see no spiritual value in the complexity of human social relations. 'Primitive Christianity', says Naumann in his Briefe Ü ber Religion, 'attached no value to the preservation of the

State, law, organization, production. It simply does not reflect on the conditions of human society.' And Naumann concludes: 'Hence we either dare to aim at being without a state, and thus throwing ourselves deliberately into the arms of anarchy, or we decide to possess, alongside of our religious creed, a political creed as well.' Thus the Qur'an considers it necessary to unite religion and state, ethics and politics in a single revelation much in the same way as Plato does in his Republic.

The important point to note in this connexion, however, is the dynamic outlook of the Qur'an. I have fully discussed its origin and history. It is obvious that with such an outlook the Holy Book of Islam cannot be inimical to the idea of evolution. Only we should not forget that life is not change, pure and simple. It has within it elements of conservation also. While enjoying his creative activity, and always focusing his energies of the discovery of new vistas of life, man has a feeling of uneasiness in the presence of his own unfoldment. In his forward movement he cannot help looking back to his past, and faces his own inward expansion with a certain amount of fear. The spirit of man in its forward movement is restrained by forces which seem to be working in the opposite direction. This is only another way of saying that life moves with the weight of its own past on its back, and that in any view of social change the value and function of the forces of conservatism cannot be lost sight of. It is with this organic insight into the essential teaching of the Qur'an that to approach our existing institutions.

No people can afford to reject their past entirely, for it is their past that has made their personal identity. And in a society like Islam the problem of a revision of old institutions becomes still more delicate, and the responsibility of the reformer assumes a far more serious aspect. Islam is non-territorial in its character, and its aim is to furnish a model for the final combination of humanity by drawing its adherents from a variety of mutually repellent races, and then transforming this atomic aggregate into a people possessing a self-consciousness of their own. This was not an easy task to accomplish. Yet Islam, by means of its well-conceived institutions, has succeeded to a very great extent in creating something like a collective will and conscience in this heterogeneous mass. In the evolution of such a society even the immutability of socially harmless rules relating to eating and drinking, purity or impurity, has a life-value of its own, inasmuch as it tends to give such society a specific inwardness, and further secures that external and internal uniformity which counteracts the forces of heterogeneity always latent in a society of a composite character.

The critic of these institutions must, therefore, try to secure, before he undertakes to handle them, a clear insight into the ultimate significance of the social experiment embodied in Islam. He must look at their structure, not from the standpoint of social advantage or disadvantage to this or that country, but from the point of view of the larger purpose which is being gradually worked out in the life of mankind as a whole. Turning now to the groundwork of legal principles in the Qur'an, it is perfectly clear that far from leaving no scope for human thought and legislative activity the intensive breadth of these principles virtually acts as an awakener of human thought. Our early doctors of law taking their clue mainly from this groundwork evolved a number of legal systems; and the student of Muhammadan history knows very well that nearly half the triumphs of Islam as a social and political power were due to the legal acuteness of these doctors.

'Next to the Romans', says von Kremer, 'there is no other nation besides the Arabs which could call its own a system of law so carefully worked out.' But with all their comprehensiveness these systems are after all individual interpretations, and as such cannot claim any finality. I know the 'Ulema of Islam claim finality for the popular schools of Muhammadan Law, though they never found it possible to deny the theoretical possibility of a complete Ijtihad. I have tried to explain the causes which, in my opinion, determined this attitude of the 'Ulema; but since things have changed and the world of Islam is confronted and affected today by new forces set free by the extraordinary development of human thought in all its directions, I see no reason why this attitude should be maintained any longer.

Did the founders of our schools ever claim finality for their reasonings and interpretations? Never. The claim of the present generation of Muslim liberals to reinterpret the foundational legal principles, in the light of their own experience and the altered conditions of modern life is, in my opinion, perfectly justified. The teaching of the Qur'an that life is a process of progressive creation necessitates that each generation, guided but unhampered by the work of its predecessors, should be permitted to solve its own problems. You will, I think, remind me here of the Turkish poet Êiya whom I quoted a moment ago, and ask whether the equality of man and woman demanded by him, equality, that is to say, in point of divorce, separation, and inheritance, is possible according to Muhammadan Law. I do not know whether the awakening of women in Turkey has created demands which cannot be met with without a fresh interpretation of foundational principles. In the Punjab, as everybody knows, there have been cases in which Muslim women wishing to get rid of undesirable husbands have been driven to apostasy.

Nothing could be more distant from the aims of a missionary religion. The Law of Islam, says the great Spanish jurist Imam Shatibâin his al-Muwafiqat, aims at protecting five things - Dân, Nafs, 'Aql, Mal, and Nasl. Applying this test I venture to ask: 'Does the working of the rule relating to apostasy, as laid down in the Hedayah tend to protect the interests of the Faith in this country?' In view of the intense conservatism of the Muslims of India, Indian judges cannot but stick to what are called standard works. The result is that while the peoples are moving the law remains stationary. With regard to the Turkish poet's demand, I am afraid he does not seem to know much about the family law of Islam. Nor does he seem to understand the economic significance of the Qur'anic rule of inheritance. Marriage, according to Muhammadan Law, is a civil contract. The wife at the time of marriage is at liberty to get the husband's power of divorce delegated to her on stated conditions, and thus secure equality of divorce with her husband. The reform suggested by the poet relating to the rule of inheritance is based on a misunderstanding. From the inequality of their legal shares it must not be supposed that the rule assumes the superiority of males over females. Such an assumption would be contrary to the spirit of Islam. The Qur'an says:

And for women are rights over men similar to those for men over women' (2:228). The share of the daughter is determined not by any inferiority inherent in her, but in view of her economic opportunities, and the place she occupies in the social structure of which she is a part and parcel. Further, according to the poet's own theory of society, the rule of inheritance must be regarded not as an isolated factor in the distribution of wealth, but as one factor among others working together for the same end. While the daughter, according to Muhammadan Law, is held to be full owner of the property given to her by both the father and the husband at the time of her marriage; while, further, she absolutely owns her dower-money which may be prompt or deferred according to her own choice, and in lieu of which she can hold possession of the whole of her husband's property till payment, the responsibility of maintaining her throughout her life is wholly thrown on the husband.

If you judge the working of the rule of inheritance from this point of view, you will find that there is no material difference between the economic position of sons and daughters, and it is really by this apparent inequality of their legal shares that the law secures the equality demanded by the Turkish poet. The truth is that the principles underlying the Qur'anic law of inheritance - this supremely original branch of Muhammadan Law as von Kremer describes it - have not yet received from Muslim lawyers the attention they deserve. Modern society with its bitter class-struggles ought to set us thinking; and if we study our laws in reference to the impending revolution in modern economic life, we are likely to discover, in the foundational principles, hitherto unrevealed aspects which we can work out with a renewed faith in the wisdom of these principles.

b. **The Àadâth** - The second great source of Muhammadan Law is the traditions of the Holy Prophet. These have been the subject of great discussion both in ancient and modern times. Among their modern critics Professor Goldziher has subjected them to a searching examination in the light of modern canons of historical criticism, and arrives at the conclusion that they are, on the whole, untrustworthy. Another European writer, after examining the Muslim methods of determining the genuineness of a tradition, and pointing out the theoretical possibilities of error, arrives at the following conclusion:

'It must be said in conclusion that the preceding considerations represent only theoretical possibilities and that the question whether and how far these possibilities have become actualities is largely a matter of how far the actual circumstances offered inducements for making use of the possibilities. Doubtless, the latter, relatively speaking, were few and affected only a small proportion of the entire Sunnah. It may therefore be said that . . . for the most part the collections of Sunnah considered by the Moslems as canonical are genuine records of the rise and early growth of Islam' (Mohammedan Theories of Finance). For our present purposes, however, we must distinguish traditions of a purely legal import from those which are of a non-legal character. With regard to the former, there arises a very important question as to how far they embody the pre-Islamic usages of Arabia which were in some cases left intact, and in others modified by the Prophet. It is difficult to make this discovery, for our early writers do not always refer to pre-Islamic usages.

Nor is it possible to discover that usages, left intact by express or tacit approval of the Prophet, were intended to be universal in their application. Shah WalâAllah has a very illuminating discussion on the point. I reproduce here the substance of his view. The prophetic method of teaching, according to Shah WalâAllah, is that, generally speaking, the law revealed by a prophet takes especial notice of the habits, ways, and peculiarities of the people to whom he is specifically sent. The prophet who aims at all-embracing principles, however, can neither reveal different principles for different peoples, nor leaves them to work out their own rules of conduct. His method is to train one particular people, and to use them as a nucleus for the building up of a universal Sharâ'ah. In doing so he accentuates the principles underlying the social life of all mankind, and applies them to concrete cases in the light of the specific habits of the people immediately before him. The Sharâ'ah values (AÅkam) resulting from this application (e.g. rules relating to penalties for crimes) are in a sense specific to that people; and since their observance is not an end in itself they cannot be strictly enforced in the case of future generations.

It was perhaps in view of this that Abë Àanâfah, who had, a keen insight into the universal character of Islam, made practically no use of these traditions. The fact that he introduced the principle of IstiÁsan, i.e. juristic preference, which necessitates a careful study of actual conditions in legal thinking, throws further light on the motives which determined his attitude towards this source of Muhammadan Law. It is said that Abë Àanâfah made no use of traditions because there were no regular collections in his day. In the first place, it is not true to say that there were no collections in his day, as the collections of 'Abd al-Malik and Zuhrâ were made not less than thirty years before the death of Abë Àanâfah. But even if we suppose that these collections never reached him, or that they did not contain traditions of a legal import, Abë Àanâfah, like Malik and AÁmad Ibn Àanbal after him, could have easily made his own collection if he had deemed such a thing necessary.

On the whole, then, the attitude of Abë Àanâfah towards the traditions of a purely legal import is to my mind perfectly sound; and if modern Liberalism considers it safer not to make any indiscriminate use of them as a source of law, it will be only following one of the greatest exponents of Muhammadan Law in Sunni Islam. It is, however, impossible to deny the fact that the traditionists, by insisting on the value of the concrete case as against the tendency to abstract thinking in law, have done the greatest service to the Law of Islam. And a further intelligent study of the literature of traditions, if used as indicative of the spirit in which the Prophet himself interpreted his Revelation, may still be of great help in understanding the life-value of the legal principles enunciated in the Qur'an. A complete grasp of their life-value alone can equip us in our endeavour to reinterpret the foundational principles.

c. **The Ijma-** The third source of Muhammadan Law is 'Ijma' which is, in my opinion, perhaps the most important legal notion in Islam. It is, however, strange that this important notion, while invoking great academic discussions in early Islam, remained practically a mere idea, and rarely assumed the form of a permanent institution in any Muhammadan country. Possibly its transformation into a permanent legislative institution was contrary to the political interests of the kind of absolute monarchy that grew up in Islam immediately after the fourth Caliph. It was, I think, favourable to the interest of the Umayyad and the Abbasid Caliphs to leave the power of Ijtihad to individual Mujtahids rather than encourage the formation of a permanent assembly which might become too powerful for them. It is, however, extremely satisfactory to note that the pressure of new world-forces and the political experience of European nations are impressing on the mind of modern Islam the value and possibilities of the idea of Ijma'.

The growth of republican spirit and the gradual formation of legislative assemblies in Muslim lands constitute a great step in advance. The transfer of the power of Ijtihad from individual representatives of schools to a Muslim legislative assembly which, in view of the growth of opposing sects, is the only possible form Ijma' can take in modern times, will secure contributions to legal discussion from laymen who happen to possess a keen insight into affairs. In this way alone can we stir into activity the dormant spirit of life in our legal system, and give it an evolutionary outlook. In India, however, difficulties are likely to arise for it is doubtful whether a non-Muslim legislative assembly can exercise the power of Ijtihad. But there are one or two questions which must be raised and answered in regard to the Ijma'. Can the Ijma' repeal the Qur'an? It is unnecessary to raise this question before a Muslim audience, but I consider it necessary to do so in view of a very misleading statement by a European critic in a book called Mohammedan Theories of Finance - published by the Columbia University.

The author of this book says, without citing any authority, that according to some Hanafâ and Mu'tazilah writers the Ijma' can repeal the Qur'an. There is not the slightest justification for such a statement in the legal literature of Islam. Not even a tradition of the Prophet can have any such effect. It seems to me that the author is misled by the word Naskh in the writings of our early doctors to whom, as Imam ShaÇibâë points out in al-Muwaffiqat, this word, when used in discussions relating to the Ijma' of the companions, meant only the power to extend or limit the application of a Qur'anic rule of law, and not the power to repeal or supersede it by another rule of law. And even in the exercise of this power the legal theory, as 'Amâdâ- a Shafi'â doctor of law who died about the middle of the seventh century, and whose work is recently published in Egypt - tells us, is that the companions must have been in possession of a Sharâ'ah value (Àukm) entitling them to such a limitation or extension.

But supposing the companions have unanimously decided a certain point, the further question is whether later generations are bound by their decision. Shaukanâ has fully discussed this point, and cited the views held by writers belonging to different schools. I think it is necessary in this connexion to discriminate between a decision relating to a question of fact and the one relating to a question of law. In the former case, as for instance, when the question arose whether the two small Sërahs known as Mu'awwidhatan formed part of the Qur'an or not, and the companions unanimously decided that they did, we are bound by their decision, obviously because the companions alone were in a position to know the fact. In the latter case the question is one of interpretation only, and I venture to think, on the authority of Karkhâ, that later generations are not bound by the decision of the companions. Says Karkhâ: 'The Sunnah of the companions is binding in matters which cannot be cleared up by Qiyas, but it is not so in matters which can be established by Qiyas.'

One more question may be asked as to the legislative activity of a modern Muslim assembly which must consist, at least for the present, mostly of men possessing no knowledge of the subtleties of Muhammadan Law. Such an assembly may make grave mistakes in their interpretation of law. How can we exclude or at least reduce the possibilities of erroneous interpretation? The Persian constitution of 1906 provided a separate ecclesiastical committee of 'Ulema - 'conversant with the affairs of the world' - having power to supervise the legislative activity of the Mejlis. This, in my opinion, dangerous arrangement is probably necessary in view of the Persian constitutional theory. According to that theory, I believe, the king is a mere custodian of the realm which really belongs to the Absent Imam.

The 'Ulema, as representatives of the Imam, consider themselves entitled to supervise the whole life of the community, though I fail to understand how, in the absence of an apostolic succession, they establish their claim to represent the Imam. But whatever may be the Persian constitutional theory, the arrangement is not free from danger, and may be tried, if at all, only as a temporary measure in Sunnâ countries. The 'Ulema should form a vital part of a Muslim legislative assembly helping and guiding free discussion on questions relating to law. The only effective remedy for the possibilities of erroneous interpretations is to reform the present system of legal education in

Muhammadan countries, to extend its sphere, and to combine it with an intelligent study of modern jurisprudence.

d. **The Qiyas-** The fourth basis of Fiqh is Qiyas, i.e. the use of analogical reasoning in legislation. In view of different social and agricultural conditions prevailing in the countries conquered by Islam, the school of Abë Àanâfah seem to have found, on the whole, little or no guidance from the precedents recorded in the literature of traditions. The only alternative open to them was to resort to speculative reason in their interpretations. The application of Aristotelian logic, however, though suggested by the discovery of new conditions in Iraq, was likely to prove exceedingly harmful in the preliminary stages of legal development. The intricate behaviour of life cannot be subjected to hard and fast rules logically deducible from certain general notions. Yet, looked at through the spectacles of Aristotle's logic, it appears to be a mechanism pure and simple with no internal principle of movement. Thus, the school of Abë Àanâfah tended to ignore the creative freedom and arbitrariness of life, and hoped to build a logically perfect legal system on the lines of pure reason.

The legists of Àijaz, however, true to the practical genius of their race, raised strong protests against the scholastic subtleties of the legalists of Iraq, and their tendency to imagine unreal cases which they rightly thought would turn the Law of Islam into a kind of lifeless mechanism. These bitter controversies among the early doctors of Islam led to a critical definition of the limitations, conditions, and correctives of Qiyas which, though originally appeared as a mere disguise for Mujtahid's personal opinion, eventually became a source of life and movement in the Law of Islam. The spirit of the acute criticism of Malik and Shafi'â on Abë Àanâfah's principle of Qiyas, as a source of law, constitutes really an effective Semitic restraint on the Aryan tendency to seize the abstract in preference to the concrete, to enjoy the idea rather than the event. This was really a controversy between the advocates of deductive and inductive methods in legal research. The legists of Iraq originally emphasized the eternal aspect of the 'notion', while those of Àijaz laid stress on its temporal aspect. The latter, however, did not see the full significance of their own position, and their instinctive partiality to the legal tradition of Àijaz narrowed their vision to the 'precedents' that had actually happened in the days of the Prophet and his companions.

No doubt they recognized the value of the concrete, but at the same time they eternalized it, rarely resorting to Qiyas based on the study of the concrete as such. Their criticism of Abë Àanâfah and his school, however, emancipated the concrete as it were, and brought out the necessity of observing the actual movement and variety of life in the interpretation of juristic principles. Thus the school of Abë Àanâfah which fully assimilated the results of this controversy is absolutely free in its essential principle and possesses much greater power of creative adaptation than any other school of Muhammadan Law. But, contrary to the spirit of his own school, the modern Hanafâ legist has eternalized the interpretations of the founder or his immediate followers much in the same way as the early critics of Abë Àanâfah eternalized the decisions given on concrete cases. Properly understood and applied, the essential principle of this school, i.e. Qiyas, as Shafi'â rightly says, is only another name for Ijtihad which, within the limits of the revealed texts, is absolutely free; and its importance as a principle can be seen from the fact that, according to most of the doctors, as Qadâ Shaukanâ tells us, it was permitted even in the lifetime of the Holy Prophet.

The closing of the door of Ijtihad is pure fiction suggested partly by the crystallization of legal thought in Islam, and partly by that intellectual laziness which, especially in the period of spiritual decay, turns great thinkers into idols. If some of the later doctors have upheld this fiction, modern Islam is not bound by this voluntary surrender of intellectual independence. Zarkashâ writing in the eighth century of the Hijrah rightly observes:

'If the upholders of this fiction mean that the previous writers had more facilities, while the later writers had more difficulties, in their way, it is, nonsense; for it does not require much understanding to see that Ijtihad for later doctors is easier than for the earlier doctors. Indeed the commentaries on the Koran and Sunnah have been compiled and multiplied to such an extent that the mujtahid of today has more material for interpretation than he needs'.

This brief discussion, I hope, will make it clear to you that neither in the foundational principles nor in the structure of our systems, as we find them today, there anything to justify the present attitude. Equipped with penetrative thought and fresh experience the world of Islam should courageously proceed to the work of reconstruction before them. This work of reconstruction, however, has a far more serious aspect than mere adjustment to modern conditions of life. The Great European War bringing in its wake the awakening on Turkey - the element of stability in the world of Islam - as a French writer has recently described her, and the new economic experiment tried in the neighbourhood of Muslim Asia, must open our eyes to the inner meaning and destiny of Islam. Humanity needs three things today - a spiritual interpretation of the universe, spiritual emancipation of the individual, and basic principles of a universal import directing the evolution of human society on a spiritual basis.

Modern Europe has, no doubt, built idealistic systems on these lines, but experience shows that truth revealed through pure reason is incapable of bringing that fire of living conviction which personal revelation alone can bring. This is the reason why pure thought has so little influenced men, while religion has always elevated individuals, and transformed whole societies. The idealism of Europe never became a living factor in her life, and the result is a perverted ego seeking itself through mutually intolerant democracies whose sole function is to exploit the poor in the interest of the rich. Believe me, Europe today is the greatest hindrance in the way of man's ethical advancement.

The Muslim, on the other hand, is in possession of these ultimate ideas of the basis of a revelation, which, speaking from the inmost depths of life, internalizes its own apparent externality. With him the spiritual basis of life is a matter of conviction for which even the least enlightened man among us can easily lay down his life; and in view of the basic idea of Islam that there can be no further revelation binding on man, we ought to be spiritually one of the most emancipated peoples on earth. Early Muslims emerging out of the spiritual slavery of pre-Islamic Asia were not in a position to realize the true significance of this basic idea. Let the Muslim of today appreciate his position, reconstruct his social life in the light of ultimate principles, and evolve, out of the hitherto partially revealed purpose of Islam, that spiritual democracy which is the ultimate aim of Islam.

3

Muslim Religious Experience

A good place to start in understanding experience is to look closely at what the word itself means and how it is used. The Oxford Dictionary has this to say of experience:

'Actual observation of facts or events; knowledge resulting from this...an event that affects one...fact, process, of being so affected as I learnt by experience...state, phase, of religious emotion'.

If we think about this, several things become clear. Experience is personal. It refers to something we go through, like an event. Experience is also linked to observation and reflection. That is, after we have observed an event, we think about what it meant and this brings us knowledge of something important. In other words, as the quote itself says, through experience we learn something.

Experience is also used as a verb (a 'doing word'). In this case, the Oxford Dictionary explains that to experience is to:

'Meet with, feel, under-go (pleasure, treatment, fate); learn, find'.

If we think about it for a moment, when we say we experience something we usually mean one of the things mentioned above. So to experience something is more than a mental exercise; emotion (how that event feels) is absolutely essential. We can also see, once again, that experience is deeply connected with learning. This will be an important idea to remember when we come to look at 'religious' experience. This is because a religious experience usually involves a person learning something about the nature of the world, themselves, or life in general. We can add to these ideas by looking at how the word experience is used. A good way of doing this is by looking at a Thesaurus. The word thesaurus comes from a Latin word meaning 'treasury' and so; in this case, it is a treasury of words. It lists words which mean the same thing (called synonyms) and those which mean the exact opposite (called antonyms).

The Collins Thesaurus lists some of the following words under the heading 'experience':

'Experience, noun,

1. Contact, doing, evidence, exposure, familiarity, involvement, know-how, (informal), knowledge, observation, participation, practice, proof, training, trial, understanding.
2. Adventure, affair, encounter, episode, event, happening, incident, occurrence, ordeal, test, trial ...verb.
3. Apprehend, become familiar with, behold, encounter, endure, face, feel, go through, have, know, live through, meet, observe, participate in, perceive, sample, sense, suffer, sustain, taste, try, undergo'.

Taken together, these synonyms suggest that experience is about knowledge, understanding and personal contact. They also clearly show that experience is about learning. These quotes may also help us to understand what experience actually is more fully:

'Trust one who has gone through it' Virgil, Aeneid.

'All experience is an arch to build upon' Henry Brooks Adams, The Education of Henry Adams.

'What poor education I have received has been gained in the University of Life' Horatio Bottomley.

'If you have lived one day you have seen everything; one day is the same as all the others' Montaigne, Essais.

'Experience is the best teacher'

'No, the burned hand teaches best. After that, advice about fire goes straight to the heart' Gandalf in Lord of the Rings.

'The man said, "You have spoken the truth. Now, tell me about spiritual excellence (ihsan)." The Prophet (peace and blessings be upon him) replied, "It is to serve Allah as though you behold Him; and if you don't behold him, (know that) He surely sees you." Prophet Muhammad (alaihi al-salatu wa al-salam).

Experience is, therefore, an essential part of how human beings learn. It is deeply personal (or subjective) in that it is related to the way an individual thinks, feels and understands. In some ways, it is also about a person's path through life, and what they have understood that path to mean.

As we have seen, experience is a deeply personal experience. To use academic terminology, it is deeply subjective. We have looked at this term briefly in class. The Oxford Dictionary defines subjective in this way: 'belonging to, of, and due to, the consciousness or thinking or perceiving subject or ego as opposed to real or external things'

This is perhaps a rather confusing definition, although it does point to the personal nature of the word. The Collins Thesaurus offers us some interesting synonyms: 'subjective biased, emotional, idiosyncratic, instinctive, intuitive, nonobjective, personal, prejudiced'

A subjective experience is therefore a personal and intuitive experience, with the understanding that it can also be biased and based largely on emotion. Objective, by contrast, is defined by the Oxford Dictionary as:

'Belonging not to the consciousness ...external to the mind, real ...dealing with outward things and not with thoughts and feelings ...actual facts uncoloured by ...feelings or opinions'

Objective experience is, by this definition, said to be based upon facts in the real world, rather than upon our own thoughts, feelings and opinions. Scientific knowledge is often described as objective; in that it attempts to use experiments to describe things as they are (this kind of knowledge is called empirical knowledge). It is easy, perhaps, to focus solely on objective knowledge and to believe that subjective experience is of little or no serious account. However, subjective experience is very important in understanding how religion feels.

Ways of Studying Religion

Having looked at experience, we can now look more closely at Ninian Smart's 'Dimensions of Religion'. Professor Ninian Smart was an important scholar of Religious Studies. Having studied religion for many years, Professor Smart felt that we could understand religion more fully by thinking about its different aspects (which he called 'dimensions').

Professor Smart felt that religions could be studied in seven main ways:

i. The Practical or Ritual Dimension

That is, every religious tradition involves doing certain things, or certain practices. In the case of Islam, the five daily prayers (salat) are a good example (as are the other 4 pillars). It is important to remember when studying religious traditions that religion is more than ideas or concepts, it is also about doing things. According to the Oxford Dictionary, a ritual is a 'prescribed order of performing religious service'. In other words, the ritual dimension of a ritual is its set way of doing things. It is also the practical application of religious teachings. In the case of Islam, zakat is the practical expression of the religious concept of charity (sadaqa).

ii. The Experiential or Emotional Dimension

Professor Smart speaks of this area in the following manner: 'We have only to glance at religious history to see the enormous vitality and significance of experience in the formation and development of religious traditions. Consider the visions of the Prophet Muhammad, the conversion of Paul, the enlightenment of the Buddha'.

In other words, the experiential dimension of religion refers to the personal experiences of founding figures. It also refers to the subjective quality of these experiences. Because religious experience is so deeply personal, it is important to understand what they mean for religious traditions in general. For example, Islam would look very different indeed if the Prophet (alaihi al-salatu wa al-salam) had not met with the angel Gabriel.

Experience, as we have seen above, is also about how a religious event feels. That is, it is also about emotion. When we listen to the Qur'an, for example, we are supposed to feel awe at the majesty of God. We are also supposed to understand our own shortcomings (and thus to repent for our mistakes). Experience, reflection and emotion are also deeply connected to conversion.

iii. The Narrative or Mythic Dimension

The experiences of prophets, saints and other such figures are often passed on through stories and tales (or narrative). Such narratives attempt to express the feeling and meaning of an event. This is why Smart refers to such stories as a channel.

These stories may be 'true' or they may 'not'. That is, they may be true in different ways. Some religious stories refer to creation and as such, are before history (that is, they are before time and the world began). In this case, they are called myths. Some stories are about the founder themselves and others are about others who followed that religion. We will look at some examples of this when we look at Sufism.

The narrative dimension of religion is therefore about religious stories, what they mean and what they are used for.

iv. The Doctrinal and Philosophical Dimension

The Oxford Dictionary defines doctrine as: 'what is taught, body of instruction; religious, political, scientific ... belief, dogma, or tenet'. That is, doctrine is a body of learning or a way of understanding things. Religious doctrine is therefore a body of religious learning, or a way of understanding religious matters (such as God, life after death, ethic values and so on). Doctrine is therefore an organised system of knowledge. The doctrinal dimension of religion is therefore how experience and narrative are put together to form a body of learning. That is, it is relates an organised expression of these experiences (and the stories told to pass them on to others). In Islam, a good example of religious doctrine is aqida. Aqida refers to statements about the nature of God (tawhid), prophet hood (nubuwwa), life after death and resurrection (akhira) and other such things. I have given you several examples of these statements (sometimes called 'creeds' in English).

The Oxford Dictionary refers to philosophy as:

'Love of wisdom or knowledge, esp. that which deals with ultimate reality, or with the most general causes and principles of things; natural philosophy, study of natural objects and phenomena; moral philosophy, study of principles of human action or conduct; a philosophical system; system for the conduct of life...'

The philosophical dimension of religion refers therefore to religious ways of thinking about ultimate realities, ethics and the world around us. As with doctrine, philosophy also refers to an organised system of thought and expression (or to organised ways of thinking and talking). Religious doctrines and philosophies are thus attempts to analyse the meanings of experiences and stories and to put those ideas into an organised structure. Doctrines emerge, according to Professor Smart, because religions have to adapt to 'social realities' and also to the intellectually gifted (who seek deeper understandings of why things are the way they are).

v. The Ethical and Legal Dimension

Narrative and doctrine help structure experience, and thus give rise to a concrete worldview. Such worldviews are often expressed in terms of religious law and ethics. Legal teachings relate to what a follower must and must not do. That is they set out boundaries of acceptable and unacceptable behaviour. In Islamic language Muslims speak of the halal and the haram (or to things we are allowed and not allowed to do). Within the Islamic tradition, ideas about what is acceptable and what is unacceptable behaviour go to make up the Shariah. As we are perhaps all aware, the Shariah is an important part of Islam. Why? Well, one reason is that the Shariah offers Muslims a concrete system to follow, an organised system of ideas about how (and how not) to act.

If law refers to what a person must and must not do, then ethics refers to what a person should and should not do. The Oxford Dictionary explains ethics in the following way:

'relating to morals, treating of moral questions ... science of morals ... moral principles, rules of conduct, whole field of moral science'.

Morals are defined by the dictionary in this way:

'Concerned with character or disposition, or with the distinction between right and wrong; power or distinguishing between right and wrong...dealing with the regulation of conduct'.

Ethics is concerned with morality, which is about working out what is good and what is bad. It is also a system for working these things out. In the Islamic tradition, actions are often ranked into five main categories, each of which refer to their moral value. These are, in order:

i. Obligatory (fard/wajib)
ii. Recommended (mandub)
iii. Permitted (mubah)
iv. Disliked (makruh)
v. Forbidden (haram)

In other words, the ethical dimensions of religion refer to how to judge the moral worth of actions, according to a particular religious teaching.

vi. The Social and Institutional Dimension

It is important to remember, as Professor Smart reminds us, that 'every religious movement is embodied in a group of people, and that is very often rather formally organised'. In Christian terms, this means the Church. In Islamic terms, Muslims are organised into the Ummah, or 'nation' of Islam. Furthermore, within these broad groups, there are often smaller groups. These are sometimes referred to as 'schools of thought', sects and sometimes 'cults' (although we should be careful how we use such words). That is, there are often several different schools of thought within a single religion. Within Christianity, for example, there are a great many different denominations, such as Catholicism and Protestants. In the Islamic tradition, the main denominations are the Sunni and Shi`a communities.

Each community (which is, in its own turn, made of smaller groups still) has its own ideas regarding religious history, the interpretation (exegesis) of the Qur'an and other such things. When thinking about religion, and ways of studying it, it is important to understand how it works amongst people. Thinking about the social aspects of religion forms the basis of the discipline called the sociology of religion. The institutional dimension of religion refers to the formal structures of that community. Within the Islamic tradition, the community is led by the scholars/imams (ulema), whilst the Christian tradition has an ordained priesthood. It is also important to understand the impact that saints and mystics can also have. These charismatic individuals claim a special relationship with God (based upon their experiences). They are also sometimes felt to have a certain aura. One of the key areas of this module will explore mystical experiences. In this section, we will also consider what such experiences mean for religious authority.

vii. The Material Dimension

According to Smart, social and institutional dimensions are often given concrete expression. This means that another important way of studying religion involves understanding material form. Different religions express their experiences in all sorts of ways. Christianity has a rich and long-lived tradition of art, in particular of depicting Jesus. Islam, by contrast, has avoided depictions of God. Even here, though, Islam has a very rich tradition of religious art: calligraphy, architecture and Qur'anic decoration are important examples of this practice.

Religious buildings are another way of studying the material dimension. Hindu temples, Christian churches and Islamic mosques all reveal important things about each religion and its teachings. Religions often have their own sacred spaces. These are usually significant in some way. Jerusalem is sacred to Judaism as it is connected with Abraham, David and Solomon. The temple at Bodh Gaya is sacred to Buddhism as it is believed to be the place where the Buddha achieved enlightenment. In Islam, Mecca, Medina and Jerusalem are the most important sacred spaces (although there are others too). This highlights another important fact: religions may share the same sacred space. It also demonstrates another crucial idea: within religious traditions, different schools of thought may have different sacred spaces. Thus Shi'a Islam places great emphasis on the sacredness of Najaf (the burial place of Ali) and Karbala (the site of the murder of Imam Hussein), whilst Sufis revere the tombs of important saints, such as Abd al-Qadir al-Jilani in Baghdad, Jalaluddin Rumi in Konya, Turkey and Shahbaz Qalandar Lal in Sehwan Sherif in Pakistan.

Knowledge and Experience in the Islamic Tradition

'The Messenger of God (sall Allahu alaihi wa salem) said, "To acquire some useful knowledge is of greater merit than to perform a hundred devotional prayers voluntarily" (Related by Ibn Majah).

'The Messenger of God (sall Allahu alaihi wa salem) said, "A Muslim never gives a fellow Muslim a better gift than wisdom through which God increases him in guidance or turns him away from harmful behaviour" (Recorded by al-Baihaqi).

These two hadith (Prophetic Traditions) both underline the importance of knowledge and wisdom in Islamic thought. There are many similar traditions in which learning and the knowledge gained from learning are praised. For example, the Prophet (alaihi al-salatu wa al-salam) said:

'Pursue knowledge even to China, for its pursuance is the sacred duty of every Muslim' (Related by Ibn Abd al-Barr).

If pursuing knowledge is important in Islam, it is also important to understand what knowledge is. The word translated as 'knowledge' is ilm. Ilm is an important concept in the Islamic tradition. However, it is deeper and broader than mere information. Ilm is knowledge and wisdom based upon practice. To have ilm is not merely to know something, it is to understand what you know and then to put it into practice. In other words, ilm equals knowledge, wisdom and experience.

This is why the Prophet (alaihi al-salatu wa al-salam) is reported to have sought refuge with God from knowledge that was not beneficial. There is also a very interesting Qur'anic verse:

'So high [above all] is Allah, the Sovereign, the Truth. And, [O Muhammad], do not hasten with [recitation of] the Qur'an before its revelation is completed for you, and say, "My Lord, increase me in knowledge [rabbi zidni ilma]' (Surah Ta Ha 20:114)

Unfortunately, in the Pakistani context, this issue is, more often than not, brought to public attention through books with evocative titles but poor analytical content. Since 2001, it has caught the imagination of apocalyptic and often conceited interpretations (based on a handful of Islamist propagandists' dreadful claims) rather than PhD candidates, the latter explaining only to a certain extent the former. Consequently, the so-called 'Talibanization' of Pakistani society—now almost a decade old, if slightly rusty—is still fashionably perceived as having been brought about by a rogue Islamic state, frozen-in-time ulama, so-called tribal chiefs, unthinking, madrasa-trained students, and submissive women.

What Magnus Marsden successfully challenges is precisely the notion that Pakistan 'is a place brimming with unthinking village conformists and, thus, inevitably in the grip of Islamising fanatics'. If only one reason to read Living Islam was to be given, then, it is for the book's challenging account of how people pressurized in their day-to-day life by radical reformist preachers perceive and interact with what they label the 'bearded ones', 'narrow-minded' or 'hardened' Muslims. The puritan form of Islamization pursued by the Muttahida Majlis-e-Amal (MMA, the Islamist coalition in power in the North West Frontier

Province), similar in many ways to the Taliban's as far as its fight against profane culture is concerned, is regarded by the people Marsden met, 'Ismai'lis, as well as many Sunnis... as a threat to their way of being Muslims'.

This is all the more important because the area on which he focuses, the Chitral region bordering Afghanistan, is known to the scientific community at best only for its widely studied Kalash valleys, and at worst, to the general public for its association with the Taliban (who mobilised there, as the author mentions it), Bin Laden (whose presence in Chitral has been alleged by 'FBI sources' since 2003), or sectarian violence against its 30%-strong Ismai'li community. There are, nonetheless, far stronger reasons to read this book carefully. Its quality is the result of an intense personal but professional involvement with the area studied. For almost ten years, Marsden (presently Graduate Officer in Research at the Centre of South Asian Studies at the University of Cambridge) periodically visited Chitral, first, to teach English and learn the local language (Khowar) of this non-Pashto-speaking area, and eventually to conduct fieldwork for his PhD thesis. Interestingly, the subject of his thesis, on which the book is based, was suggested by companions during his discussions with them in Chitral itself. It thus articulates their own lines of questioning: exploring the reaction to and understanding of the growing influence of 'Islamizing forces' in their lives.

Years of carefully observing rural and urban life, listening to inhabitants discuss their anxieties and pleasures, and building individual bonds with them, have finally been translated into this sensitive and, in many respects, highly original work. Marsden takes us on an unusual journey—scientific but also literary and poetic—towards a better understanding of the 'critical responsiveness to 'Islamization'' in a rural Muslim society that is nonetheless infused with a deep knowledge of Islamic doctrine and respect for Islamic practices.

This allows him a wider spectrum of inquiry: the multidimensional vision of what a 'world made perfect by religion' encompasses in this particular social setting. This subtle anthropological study is also important because it has a strong thesis to defend—a phenomenon exceptional enough not to be passed over in silence. Its scientific stake (pari scientifique) can be rephrased as follows: to understand how Chitral's people handle the pressure to Islamize them requires a 'consideration of people's conceptions and experiences of the life of the mind, intellectual activity and emotional sensitivity'. This involves analytical variables that are still underestimated by sociological studies of Muslim societies' reaction to Islamism.

The relevance of Marsden's statement goes well beyond the Chitral case study: if 'being a Muslim in Chitral involves dynamic and creative processes, that reflect a complex interaction of decision-making, intellectual energy, debate and critical discussion, and ideally balanced levels of affect and emotion', this is unquestionably true for 'being a Muslim' in many other parts of Pakistan and elsewhere. It remains that this scientific intuition—impressive for the 22- or 23-year-old PhD candidate that Marsden was when he started studying the region in 1995—is all the more commanding because it springs from his own empirical observations. Indeed, what initially surprised him was the important role that music, poetry, and travel played in Muslim life in Chitral.

More decisively, he was struck by the level to which intellectual and emotional refinement was not only valued by people—men as well as women; urban residents in Chitral's main city, Markaz, as well as rural villagers, particularly in Rowshan; and even by the most 'extremist' among them, such as young ulama (dashman) trained in Peshawar's Deobandi madrasa or the Jamaat-i-Islami's sympathizers—but how it was also a decisive component in their questioning and debating the norms of spirituality and religious behaviour that they are called upon to change. The author defends his main thesis through a narrative choice, which constitutes, as well, a discrete but significant contribution to the anthropology of Islam. First, the book includes many unpublished or even un-translated beautiful verses of Khowar poetry.

Second, it is written as if, and rightly so, the only way to convey the 'complex nature' of Chitrali society's 'subjectivity' (or that of any Muslim society for that matter) is by letting the reader 'meet' some of the thought-provoking individuals he encountered. Without either attempting to categorize these characters or filling pages with unending quotations, he gracefully suspends his analysis and lets his object unveil itself. In other words, Marsden belongs to the small category of researchers who take seriously the explicit enunciations of their interviewees, of people such as Israr, an uneducated caretaker of a primary school, an alcohol drinker and hashish smoker, but considered by the villagers a 'deep thinker' for his contentious but thought-provoking comments on Islam. This is also true for the striking Arkhon sahib, a Deobandi alim and member of the Tablighi Jamaat, committed to purifying village life from immorality but who carefully explains how and why making amulets is permissible.

Marsden also introduces us to his friends' thoughts and feelings: Farhan, who educates his wife despite criticism from the other villagers, because he is convinced that his marriage will only be successful if she is able to talk about 'more interesting things than the health of her cows'; Aftab, the clean-shaven, onetime member of the Jamaat-i-Islami who is vocal in his criticism of the Taliban for their 'surface level interpretation of Islam' (and was once humiliated by one of their zealots who smeared black soot over his face in a public bus); Majid who, on the contrary, considers the Afghan militia the only true example of an 'Islamic system' yet enjoys passionate discussions on the meaning and place of Islam with his companions. There is also Mufti, follower of an Islamist party and a musical performer who thrills his audience by imitating and mocking mullahs and super-conservative Islamists, and was even threatened by Chitral's ulama with the charge of blasphemy.

And finally, there is the unforgettable Shabnam, the young Ismai'li village woman whose religious fervour was so strong that she braved her family's taboos and purdah to secretly go on a long journey alone just to 'catch a glimpse' of the Aga Khan in a nearby city. Why then do the people of Chitral, both Sunni and Isma'ili, understand a 'Muslim life' as one that has to be 'intellectually vibrant and emotionally significant' to be commendable? To address this particularly inventive problématique, and after presenting the multiple facets of village life, the book deals with the place of affection and emotions in living a moral Muslim life in a village, the pleasure taken from debating and 'the play of the mind', the shaping of new Muslim identities in musical gatherings in an urban setting, the multidimensional ways in which villagers think about the status and the role of 'men of learning and piety', and finally, sectarian relations and conflict between Sunnis and Ismai'lis. Instead of giving a summary of each chapter, I will focus on the methodological originality of Living Islam. Marsden embarks on an ambitious yet beguiling three-layered scientific task.

First, he aims to show how the interplay between intellect, the emotions, and body informs people's moral judgements and ideas of what a 'Muslim life' is or should be. As he puts it, 'in order to understand the full complexities of Muslim thought and identity, it is not possible to simply ask how Muslims think about the claim of faith: what is needed, rather, is an appreciation of the ways in which Muslims engage—intellectually and emotionally—with different classes of religious knowledge, and, importantly, to recognise that they often do so in deeply critical ways'. This thread leads to an important finding: the conventional way of classifying 'types of Muslims' (Islamist, traditionalist, fundamentalist, neo-fundamentalist, strict, modernist, liberal, Sufi, anti-Sufi, etc.) is simply untenable as far as Chitral's Muslims are concerned.

The people we 'meet' in Marsden's book are, as mentioned previously, revivalist Deobandi scholars who make love amulets, reformist Jamaat-i-Islami supporters who cultivate their reputations for being Sufis and love poets, musical performers (such as The Nobles band) who not only play and pray in the same space but also try to 'civilise' their fellow Muslims by 'broadening their minds'. It is undoubtedly refreshing to be called to recognise that 'Islamization is something other than a one-dimensional process of purification or standardisation'. In fact, the division that makes sense, as far as Rowshan villagers' conception of the different ways of being Muslim is concerned, is not 'reformist' versus 'liberal' but 'open-minded' versus 'narrow-minded'. This crucial distinction, which transcends other systems of categorization (educated/uneducated, young/old, men/women, Sunni/Ismai'li, etc.) is complex and subtle, and analyzed beautifully.

To be 'open-minded' is not to conform to a set of standards and by no means synonymous with 'Westernization'. Its sense is precisely shaped by the importance and value people give to the 'play of the mind', to genuine yet balanced emotions, and to tactfully yet cleverly expressive bodies. Therefore, those who are able to engage in critical conversation (and as such, to show a 'momentary indifference' towards 'personal religious belief'), to write moving and thought-provoking poetry, or to sing and dance to it, are viewed as closer to Islam than 'folks who have low thoughts about women and purdah, /…/ read too many religious books, and /…/ are over-emotional about religion'. In other words, living a mindful Muslim life means being 'intelligent' and this, in the view of Rowshan's residents, 'requires not only a fast mind /.../ but also a heightened sense of bodily feeling and intuition [and being able] to go beyond the surface-level words and get the sounds of the heart, for it is in the hidden depths of the heart that true thoughts are to be found'. This perception results from the strong influence Sufism enjoys in Chitral ('Islam is the knowledge of the heart', says a Chitrali man working in a carpet shop in Karachi to the author), but it is also linked to a lesser known dimension of Islamic morality. Its exploration constitutes the second scientific task of Living Islam, namely how the interplay between mind, emotions, and body is itself determined by a firm but variable distinction between the open and the hidden.

This includes an analysis of the difference between the home (ideally, the locus of affection and security) and outside environment (a place of tension and anxiety). However, the analysis goes beyond this common distinction, which addresses the village's moral and emotional landscape. Here, Marsden offers a remarkable anthropological examination of children's role (his account of the 'devilish' children who can turn villagers' relations 'upside-down' by disclosing secrets to which they have access in private homes, or who can become 'scoundrels', is an intellectual gem). He also discusses parental love, women's moral evaluations, illicit cross-gender friendships, education, and migration. The way people make moral valuations about these issues is structured by the necessity to maintain 'proper levels of emotion and affection' and by constantly negotiating the division between the hidden and open, secrecy and revelation, the inside and outside. Indeed, the hidden and open offer two sets of moral standards. This explains why a 'true Muslim' is commonly perceived in Rowshan not as someone who practices his religion regularly, but as someone who is sincere, compassionate, and self-sacrificing.

If the experience of undisclosed thoughts and emotions, secret knowledge and the 'everyday tactics of concealment' is an ongoing feature of Rowshan's moral life, then how and what to reveal or hide requires a constant decision-making process. This brings us to the third noticeable dimension of Marsden's anthropological exploration: how the complex triangle between the mind, heart, and body shapes not only moral valuations but also many practical dimensions of people's lives. Indeed, how to behave with the opposite sex, interact with neighbours and other religious communities, protect and enrich friendship, enjoy a satisfying family life, acquire an education (and what kind), conduct business (which could also be religious), and entertain are all crucial aspects where the meaning and the quality of a 'Muslim life' are not only put to the test but also thoroughly pondered on by Chitral's people.

The proper balances between mind, feelings, and body, as well as between the seen and the unseen, are key variables at play in making these day-to-day decisions. However, this is also a highly anxiety-provoking (anxiogène) process. A wrong decision, and especially one in small settings such as Markaz and Rowshan, can dramatically upset individual as well as social harmony, bringing shame and disrespect at a personal level or arousing sectarian tensions. The emphasis on anxiety is one of the most innovative and interesting topics of the book, although regrettably, it is discussed more implicitly than explicitly. The book's methodological choices are of particular significance: because they focus on dimensions other than religious practice, and on spaces other than the mosque or madrasa, they enable its author to challenge brilliantly the usual assertion that Islamic morality is, above all, about piety.

Debates in courtyards, buses, orchards and shops, musical gatherings, children's playful walks in the street, teachers' addresses in schools, men's greetings to each other at the bazaar, are among the many unusual sites from which the 'bodily experience, creative intellectual activity and sensory modes in contexts that appear to be something other than 'religious' are explored to illuminate the full complexity of the ways people construct Muslim personhood, and create and respond to revivalist visions of the Islamic tradition'. Living Islam's reading of sectarian conflict also brings forth valuable observations and innovative analysis. The issue is tackled from an unusual angle: how can the 'value of social harmony as well as discourses of difference' take shape simultaneously? In the first instance, sectarian violence in Chitral can be explained by tangible factors, that Marsden analyses in chronological detail, such as land disputes and individual politicized preachers (such as one of the provincial leaders of the Jamiat-i-Ulama-i-Islam [JUI]).

However, this is an inadequate explanation and the author recalls that violence grew out of underlying tensions between Sunnis and Ismai'lis regarding conceptions of women and purdah, religious education, and the status of the Sunni ulama. Actually, it is Marsden's anthropological focus on open/hidden dialectics and the normative evaluation of emotions, which offers the most interesting hypothesis regarding sectarian violence. This can be read as a useful addition rather than an alternative (as the author claims) to reading sectarian distinctions as being mainly fuelled by modern styles of education and mass literacy, which have 'objectified' and transformed Islam into a 'system' of different 'doctrinal clusters'. Living Islam shows that sectarian violence in Chitral has less to do with standardized education than with 'underlying anxieties about inner dimensions of life and self shared by both Ismai'lis and Sunnis'. This is so because not only is the division between open and secret knowledge at the heart of doctrinal differences between the two communities but, more importantly, because it is a critical dimension of the way in which the boundary between Ismai'lis and Sunnis in the village is constructed and maintained.

Indeed, Marsden maintains that many Sunnis in Rowshan and Chitral are torn between their conception of the village as one moral unit and pressure from Sunni authorities to display stronger religious commitment and feelings (even to convert Ismai'lis to the Sunni tradition). This is a crucial issue: such pressure means not only demarcating stronger boundaries between themselves and their Ismai'li neighbours but also being forced to constantly situate themselves in terms of the place that this boundary occupies in their lives. It implies, for instance, being compelled to make, again, stressful decisions regarding such routine activities as eating each other's food, attending each other's weddings, inviting or not inviting one's best friends to a religious event when s/he belongs to another tradition, etc.

Yet, Living Islam also shows that 'many Chitral Muslims negotiate religious difference through skilled mindful work on a daily basis, and one result of this is the generally peaceful nature of Ismai'li-Sunni relations in Chitral', notwithstanding episodes of terrifying violence. Insisting on factors that have the potential to prevent or diffuse violence, in settings where strong Ismai'li minorities cohabit with Sunnis, is another very valuable scientific as well political contribution of Living Islam. It reminds us that, at the village level (still widely conceptualized as a single moral unit), Ismai'lis and Sunnis join together in shared sources of faith and value as well as in the common pleasure of the play of mind and creative musical and intellectual performance. More strongly, Marsden underlies that Rowshan's concern about 'a thoughtful life of plurality' and 'the danger of excessive displays of inauthentic emotion' can act as a safeguard against sectarian violence.

The book offers other important empirical findings of interest to a wide range of researchers on Islam. Those working on Sufism will learn that the Sufi tradition in Chitral, surprisingly, 'focuses on intellectual and emotional engagement with Sufi texts and ideas, rather than ecstatic worship at shrines and affiliation to formalised Sufi lodges and brotherhood'. Those studying madrasa education will be interested to discover that, while it is valued by Chitral's people, it is also critically judged for its potential to upset 'young minds' balance between reason and emotion'. Social scientists studying 'jihadism', - and already suspicious of either the simplistic equation between poverty, lack of education, and the call for armed jihad or the assumed parental authorization that jihadist organizations claim they get before sending their recruits onto the battlefield -, might be satisfied with the following tale of an uneducated woman from Rowshan.

Worried that her younger son, studying in a Jamaat-i-Islami madrasa in Lahore, could go off to become a suicidal martyr in Kashmir, she sent her elder son to reason with him. What she was thoughtfully trying to do was redirect the young madrasa student's mental process towards his mother's love and care, fully aware that 'pernicious religious emotion' could lead him 'to deny family affective ties, act thoughtlessly and unreasonably'. Brilliant as it is, Living Islam has, like any other first academic work, certain shortcomings. There are recurring editorial mistakes. The book's outline is also a little confusing: we go back and forth between the village of Rowshan (not even located in the only given map of Chitral district) and Markaz city. If this distinction is important enough to determine the plan of the book, then a comparison of the difference and similitude between rural and urban 'ways of being Muslim' is surely lacking.

One also wonders why the author felt compelled to include such an encyclopaedic bibliographic and footnotes' apparatus. Its actual utility is doubtful as most of the references mentioned are brushed aside in footnotes as mere comparative elements. At the content level as well, some critical observations can be made not so much on the book's empirical findings (only an anthropologist working on

Pakistan's NWFP region could seriously evaluate these) as on its methodology, tone, and some analytical fault-lines. Although the work is otherwise methodologically very strong, the level of analysis remains strangely undefined and ambiguous all through the book. It seems that Marsden has not really been able to choose between the individual and the collective agent; the passage from one to the other is taken for granted. This leads to self-contradictions.

While he, somewhat condescendingly, calls upon his peers to recognize the importance 'of the independent self as a category for anthropological analysis', he often makes generalizations about 'the Rowshan people', 'the Chitral people', 'Sunnis', 'Ismai'lis', and 'Muslims', on the basis of a dozen individual cases. Generalizations are almost unavoidable and, in fact, welcome, but they should be based on a middle ground: in between isolated cases and 'the people', there are certainly distinct groups that can be identified by anthropological, sociological, political, or psychological indicators. The methodological mist is thickened further by abrupt explanations concerning certain crucial choices such as the decision not to explore the role that status distinctions play in the everyday religious and social lives of villagers; this is a critical component one would expect, even more so as it is presented as a 'source of considerable tension in present-day Rowshan'.

However, we are not only told that it was 'difficult to do so', but that, 'for ethical reason[s]', the author has decided not to focus on it. Without further explanation, one can only wonder what these 'ethical' reasons are. Living Islam also has, at some points, a tendency to essentialize its object. While Marsden is fully aware of the risk, when he states that a question of central importance for his book is 'how far ... the striking levels of intellectual vibrancy documented here [are] a reflection of Chitral's location within a unique frontier zone, or to what degree ... they challenge assumptions about the nature of religious thought and identity in rural localities in Pakistan and, indeed, other Muslim countries generally', he gives only an implicit answer, and one is left with the impression that the 'Chitrali Muslim' is an exclusive case compared to what is referred to in the book as 'down Pakistan'.

It is certainly not expected of the author to test how far his main findings are valid or typical for the entire country (a claim methodologically indefensible), but interacting with Pakistani society in other parts of the country or at least comparing his observations with other anthropological works on Pakistan would surely have helped him realise that many kinds of behaviour and opinions that he attributes to Chitral's peculiar geographical, social, and intellectual set-up are indeed very much in evidence elsewhere in the country. Anyone who has spent a significant amount of time in Pakistan (or in any other Muslim country) is not likely to be particularly impressed by the repeated and predictable assertion about the 'complex and multi-dimensional ways of being Muslim'.

The exemplary cases that the author analyzes are, in fact, an easily observable reality in Pakistan, from amulet-making Deobandi ulama encountered in Karachi and children playing cricket in a madrasa courtyard in Gujranwala, to a Lahore-based Islami Jamiat-i-Tulabah (the Jamaat-i-Islami's student wing) celebrating the urs of his pir once back in his family's village. Thus, if Marsden is absolutely right in criticizing the conventional classification of 'Muslims' (Islamists, liberals, etc.), he is wrong in assuming that only his case study proves how untenable they are. These rigid categories have indeed badly spoiled our understanding of the syncretistic traditions and the ambiguities of reformism in South Asian Islam as a whole. Imtiaz Ahmed, Barbara D. Metcalf, Vali Reza Nasr, and Yoginder Sikand, among others, have already made this point quite strongly. There are other analytical conclusions that could have been usefully enhanced by a comparative approach, not with Mali or Lebanon as Marsden does, but with other parts of Pakistan. One case in point is his analysis of sectarianism. For instance, the concrete factors that he identifies as being at the root of sectarian violence—land disputes and politicized preachers—have indeed already been emphasized in other studies of sectarianism in Pakistan. They also account for many acts of violence against Christians in Punjab.

Another case in point is Living Islam's discussion on the place occupied by the body in Chitrali people's perception. Again, in many other regions of Pakistan, it is also seen as 'something that bears the imprint of thought'. To limit myself to a place I know better, I often heard in Punjab that a disobedient daughter is ziddi-patli (stubborn and thin), as if her flesh was to be eaten by her 'selfish' thoughts. Similarly, women's dress and body language, men's gaze, and learned men's beard, are all the subject of 'stimulating discussion and emotional response' in which, and as much as in Chitral, Islamic morality is evaluated as a matter not of disciplinary practices but rather of the sincerity of one's intention (is the girl's niqab a disguise for meeting a lover incognito? is the maulwi's beard a cover hiding a big belly filled thanks to the devotees' money?).

It is also surprising that Richard Kurin's work, one of the rare sources available on the subject Marsden focuses on, is not even mentioned, although it shows how, in a central Punjab village during General Zia's time (and one that probably had a much lower level of literacy than in today's Chitral), what a valuable yet practicable 'Muslim life' could and should be. This was the focus of lucid discussion, as much as the relationship with religious authorities was subjected to funny tales. Actually, people's multidimensional perception of 'men of piety', on which the book rightly insists, is a general feature of any society where commitment to one's faith remains a central dimension of public life and is subjected to outsiders' moral valuation. To be sure, there are still hundreds of popular jokes in today's Pakistan about rigid and hypocritical displays of religious piety or licentious maulwis, which echo the amusement of Rowshan's people on observing the change in the young dashmanan's (learned man) bodily comportment.

Valuing intellectual creativity and the ability to sound the truth of the heart is far from being a distinct feature of a Muslim life only in Chitral; it is the strongest repellent to authoritarian, puritanical, and Wahhabi-oriented Islamization in many other parts of the country. Twenty years ago, Kurin was already asserting that the ability of Pakistani rural society to defy attempts to be 're-Islamized' was informed by people's perception of Islam as more of a core symbol than a specific theology or body of practice. Indisputably, Marsden stretches the argument much further and to deeper spheres; intellectual creativity, for instance, is an analytical variable, which was totally absent from Kurin's work. Yet, his focus on people's resistance to government-sponsored Islamization in Pakistan's rural areas is not as pioneering as he claims it to be.

In some parts of the book, a certain lack of intellectual humility also tends to damp the intense pleasure of reading its otherwise extremely fine analysis. This is not only confirmed by repetitive mention of the author's name in interviewees' quotations but also by lines such as 'I was able to make broad arguments about religious life and morality' or 'my account of Muslim life in Chitral differs, then, in striking and substantial ways from other treatments of the nature of Islamic tradition in contemporary Muslim-majority settings. Thus, this book's findings pose significant questions concerning /.../ how it is possible to account for diversity in the contemporary Muslim world'. Is the author really the first anthropologist to reflect upon 'diversity in the contemporary Muslim world'?

The reader is also led to believe, especially in the book's

introduction and conclusion, that Marsden has succeeded in challenging, and putting back on the right track, this impressive list of disciplines: the 'anthropology of religion', 'of Islam', 'of Islamic education', 'of sociality in Pakistan', 'of emotion, thought, the intellect, personality and morality', 'of ethics', and 'of cross-gender relations', as well as 'broader philosophical and political concerns about morality, political violence and religious tolerance', without omitting 'social sciences debates' on 'political Islam', 'so-called religious conflict', and 'the post colonial development state' (all statements extracted from the book). This can probably be explained by the fact that Living Islam is derived from a PhD thesis, an intellectual exercise whose introduction is generally bound to make catchy yet unattainable claims. Obviously, the demonstration cannot do, and could have never done, justice to over-ambitious promises spread through so many academic fields.

Living Islam's approach to the state is a case in point. While the author promises to contribute to a better understanding of the role played by 'the state and the machinery of state level politics' in communal violence and 'as a source of moral norm in South Asia', these dimensions are in fact absent from his analysis. The state 'appears' here and there in the shape of a local policeman or a soldier, but it is not discussed in any serious and systematic manner. This is regrettable because, undoubtedly, the state has to be 'brought back' into the study of sectarian conflict, not just as an instrumentalist policymaker (consider Zia's policies) but in implementing 'harsh regimes of political and religious subjection', in the way it represents 'minorities' (in textbooks and censuses), labels political tensions, represses its discontents, and implements conflict management.

This approach could have been usefully articulated to the local and personal level on which Marsden has invaluable empirical material.

The book's treatment of morality and emotion is similarly frustrating. Both are key variables but neither are theoretically discussed nor defined, merely taken as given. Consequently, moral categorizations regarding Islam (sahi, ja'ez, haram, etc.) are quoted as being interchangeable, although they are not. Similarly, if anxiety (pareshani), a feeling mentioned an innumerable number of times, is rightly understood as informing the very praxis of Chitrali Muslims, this is asserted, not demonstrated. How does anxiety not simply accompany, or colour, judgement and reasoned decisions, but is, actually, at the heart of the very process of shaping one's aspirations, defining choice, and constructing moral preferences?

This critical question is not answered, perhaps because addressing it would have inevitably pushed the author towards an interdisciplinary dialogue between anthropology, sociology, and psychoanalysis, one that he would prefer to avoid (as most social scientists persist in doing) even though another method of including the emotional variable in social science, without being tautological or merely descriptive, has yet to be invented. This is all the more regrettable as Marsden's ambition is, as he puts it, to 'demonstrate how it is possible to present anthropology of the embodied experience of thought'. This light treatment of the emotional variable is particularly manifest in Marsden's analysis of sectarianism. It emphasises that 'heightened states of religious emotion' and 'shared anxieties' are 'at the heart of the Sunni-Ismai'li conflict'.

This is an enticing hypothesis. But, although emotion and stress are made causal variables, the causal link is nowhere explained. For instance, we are told—and this is a decisive point—that it is not pressure from the radical ulama as such that people identify as the main root of sectarian violence, or even their inflammatory speeches in mosques, but instead the listeners' inability to control their emotional state or to maintain their critical intellectual activity so as to be able to see the 'real motivations behind the making of these speeches'. This is a useful reminder of the urgent need to include the individual subject in our understanding of 'Islamization' in Pakistan - of the need to articulate the macro to the micro level, a missing link in current theories of Islamist militancy – but, unfortunately, the thesis further is not stretched further. Therefore, Marsden succeeds in studying how people perceive sectarian tensions, rather than he explains what really generates them.

Finally, what is proclaimed as being a strongly critical appraisal of available studies on political Islam is indeed the weakest part of Living Islam? This is because the book fights the wrong enemy: Gilles Kepel and Olivier Roy are virtually the only references discussed, although they are neither specialists on Pakistan nor anthropologists. One wonders why, for instance, in a critical appraisal of the assessed role of madrasa education in Pakistan, only Kepel's opinions are quoted, rather than Jamal Malik's or Muhammad Qasim Zaman's (social scientists who are surely far more recognized authorities on the subject). It is also a little odd to criticize Roy's main thesis, namely the failure of political Islam, on the ground that it does not 'appreciate the extent to which religion and politics have fused even in the Western political entities'. In the same vein, why accuse him of failing to understand that the political and cultural diversity of Muslim societies explain the neo-fundamentalist movements' inability to bring about a homogenization of thought and practice?

Roy has never claimed to look at the societal response to Islamism but at its intrinsic ideological failure (much as Marsden chooses to focus on the former and consciously ignores the latter). Therefore, reproaching him to ignore the 'voices of Muslims who are themselves critical of emergent styles of Muslim thoughts and identity' is quite irrelevant. Unsurprisingly, therefore, Marsden's own analysis of Islamism or fundamentalism is quite disappointing. Firstly, he contradicts himself: after strongly criticizing Kepel for stating that madrasas 'brainwash' students and give them 'retrograde' worldviews, he himself explains that the very limited number of boys from Rowshan studying in madrasas is based on the villagers' perception that these institutions create 'narrow-minded' and 'brainwash' students . Secondly, 'Chitral's extremists' remain not only an elusive scientific category but also a faceless figure all through the book.

It is indeed surprising that the author, who seems to have conducted a lot of interviews and informal discussions, does not include any talks with the young dashmanan he mentions so frequently. This would have helped us grasp the perceptions held by local proponents of the need to politicize Islam (or Islamize politics). Instead, they are approached by default or in absentia through the many ways that people perceive them or, at best, through the comments of a young madrasa student's brother. The voice of only one local supporter of the Jamaat-i-Islami is heard briefly, and that too, only on poetry and music; a strict old Deobandi alim is cited, but again, only on amulet making. Moreover, being a Jamaati or Deobandi alim is of course different from being an active supporter of the Taliban! For this reason, Marsden's statement that, his 'book is also a contribution to the anthropological understanding of the form taken by the so-called 'Islamic revival' in the contemporary Muslim world' is hardly tenable.

The author could have been content enough to contribute—which he unquestionably does—to two very important fields of research: one, the anthropology of rural Islam, and two, Muslims' responsiveness to reformist movements. As he rightly points out, the intellectual life of village Muslims has very rarely been the focus of anthropological research and, as far as Pakistan is concerned, has never been explored until his own attempt to do so. In addition, this is the first extensive anthropological work on societal responsiveness to 'Islamization' in Pakistan. 'I have shown', writes Marsden 'that /.../ the Chitral people I know all felt that the life of a good Muslim is a mindful life, in which the play of refined and emotionally sensitive thought processes is and should be a critical element of everyday human interaction'.

This is indisputably a crucial input to our understanding of 'Muslim personhood' in a world where, as the author rightly recalls, faith counts. Anyone interested in Pakistani society should also pay close attention to one of the book's main findings: the perceived deficiencies in village morality, something local people lament so deeply, are rarely accounted for in terms of 'failure to conform to Islamic values'. Lack of parental care or suffocating parenthood, poverty, unemployment, and boredom are all blamed for this. The present study of people's 'normative assessments' regarding Islam is, therefore, an extremely important reminder that Islamic morality is not only a much more complex and intricate sphere than the Taliban's programme of 'preventing vice and promoting virtue', but also that many Muslims are fully aware of it. For all these reasons, Living Islam undoubtedly joins the very selective group of groundbreaking academic books recently published on Islam in Pakistan. It deserves to become a 'classic' and I sincerely hope it will be.

4

Islamic Religious Foundations

As we already approach the twenty-first century, few challenges loom larger in the search for justice and world peace than the achievement of mutual understanding among nations, cultures, and religious traditions. For people who profess faith in a sovereign God, few responsibilities are more urgent than that of moving toward a sympathetic appreciation of other faiths. The more our world grows, the more rapidly it seems to shrink, so that we must at the very least learn to cope with the fact of diminishing religious and cultural elbowroom. One of the increasingly visible features on the international landscape is the religion known as Islam, with it's nearly three-quarters of a billion adherents.

A major question for Christians with respect to Islam is this: How can we begin to learn about so massive and expansive a phenomenon without resorting to the convenient but unjust stereotypes one hears so often, caricatures that amount to little more than a new form of religious bigotry or racism? Three more specific questions present themselves. First, what do Muslims have in common with other avowedly religious people across the world? Second, how do Muslims define themselves as a distinct community of faith unique among religions? And third, what possibilities for spiritual growth has Islam offered historically to the individual believer? The image of a spiritual journey will provide a framework within which to respond to these questions. As citizens of the world, Muslims discern God's signs in nature, the broad terrain on which they journey. As members of a unique community of faith, they discover God's signs preeminently in their scripture, the Qur'an, and in their history; this scripture and history map out for them the main road, the "straight way."

As individual believers, Muslims look for God's signs within themselves, where the signs mark off the path each person must walk before God. In all three instances the signs are illumined by the light of God's all-encompassing revelation. Believers strive to respond to that revelation by taking one more step across the terrain of creation, down the "straight way" of Islam's special history, and along the path of personal sanctification and self-knowledge, all in a journey back to the Lord of the universe. Both the imagery of God's threefold revelation and that of journey and light are rooted in the Qur'an. "We will show them Our signs on the horizons and in their very selves, until it becomes clear to them that it is the Truth". And: "On the earth there are signs for those of firm faith, and in your very selves. Will you not then see?". In addition, the Arabic term that is used for "verse" of scripture (ayah) also means "sign," thus suggesting that the Qur'an also is one great sign replete with more specific signs. In response to each of the three questions I have posed above, I will introduce further texts of the Qur'an that unite all three elements of the imagery of journey, sign, and light.

If readers are willing to accept the possibility that God has spoken, and continues to speak, to human beings who are not Christians, let them read on. My premise here is that, for reasons known only to the Creator, God has desired to make his word known to a faith community whose members call themselves Muslims. He is not some "other" God who speaks Arabic, Persian, Turkish, and a host of other tongues which Muslims speak all over the globe. For the Arabic word Allah simply means "God," the very Deity to whom we pray. Now to the first question: How do Muslims perceive and respond to God's signs on the horizons?

Signs on the Horizons

Behold, in the heavens and the earth is signs for those who believe. And in your creation, and all the wild creatures He has scattered over the earth, are signs for a people of firm faith. And the alternation of night and day, and the sustenance that God sends down from the sky, quickening thereby the earth after her death, and the ordering of the winds — these are signs for a people who understand. Divine revelation in nature appears in Islam's scripture as the "terrain" on which the journey of humanity takes place, the heavens and the earth as alluded to in the word horizons. Human response at this level we may characterize as a universal or cosmic experience expressed in a creation — inspired language and system of symbols that describe the journey of all creation from God and back to God.

According to an Islamic tradition, called a "Sacred Saying," God once said: "I was a hidden treasure and I desired to be known, so I created the world." In that world all nonhuman creatures are essentially "muslim" in that they "surrender" to God by their very nature. Human beings must make the choice as to whether they will surrender. Once they choose to submit and respond gratefully (thus becoming muslims through their response of "islam", human beings rather naturally express their response in ritual and symbol that are at once common to other religious traditions and also distinctively Islamic. In themselves these practices are not uniquely Islamic, but they bear an Islamic stamp to the extent that they are integral to the faith-response of a community explicitly gathered by God's revelation as delivered through Muhammad in the Qur'an.

This aspect of Islamic religious experience we will take up in the next segment of this discussion. For now, let us look at some of the ritual and symbolic ways in which Muslims express their response to the "signs on the horizons." Fasting is a nearly universal religious practice. Each year, during the lunar month of Ramadan (movable in relation to our calendar), Muslims break their regular life-patterns by abstaining from food and drink from dawn to sunset each day, a period that averages fifteen to seventeen hours. The discipline of refraining from creation's means of sustenance is a reminder of one's greater need of God, a need that even creation itself cannot fill. It presupposes that one is also refraining from forbidden words and actions and thoughts, such as envy or hatred. Compassion for those who habitually suffer from hunger, greater ability to go against one's own less noble tendencies, and the removal of obstacles in one's relationship to the Creator are among the most desired effects of the fast.

Almsgiving likewise is commonly practiced among religious people the world over. Muslims have the conviction that creation is not a permanent possession, but merely given to humankind as a "loan." That conviction prompts the response of sharing God's own wealth. Muslims "give God a loan" in return and seek to steward creation by giving freely what they have freely received. The root meaning of the word for almsgiving in Arabic, zakat, is "to purify oneself," in the sense that one must strive never to lay claim to what belongs only to God. One must not "overflow one's banks" by imagining he or she is the source or owner of created goods. Almsgiving is therefore meant not to give a person the good feeling of being generous, but to remind the Muslim of who first gave all to him or her. Before each of the five daily prayers, Muslims perform a ritual ablution. It is another facet of the purification that almsgiving presupposes. The action involves the use of that universal symbol of cleansing – water. But if water is not available, one may use sand or pebbles. The important thing is to make use of some earthy object as a physical reminder of the overall, inner and outer, purification that is itself an integral part of a proper relationship with God and his creation.

Daily ritual prayer with its orientation toward Mecca is another way of expressing a right relationship to the created world. Mecca is a symbolic axis of the world, a spiritual center, the meeting place of heaven and earth from which all creation radiates. Orientation to one of the cardinal points of the compass or to a particular "spiritual center" (such as Jerusalem in Judaism, for example) is evidenced in many major religious traditions. When Muslims pray together on Friday at noon, or whenever they gather in a mosque for congregational prayer, they express their right relationship with each other by lining up in rows as they face Mecca. Finally, the five daily ritual prayers sanctify time as well as space, as a round of concrete reminders that morning, noon, and night are a gift of God. Pilgrimage to Mecca, ideally to be made once in a lifetime if one possesses good health and sufficient means, is meant to acknowledge the unity and absolute equality of all. It is the symbol par excellence of the journey of God's people back to the source. Including such rituals as change of garb and cutting of hair, the journey gives physical expression to the need for a change of heart and mind. Pilgrim goals vary from one religion to another, but they are all symbolic of the journey to the center of creation.

According to Qur'an 6:39, "those who reject Our Signs are deaf and dumb and in profound darkness. God allows going astray whom He will, and He places on the Straight Way whom He will." One of the Qur'an's most beautiful images provides both a background and a foreground against which to appreciate the Muslim response to signs on the horizons:

God is the Light of the heavens and the earth. The likeness of His Light is as a Niche [the symbol of orientation to Mecca on the back wall of every mosque, as well as a symbol of the human heart] in which there is a lamp. The lamp is within a glass which is like a shining star enkindled from a blessed olive tree, neither of East nor West, whose oil would glow almost of it even if no fire touched it. Light upon Light! And God guides to His Light whom He will.

The Qur'an as Sign

These are the signs [verses] of the clear Scripture. We have sent it down as an Arabic Qur'an. Perhaps you will understand. (Qur'an 12:1-2)

Muslims believe, as do Christians, that the most significant events in human history are precisely those events that define their history. If the "signs on the horizons" describe the terrain in which God reveals himself, the historical fact of the Qur'an as revealed to Muhammad between 610 and 632 is for Muslims the opening to the main road on which they as a community journey. "Lead us along the Straight Way," Muslims pray five times daily and on the many other occasions when they recite the opening chapter of the Qur'an. One might describe Muslims' response to God's revelation in "an Arabic Qur'an" as a communitarian experience expressed in a confessional (or kerygmatic) language and symbol-system. Their experience is that of being Muslims in a world where most people are not. Terms of membership are definitive; although there is a good deal of latitude in practice, for we are talking about a tradition that crosses many ethnic and cultural boundaries, they call for a deliberate choice either for or against membership.

How do Muslims define themselves as a unique community of faith? What is distinctively Islamic about Islam? Reduced to the most fundamental terms, to be a Muslim is to adhere to God's revelation in the Qur'an as spoken by the Prophet Muhammad. "We have sent a Messenger into your midst and from among you, to recite [that is, make a Qur'an, a recitation] to you Our Signs . . . and to teach you the Book and Wisdom" (Qur'an 2:151). But if the matter were all that simple, I would probably not have written this article, and surely no one would be reading it. History has a way of making life enormously complicated. During the course of nearly fourteen centuries, Islam has come to embrace a remarkable variety of cultural and ethnic entities. As the world of Islam expanded, it became more and more evident to Muslims that neither the text of the Qur'an, nor the paradigmatic words and deeds of Muhammad enshrined in the community's collective memory, corresponded item for item with the new issues that surfaced with changing times and circumstances.

Therefore, the two prime sources of Islamic tradition, the scripture and the Prophetic Example (called the Sunnah in Arabic), had to be adapted and reinterpreted continually. Islam's religious history is the composite story of how those adaptations and reinterpretations have unfolded. In order to appreciate something of the Islamic experience of unity in diversity, it will be necessary to explore some of the implications of Muslims' evolving understandings, first, of the Prophet Muhammad and the issue of leadership and authority as it arose after the Prophet's death; and, second, of the Qur'an and the problems attendant on the need to implement it in daily Islamic life. I shall introduce each of these considerations with an appropriate text from the Qur'an, so as to situate both the Prophet and the Qur'an in the context of our journey, sign, and light imagery. We turn, then, to the role of the Prophet and the question of community leadership.

He [God] is the One Who sends manifest Signs to His servants, that He might lead you from the depths of darkness into the Light ... O you who believe! Be mindful of your duty to trust in His Messenger, and He will bestow on you a double portion of His Mercy: He will provide for you a Light by which you shall walk and He will forgive you ... (Qur'an 57:9 and 28)

It was one thing to trust in God's messenger while he lived; it was yet another to know whom to trust as Muhammad's successor. Muhammad's death thrust the young Muslim community into a protracted debate over the criteria of legitimate succession, a debate that gave rise to a diversity of opinion that would also have serious implications for the practical implementation of Qur'anic legislation, as we shall see shortly. According to sources compiled as much as two or three centuries after the Prophet's death in 632, two predominant approaches to the problem of succession emerged. One group held that the Prophet had named his son-in-law Ali to be his caliph ("successor," "vicar").

The other, convinced that Muhammad had made no such appointment, opted for an elective procedure. Abu Bakr, Muhammad's father-in-law, emerged as their choice. Ensuing developments are much too involved to detail here. In brief, the group that supported Ali came to be known as the Shi'ah (that is, party) of Ali. Those who backed Abu Bakr formed the nucleus of what is known now as the "People of the Sunnah and the Assembly," or the Sunni Muslims. The distinction between Sunni and Shiite is not the only mark of diversity within Islam. Within each of these groups there are significant subdivisions. I will mention the most important variations among Sunnis shortly, in the context of variant interpretations of the Qur'an. Here I would like to give a brief sketch of the two principal Shiite groups.

Major differences between the two largest segments of Shiite Islam crystalized around the second half of the eighth century. Until that time, both agreed that the authority to lead the community was vested in a hereditary succession of six descendants of Muhammad, beginning with Ali. In 765, the sixth Imam, or spiritual leader, died; and a dispute arose over who would be his legitimate heir. One group pledged allegiance to the sixth Imam's older son, even though he had died before his father did. They effectively terminated the official line of succession with this seventh Imam, and hence are known as "Seveners" (or Isma'ilis, after the seventh Imam, Isma'il). The Seveners are now found, for example, in East Africa, Pakistan, and India, and are headed by the Agha Khan.

A second faction chose to follow the man whom the sixth Imam designated after the death of Isma'il. This faction continued the line of succession down to the disappearance of the twelfth Imam in 873. Hence, they are now known as the "Twelvers." They constitute the vast majority of the population of Iran and about half that of Iraq. Shi'ism has been Iran's state religion since the sixteenth century. For both the Seveners and the Twelvers, religious experience has been decidedly millenialist. A strong messianic hope awaits the return of the last Imam (either the seventh or the twelfth), who will inaugurate a new age in which all believers will benefit from the Imam's redemptive suffering and that of the whole family of the Prophet.

However, to say that Shiite spirituality is very much involved with the concept of redemptive suffering is not to say that Shiites are motivated by some sort of "martyr complex," as the news media have often alleged in recent years. "Martyr complex" simply does not do justice to the willingness people have shown, in many ages and in many religious traditions, to die for what they believe in. What I have said thus far is but a superficial glance at some immensely intricate historical developments; but we must move on to consider the Qur'an. It is not fitting that God should speak to a human being except by inspiration [a technical term used for the revelation given to a prophet], or from behind a veil, or by the sending of a Messenger to reveal, by God's leave, what God wills.... And thus we have, by our command, sent an inspiration to you [Muhammad].

You knew neither what the Scripture was, nor what the Faith was. But we have made it [the Qur'an] a Light by which we guide such servants of ours as we will. And truly you [Muhammad] guide them to the Straight Way, the Way of God, to Whom belongs whatever is in the heavens and whatever is on earth.... (Qur'an 52:51-53)

The light of the Qur'an's guidance is the primary touchstone against which Muslims must judge the authenticity of their faith and action. Some texts of the scripture provide explicit regulations regarding matters of personal and social morality as well as ritual. But the Qur'an is not primarily a legislative handbook. Very early in Islamic history, local communities faced issues on which the book gave no specific ruling. The most pressing problem for the community was then, as now, how to interpret the sacred text in such a way as to preserve its spirit and still respond to new needs.

From about the late seventh century, the community as a whole began elaborating various interpretative principles and procedures. Schools of thought, each with its own peculiar emphasis on one or another aspect of legal reasoning, began to take shape. All agreed that the Qur'an and the Prophetic Example (Sunnah) were fundamental; but the schools differed in the relative stress they placed on community or scholarly consensus, private opinion, and analogical reasoning. By the end of the ninth century several distinct and formally constituted legal methodologies had come into being. Today, Sunni Muslims consider the four extant schools – the Malikite, Hanifite, Hanbalite, and Shafi'ite – equally acceptable and "orthodox." More than one school may be found in a given Islamic country, but one generally predominates; for example, Morocco, Turkey, Saudi Arabia, and Indonesia are dominated, respectively, by the schools listed above.

In cases for which no explicit solution can be found either in the Qur'an or in the Sayings of Muhammad (Hadith), the Sunni schools usually leave the final decision to scholarly or community consensus, rather than to the judgment of an individual legal authority. Shi'ites, who do not recognize the Sunni schools of law, vest overriding legal competence in some individual whom they consider to be divinely sanctioned by reason of a spiritual-genealogical link to Muhammad, via the descendants of Ali. The point I want to make is that Islam is not now, and never has been, the monolithic religion many outsiders have thought it to be. For although the historic revelation of the "straight way" demands an exclusive commitment to a single and unique community of faith, the meaning of that original call has for many centuries been variously interpreted.

Hence, it is neither fair nor accurate to equate Khomeini's approach to Islam with that of Sadat, or that of Qaddafi with that of Pakistani President Ziya al-Haqq or Wallace D. Muhammad, a leading figure in the World Community of Islam in the West. All things considered, we may say that the Islamic religious experience of God's signs in the historic scripture, revealed through the historic personage Muhammad, has been mediated through the community's ongoing experience of reinterpretation as required to keep the spirit of both the primordial revelation and the paradigmatic leader alive and growing.

Signs within the Individual

On the terrain of creation, God lays open the main road of the Muslim community's unique and exclusive history. Believers discover and set out on that road in the company of others. But Islamic tradition has not denied the individual person either the right and exhilaration or the requirement and risk of exploring and journeying alone before God. Community supports the individual's desire to acknowledge God's signs, for God has created an affection between the hearts of believers such as all the riches on earth could never effect (Qur'an 8:63); but the choice must be made and renewed in the solitary heart. The individual experiences the light of faith, which God casts into the core of his or her being, as a personalized gift, often articulated in mystical language and symbol-system. The expression is "mystical" in the sense that it describes, in Hodgson's definition of mysticism, an "inward personal experience, more or less transitory as an event but enduring in relevance, which is felt to express or lead to a special authoritative and normative relation between individual and cosmos."

The term includes much more than ecstatic experience, but it does not rule out experiences that are usually associated with the "great mystics" of any religious tradition. An important and sometimes controversial element in Islamic tradition has been the Sufi Path. Although Sufism has witnessed the development of a great variety of formally constituted religious orders, the Sufi Path is not itself an institution. It is the personal counterpart to the main road of the revealed law (called the Shariah) which circumscribes the Islamic community as a whole. Both in the more technical handbooks on Sufi doctrine and practice and in the intensely personal poetry of some of Islam's "great mystics," the individual appear as a wayfarer on a course designed uniquely for him or her. It is the journey of a love relationship between servant and Master, creature and Creator. Authors of Sufi manuals elaborated a number of psycho spiritual typologies to describe the various "stations" and "stages" along the path. But they all agree that intimate knowledge of God is the crucial ingredient in the experience. (I must point out here that I know of no clear connection between classical forms of Islamic Sufism and the "Sufi Numbers" or "Enneagrams" that have gained some popularity in recent years.)

Guidance along the path comes ultimately from God, as does the community's guidance along the main road. Sometimes, however, the wayfarer needs counsel tailored to individual temperament and gifts. The theory and practice of spiritual direction in Islam are highly developed.

That topic would require its own treatment elsewhere; but it is definitely a matter we Christians, and especially Catholic religious, could very profitably explore. Muslims not formally affiliated with religious orders, as well as members of orders, have sought and received spiritual direction from a shaykh (spiritual guide) either in person or by letter. Some of the material needed for a thorough study of the subject is beginning to be made available, and there is much more still to be edited and translated. Sufism's emphasis on individual religious experience, on the ability to recognize and interpret the "signs within the self," has had considerable influence on the broader range of Islamic popular piety.

Whether for good or ill, the growing popularity and esteem of certain early Sufi shaykhs soon transformed some of them into saints in the eyes of the people. A cult of the saints grew up, often encouraging pilgrimages to a holy person's tomb in the hope of receiving boons and miracles of all kinds. Sunni Islam has never officially sanctioned the cult of the saints the way Shi'ite Islam has recognized popular reverence at the tombs of the Imams, but both devotional practices appear very much a part of popular piety and are probably here to stay for a long time. What I have proposed here is a synthetic model. Nowhere do the primary Islamic sources analyze Islamic religious experience precisely this way.

This model is therefore a reconstruction; but the materials — the language and imagery of journey, sign, and light — are Islamic in inspiration. So long as one is aware of the limitations inherent in such models, they can be drafted appropriately into service as vehicles for cross-cultural understanding. Even so, the reader may as yet see no realistic way of setting out on the journey described in these pages. It may seem impossibly compromising, perhaps bordering on an outright betrayal of one's allegiance to Christianity. In the sequel to this article I will offer some reflections as to how twentieth-century Christians can go forth on this journey, knowing that, although it is not without its terrors, it will also have rewards as yet untold.

The Growing Religion

In the early seventh century when Islam shone forth from the land of Ishmael many flocked to its blindingly simple teachings of the uncompromising unity of God, and man's duty to live for others. It is surely one of the greatest miracles of history that from the backwater of Arabia there should have exploded a group of men, Companions of a Prophet, who within the space of a few brief decades were able to create a magnificent civilisation extending from the Pyrenees to the gates of China. Even more astonishing is the fact that this remarkable transformation came about peaceably. The Byzantine historians record of the Muslims an almost miraculous degree of religious toleration during this period, for Muslims were deeply immersed in the Qur'anic spirit of tolerance which declares, "There shall be no compulsion in religion" Qur'an, The Cow 2:256. It is almost impossible for the modern mind to comprehend some of the actions of the early Companions. When the Caliph 'Umar heard that a church had been demolished by a group of Muslims in the distant Syrian mountains and a mosque erected in its stead, he grew angry and issued an order for the demolition of the mosque, and commanded the renegade tribesmen responsible to rebuild the church with their own hands.

The Christian clergy wrote in astonishment of the new spirit of brotherhood which filled the East after the retreat of the Byzantines, who were long resented for their extortionate taxes and religious intolerance towards the Monophysite and Arian churches. The Muslim world became a place of refuge for all manner of religious dissent in Europe: Arians, Cathars, and Jews. In the same vein, that the Mongol/Tartar invaders of the thirteenth and fourteenth centuries ended up adopting the religion of the conquered, attests to the natural appeal and strength of Islam. History hardly bears out the prejudice still common in the West that Islam is to be dismissed as a religion of scimitar-waving fanatics; rather it is Europe, the land of the Inquisition, the Crusades, and the rape of the Americas, which emerges with the more sanguinary record. Islam's tolerance springs in fact from the pluralistic vision of the Qur'an. As we have already seen, Muslims recognise the genuineness of the messages of Moses and Jesus, and allow them to live in accordance with their own beliefs. To demolish a church or a synagogue, or to convert such a building into a mosque, is almost impossible under Islamic law. Thus Christian communities still flourish in the Arab world more than fourteen hundred years after the appearance of Islam. Yet one is permitted to ask: how many Muslims were suffered to remain in Andalusia after the Catholic Reconquest?

Islam the Practical Religion

Most people judge a religion by its practical effects on the lives of those who practice it, and this attitude undoubtedly does much to explain why, wherever Muslim travellers and merchants penetrated, they left in their wake communities of new believers. Far outside the limits of Islam's political sway, convert communities soon established themselves, in cities as remote as Budapest and Shanghai. The early Muslim voyagers' presence profoundly impressed those who had dealings with them, as they clearly possessed qualities which set them apart from others. Their characteristics of honesty, gentleness, and kindness to children excited curiosity and respect. A tranquility balanced by action, a life as industrious as it was prayerful. Their cities contained places of worship of the most sublime peace and symmetry, and also lively markets built right up to their walls: a perfect symbol of the Muslims society and of his vision of the universe. This equilibrium of character was the consequence of the subtle interplay of a variety of factors which resulted from the internalisation of the Qur'anic message.

Islam is a complete system of individual and collective life. There is no division between the sacred and the secular. The world is a manifestation of the attributes of the Divinity, and every human activity must ultimately reflect this. Islam provides man with a spiritual technology by which he may come to know his Creator, thereby fulfilling the function for which he was made, and it is precisely because this process is of such overriding importance that the function of society must rise above that of the provision of man's material needs and must seek to provide him with the best possible environment in which to carry out this project of self-discovery and realisation. Thus taking on the worldview of Islam has another positive implication, which is political in nature and today highly controversial. For the Muslim his belief leaves no room for arrogance and the lust for power; indeed he is enjoined to stand out against tyranny and injustice where he encounters them. The ungodly mind is always driving for the acquisition of absolute authority, which for the believer is the prerogative of God alone. Wherever he can, he endeavours to establish a government which sees itself as the mere representative of a higher power, a government whose movements are kept within the precincts of justice by its necessary commitment to the ethical ideals laid down by God.

Finding a Place in the Cosmos

As most converts to Islam will explain, the reason for their conversion is not usually pinpointed to one set reason, but several, with each individuals journey being unique. Islam has appealed to many because of its simple and intellectually satisfying creed. In the Byzantine controlled lands, Islam offered freedom from imperialist and racist oppression and the cult of priesthoods; in India, the fact of intrinsic human worth, nobility and equality attracted a society steeped in caste division; in Indonesia and Africa, Islam displaced a complex mythology which often pictured the world as alien, frightful, and full of spirits which had to be appeased and a social order which tolerated infanticide and never saw the nakedness of the body and the need to clean it. In our own day, Islam has an appeal to many in the so-called "developed" world who have become disenchanted with a mysterious and amorphous Christianity on the one hand and the insatiable demands of materialism on the other. Many also come to Islam to find liberation from racism and oppression.

The most immediately felt impact of his faith, on the newcomer to Islam, is invariably a sense of finding a place in the cosmos. The value of his life is immediately measurable by his intellect and spirit in terms of its conformity to God's will, as we are reminded of it in the Qur'an.

Direction and Discipline

For the Muslim the conviction that absolute truth is to be discovered through a certain way of life inspires an emotion of true freedom and independence. Obedience is due to God alone, and no man can hold mental sway over the believer. And as he learns to discipline himself in accordance with God's will, he begins to free himself from the blind dictates of the body, which always cries out for immediate gratification of the need for food and sex. The believer is enabled to control his physical form rather than be controlled by it. This quality, which is a prerequisite for spiritual growth, is also of inestimable worth in pursuing one's material interests.

Lack of Priesthood

In Islam there is no rite of initiation, no sacrament of belief. It is a faith of the individual, which transforms societies. And it is a faith without intermediaries, without the spiritual brokerage of a priestly class or monopolised by a formal hierarchy of clergymen; rather it cascades historically from the prophets to the generations of mankind through men and women who by their own spiritual strivings, rather than through any formal liturgical function, are inwardly invested as saints. Yet another benefit arising from the Muslim's religious orientation is the knowledge and certainty that all that takes place in his daily round is by God's leave. He is thus enabled to meet any misfortune that may overtake him far more stoically that the man of weak faith, for he knows that all things are by the will of God, which is the unfolding of His knowledge, and that, as the Prophet (PBUH) said, "When God loves His servant, He send trials upon him." Every misfortune thus takes on an aspect of purification and atonement rather than being the inexplicable and random operation of fate. This is not to be confused with the traditional belief held by many Westerners that Islam is a religion of fatalism and apathy, for Muslims are constantly exhorted by the Qur'an to act. Rather, it constitutes a means of consolation for those whose faith is pure and who perceive the workings of Providence in all the vicissitudes of life.

Racial Equality

Islam has never been the monopoly of one particular race or nation. The Prophet Muhammad (PBUH) had said to the tribesmen of Makkah, "I am the Messenger of God sent to you and to humanity at large." When we look at a map of the modern world we find that the great majority of Muslims are not Arabs, the racial community into which the Prophet (PBUH) happened to have been born. Eighty-five percent of his communities are of other stock, including Turks, Africans, Indonesians, six million Europeans, and seven million Americans. And never has there ever been any consciousness of race in Islam, for the Qur'an teaches that all are one family, and that "the most noble in God's sight is he who fears Him most." Likewise, the Prophet affirmed, "there shall be no distinction between white and black." The capacity, not for change, but for expansion, undoubtedly constitutes a key factor in Islam's continuing dynamism. For other faiths busily reforming themselves to such a degree that they would be unrecognisable to the faithful of an earlier generation, have thereby lost confidence in those spiritual and ethical teachings which by their very nature challenge the world, and may not be challenged, which transform, and are not transformed. Islam approached on its own terms and not through the distorting images of the lives of lapsed or disorientated Muslim or of the intense and hostile propaganda, will always be a potent summons to the free, rational and natural good state of man regardless of habitat and time.

5

Theology of Islam

The Five Pillars

First Pillar (Ash-Shahadah) [Two Testimonies]

La ilaha illah'Llah: There is no deity save God

Muhammadun rasulu'Llah: Muhammad is the Messenger of God.

These two phrases which punctuate and transform the Muslim life, sum up fully the theology of the Islamic religion and function as a sort of miniature creed. Every Muslim is required to affirm that "there is no deity save God" and that "Muhammad is the messenger of God." By implication more than by statement, the first testimony declares the unity of the metaphysical, while the second is the gate to what that unity implies. Full membership of the world community of Islam consists in the uttering of these two statements. Nothing more, nothing less. In Islam there is no rite of initiation, no sacrament of belief. It is the faith of the individual, who by their own spiritual strivings, rather than through any formal liturgical function, climb upwards along the spiritual ladder.

The Shahadah distinguishes between other-than-God and God himself, and it brings the former - all that appears to be 'other' - back to its origin and true identity. Perfect incomparability means that nothing can be set beside the

Incomparable. According to the Hadith Qudsi (one of the directly inspired sayings of the Prophet), "Allah was, and there was nothing beside Him"; to which Ali (the cousin of the Prophet) is said to have added: "And He is now even as He ever was." The Shahadah is not only doctrine; it is also practice - or the key to practice. Its truth is something to be assimilated and lived, which is why, when we speak of the Islamic Credo, we are speaking, not of an abstraction, but of the way in which men and women order their whole lives, their waking and their sleeping, their work and their rest, the words they use in speaking to one another and the gestures they make in loving one another, the planting of a seedling and the reaping of a crop, the turning on of a tap from which water flows and its turning off, and the life and death of all creatures.

To understand how decisive this formula is one must observe the place it occupies in the life of the ordinary Muslim, who will pronounce these words in every crisis and at every moment when the world threatens to overwhelm him, as he will when death approaches. A pious man seized by rage, will appear suddenly to have stopped in his tracks as he remembers the Shahadah, and as it were, withdraws, putting a great distance between himself and his turbulent emotions. A woman crying out in childbirth wills suddenly fall silent, remembering; and a student bowed anxiously over his desk in an examination hall, will raise his head and speak these words, and a barely audible sigh ot relief passes through the whole assembly. This is the ultimate answer to all questions.

"Truly unto Allah we belong and unto Him we return" Qur'an, The Cow 2:156

There is no Deity save God

Pure Monotheism

No object of worship save God, no conditioner of meaning apart from Him; the most perfect articulation of what lies forever beyond the reach of language. The first testimony negates the existence of each and any false god and condemns false worship as the world "illah" means "god" or whatever is worshipped, and could refer to any being, person, matter, or concept which is taken as an object of adoration or worship, whether this is done out of love or fear. But "illah" as the Qur'an cautions us could also refer to our whims or desires. To succumb or surrender totally to whims and passions is in effect to worship them and to take them as gods.

The testimony that La ilaha illah'Llah, though given outwardly through revelation as a 'reminder', can be regarded as inherent in the deepest layer of human nature. This is the encounter with Reality in the manner to which we are predisposed by our nature - and destined through our actions - to encounter. Face to face with reality in its most compelling manifestation, the 'denier' is unavoidably a 'believer'. "On the Day when the deniers are exposed to the Fire [they will be asked]: 'Is not this real?' They will say: 'Yea, by our Lord!'" Qur'an, Winding Sand-tracts 46:34 Only in dreams can the Lord be denied, only through self-deception can Reality be entirely veiled. "as for the deniers, their actions are like a mirage in a desert. The thirsty one taketh it for water, till he cometh to it and findeth it nothing, and findeth in its place Allah, who payeth him his due..." Qur'an, Light 24:39. On every horizon, at the end of every road and in every secret chamber, there is the Face, inescapable in its omnipresence; and we have to be careful that the road we take leads to the Face of Mercy and not to that of Wrath. "Wheresoever thou turnest there is the Face of Allah"- Qur'an, the Cow 2:115

It follows that there can be no graver sin for the Muslim than shirk, the 'association' of other 'gods' with God; in other words idolatry or polytheism. Idolatry and polytheism are seen, not as simple errors about the nature of reality, but as the final stage of a process of corruption or dissociation in which the human will plays a major role. Idolatry is, in essence, the worship of symbols for their own sake, whether these take the form of graven images or subsist only in the human imagination. Shirk can also take more subtle and more universal forms. It is not difficult to see that the modern scientist, not as an observer and recorder but as a theorist, is a mushrik (one guilty of 'association'), since he regards the forces of nature and all causative agencies as independent powers rather than as instruments of a single omnipotent will. So is the man who sets his heart upon some worldly prize - power or wealth, for example, in forgetfulness of the only prize worth seeking.

Muhammad is the Messenger of God

Through the second testimony of Islam, the believer confirms what was taught by every prophet before him. For according to the Qur'anic worldview, God has sent prophets to every people, and the Prophet Muhammad (PBUH) was the last of them. It could be said that the second Shahadah brings the first down to earth, and to deny the second would be to sever all connection with the first. The Prophet is by definition close to God being His messenger. He is therefore the link between Creator and creature. The Prophet Muhammad (PBUH) indicates the perfection and splendour of creation when it remains true to its Creator. He represents the human norm and is therefore the model for every Muslim. Without this model we would have no idea of how to conform, in our persons and in our lives, to the truth enunciated by the first Shahadah; and if he were a superhuman being, or an angel sent to preach to mankind, we could not attempt to imitate him and would not try to do so. It is because he is flesh and blood like us that he is able to fulfil his exemplary function, though it is said of him that he is 'man, yet not as other men but as a jowl among stones'.

Second Pillar (As-Salat) [Prayer] ...and establish the Prayer

Five times in every day the Muslim turns his back on

whatever has been preoccupying him and bows and prostrates in submission before his Creator. The regular act of Salat is a powerful aid to the constant, unceasing remembrance of the eternal presence of God. Through it, the believer constantly pulls back to this remembrance and acquires the ability to see the hand of the Lord in everything which befalls him. The Prophet Muhammad (pbuh) once compared it to a stream running by a house. "If a person were to wash in the stream," he said, "five times a day, would any dirt remain on his body?" "None," replied his Companions. And he remarked, "So it is with the five daily prayers, with which God wipes away faults." These five daily acts of devotion, which are said at dawn, noon, mid-afternoon, sunset, and in the evening, are best prayed in the company of others, but quite acceptable to pray alone.

Each of the Prayers is announced vocally in the Call to Prayer, or Adhan. The muezzin (caller to Prayer), who may be anyone from the local community, stands in an elevated place, usually the tall graceful tower known as a minaret, and sings forth the following declaration:

- God is Most Great.
- God is Most Great.
- God is Most Great.
- God is Most Great.
- I testify that there is no deity save God.
- I testify that there is no deity save God.
- I testify that Muhammad is the Messenger of God.
- I testify that Muhammad is the Messenger of God.
- Come to the Prayer.
- Come to the Prayer.
- Come to the success. Come to the success.
- God is Most Great.
- God is Most Great
- There is no deity save God.

In its directness and stark simplicity the call evokes an

instant response in those that hear it. To them it serves as a reminder that through their daily existence, with its hopes and its disappointments, there runs a thread of Divine remembrance which calls them to make their every act affirm the unity and omd with the awareness of God's grace and protection. By the same token, every moment in which we are not at prayer will become a form of Prayer itself, and we will find that in our spare time nothing seems so fulfilling and moving as facing God anew, declaring His name in humility and wonder. Thus the world in which we live will thus change in meaning for us. From being a space of taking and profit into a realm of pure service to God and to our fellow men, for as our spiritual horizons widen we will learn to take delight in selflessness.

The Conduct of Prayer

The Muslim form of prayer involves a series of bowings and prostrations, evoking the Islamic notion of the close bonding of body and spirit. There is no priest to conduct the ceremony, because there is no concept of a sacrament, in the sense of a visible sign of God's saving intervention that needs to be administered by a hierarchy. Every believer is alone before God, even when worshipping shoulder to shoulder with others.

Designated Times of Prayer

Observing the five prayers that God has laid down for us ensures that we will remember Him in times both of ease and of difficulty, and that there will never be a period of more than a few hours in which we do not turn to God. In fact the time when we least feel like praying is often when we need it most, but naturally whenever one wishes to pray one should do so, exploiting the opportunity and the inclination to the fullest.

The Social Impact of Prayer in Society

In the vision of the Qur'an, Prayer has a social impact.

As God says, Prayer distances us from evil, corruption and aggressiveness. The mechanism of this is complex, but it is nevertheless clear that as the inward voyage progresses, the one embarked upon it finds him simultaneously drawn both into and away from the society which surrounds him. He is drawn into it in the sense that he feels himself to be overflowing with the delight of closeness to God and longs to bring something of this to others, thereby consolidating further its hold within his soul as he begins to live in the service of his fellows. On the other hand, as he discovers that the best things in life are within; so he finds less and less satisfaction in pursuing those things which the lower reaches of his personality crave: good food, fast cars, power, and reputation - the list is familiar.

For each Prayer, they are "cleansing themselves with the water of heaven." If they understand their worship correctly and allow it to purify the interstices of their lives which lie between the Prayers, then each new act of devotion will not merely restore what has been lost, but will provide a step upwards on the ladder of spiritual growth. Every prayer will become more and more absorbing and more and more powerful, until our whole lives are infused with the awareness of God's grace and protection. The more complete the adorer's submission and concentration, the nearer he is to God and hence the more his external character and conduct will be under the control of his inner dictates. Thus, every moment in which we are not at Prayer will become a form of Prayer itself, a form of remembering God, and a consciousness of Him in every aspect of our lives. The world in which we live will thus change in meaning for us, from being a space of taking and profit into a realm of pure service to God and to our fellow men, for as our spiritual horizons widen we will learn to take delight in selflessness.

These two opposing forces do not, in fact, clash, as secular critics of religion would claim. Rather, they create a new and radical synthesis in the human personality. For the man or woman who is transformed by regular Prayer is also undergoing a basic change in his or her social function. No longer is such a person essentially a consumer, sleepily sucking at the teat of the materialistic golden calf; instead he shows himself concerned with improving society. This explains why to take a walk down any old street in Cairo or Damascus is to notice not only ancient and imposing mosques, but also public water fountains, schools, hospitals, and aqueducts, which are the direct result of the presence of those mosques.

The life of Prayer as understood in Islam is a fundamental challenge to the modern attitude to the individual's role in society, which is defined mainly as his contribution to the utilitarian, soulless contract of production and consumption. The Muslim life rises above this mechanical estimate of man, for Islam is founded, as it always has been, on the selfless pursuit of sanctity and of what is in society's interests, regardless of the possibility of reward.

The Significance of the Fatiha

The opening chapter of the Qur'an, sura al-Fatiha, 'The Opener', constitutes the principal text of every canonical prayer, such that if it were neglected the Prayer would be regarded as not having been performed.

The Opener

In the Name of God, the All-Merciful, the Compassionate

Praise be to Allah, the Lord of the Worlds

The All-Merciful, The Compassionate

Master of the Day of Judgement

You alone do we worship and unto You alone do we turn for help

Guide us to the Straight Path

The path of those whom You have favoured

Not those who have incurred Your wrath, nor those who are astray

In a hadith qudsi, the Prophet has narrated what God says when a person recites the sura al-Fatiha. The person says, "In the Name of God, the All-Merciful, the Compassionate", and God says, "My servant mentions Me". The servant then says, "Praise be to Allah, the Lord of the Worlds," and God says in his turn, "My servant lends Me grace." The servant then says "The All-Merciful, The Compassionate," and God replies My servant praises Me." The servant says, "Master of the Day of Judgement," and God says, "My servant glorifies Me and submits himself to Me." This first half of this chapter so far cited relates exclusively to God and the servant's invocation of His attributes. In the next half of the chapter, the servant prays with a complete sense of humility.

The servant says, "You alone do we worship and unto You alone do we turn for help," and God says, "This is shared between Me and My servant, and My servant will receive that which he asks." When the servant says, "Guide us to the Straight Path, The path of those whom You have favoured, Not those who have incurred Your wrath, nor those who are astray," God says, "All that comes back to My servant, and My servant will receive that for which he asks. Thus, the second half of this chapter is related exclusively to man. It is because of this mutual participation between God and man in this chapter, which is considered to be the heart of the Qur'an, that the canonical prayer is regarded as not having been performed if this chapter is not recited.

It is in no way insignificant that the opening of the Qur'an begins with "In the Name of God, the All-Merciful, the Compassionate", with His attributes of Graciousness and Mercy. It connects those upon whom mercy is bestowed with Him, filling them with longing for Him, and encouraging them to obey Him. This is not like the attribute of anger, had He mentioned it instead of mercy, since anger grieves men, excites fear, depresses the mind and does not delight it.

Similarly the words, "Praise be to Allah, the Lord of the Worlds" include two things. One is the basis of praise which is gratitude. This gratitude is the beginning of the straight path and as it were half of it, since practical faith has two halves - half is patience and half is gratitude.

The superiority of gratitude to patience is like the superiority of mercy to anger, because gratitude proceeds from joy, whereas patience under God's decree proceeds from fear and awe, and is not free from distress and sorrow. To walk along the straight path to God by way of love and to perform actions of love are much better than to walk along the path of fear. The words of God, "The All-Merciful, The Compassionate" the second time indicate His attribute once again. This is not to be mistaken for repetition, as there is no repetition in the Qur'an, for repetition is defined as that which does not contain any additional benefit. The mention of mercy after the mention of "Lord of the Worlds" and before mention of "Master of the Day of Judgement," has two great benefits in expounding the channels of mercy. One pays attention to creation by the Lord of all the worlds - He has created every one of these according to the most perfect and best of its kind and has given everything it needs.

In connection with this, His words, "Master of the Day of Judgement" indicates His mercy on the Day of Recompense at the time of granting the favour of perpetual kingdom, i.e. Paradise in exchange for belief in the sentence of testimony and for worship. The words, "You alone do we worship", comprise two great parts. One is worship with sincerity in relation to Him. The second is the belief that none other than God deserves worship and this is the essence of belief in divine unity. This is achieved by abandonment of belief in man's ability and power, and by the knowledge that God is alone in the execution of all works and that man is not independent by himself and without His help. Thus His words, "You alone do we worship" are an indication of making the soul beautiful by worship and sincerity, while His words, "and unto You alone do we turn for help" are an indication of its purification from belief in partnership and from paying attention to man's ability and power.

The words, "Guide us to the Straight Path" are a prayer which is the marrow of worship. These words of His make man aware of the need for entreaty and supplication to Him which form the spirit of servitude and also make man aware that the most important of his needs is guidance along the straight path, for it is by following this path that advancement towards God is accomplished. The words, "The path of those whom You have favoured, Not those who have incurred Your wrath, nor those who are astray" are a reminder of His favour to His frinds and His revenge upon, and anger towards, His enemires, in order that encouragement may be given and awe may be excited from the depth of the hearts.

Third Pillar (Az-Zakat) [Almsgiving] ...and spend out of what We have bestowed upon them.

Every human being carries the Divine amaanah or trust to transform the elements of nature into sources of nutrition and comfort, of wisdom and beauty, efficiency and enjoyment for himself and others. Built into this amaaanah or trust is the requirement on those who have been blessed with wealth and means, to spend out of their substance on those in deprivation and misery. Islam teaches people that the poor and the deprived have a "title" or a "right" in the wealth of the rich "And those in whose wealth is a recognised right for the (needy) who asks, and him who is prevented (for some reason from asking)" -Qur'an 70:24-25, and constantly exhorts the rich to meet that obligation. In this sense, the rich stand in need of the poor. If they do not fulfil this "right" of the poor, they will be called to account.

Islam distinguishes between two categories of charity: the optional form, generally termed sadaqa, and the mandatory one, the zakat. The latter constitutes the necessary revenue for the state which distributes it into those areas which might have been neglected by the "free market" system of Islamic welfare economics. While voluntary sadaqah is encouraged and its scope extended so that even the poor can offer sadaqah (in the form of a smile, for example), Islam has established the institute of zakat to make concern for the poor a permanent and compulsory duty. The word Zakat means both 'purification' and 'growth'. Our possessions are purified by setting aside a proportion for those in need, and, like the pruning of plants, this cutting back balances and encourages new growth. Thus the Zakat is the amount of money that every adult, mentally stable, free, and financially able Muslim, male and female, has to pay to support specific categories of people. It is a proportionately fixed contribution collected from the surplus wealth and earnings of the Muslim.

The Prophet (pbuh) was concerned that believers should show solidarity with the poor, and since his time, every Muslim has been expected to donate a minimum of one-fortieth of his wealth in charity every year. Traditionally an informal practice involving discreet handouts to indigent neighbours, the zakat is often administered through charities nowadays. The largest Muslim charities, such as Islamic Relief, have become important international aid agencies. Although the zakat itself is a proportionately fixed contribution, the Muslims understanding of zakat is to give out as much as possible and as frequently as he is able to. Traditionally one such implication of "spend out of what We have bestowed.." is the provision of public works by private individuals. But in addition there in the institution of the waqf, the inalienable endowment, whereby some commercial project has its profits turned over wholly or partly to a particular school or hospital in perpetuity, either by charter or through making the endowment in a written legacy.

Needless to say giving to others also exists on a more modest scale. Not everyone is able to build or donate a school or a bridge. Begging as a profession is hateful to Islam, as the Prophet (pbuh) said, "The upper hand is better than the lower," yet the genuinely poor are with us always, even in the most technically advanced industrial countries, and it is our duty to render help whenever we can. Islam teaches that charity should be given secretly, for as the Qur'an tells us, "If you give your charity openly then it is well, but you should hide it, then that is better for you, and will obliterate some of your wrong actions."

Zakat in Society

The implementation of Islamic welfare economics has historically proved highly successful. Far from being idealistic or divorced from reality, the Islamic vision of a society based on service has regularly been put into effect. In the golden centuries of Muslim civilisation, free private sector education resulted in a high literacy rate, which only began to decline during the period of colonial domination. When the armies of the Reconquest entered Cordoba, the erstwhile capital of Muslim Spain, they were astonished to find a city provided with street lighting at night and possessed of over four hundred public baths and a great library containing over half a million books. So prosperous was Islamic civilisation under Muslim economic law that a voluminous body of records details events that seem quite incredible today.

For example, an account records an exchange of correspondence between the devout eighth-century caliph 'Umar ibn 'Abd al-Aziz and his governor over the province of Iraq. In one letter, the governor complained, "Commander of the Faithful! I have given from the treasury to all in need, but some money still remains." The Caliph replied, "Seek out all those that have contracted reasonable debts, and pay off what they owe." The governor then wrote back, saying, "I have paid off every debt, but we still have a surplus." "Seek out every unmarried person," the Caliph told him, "who has insufficient money to marry, and pay their dowries and get them married." "I have already done so," came the reply, "but we still have a surplus." Finally the Caliph sent the following message: "Find out everyone who has to pay taxes and absolve him from paying them, for we have enough money for a year or two."

Categories of Zakat

The Qur'an envisages and lays down certain areas in the economy from which these revenues are to be levied, and also specifies who and what is entitled to benefit from them. The first and traditionally the most lucrative area in which the zakat is imposed, is the agricultural sector. According to the Qur'an, the landowner (not the farmer himself) is required to pay 10 % of his net profits every year to the state treasury, on condition that the crops grow readily or that the land is used solely for pasturing. However, if his land should be irrigated mechanically, through electric or diesel pumps (to give the modern equivalent), or with artesian wells, or if the land is benefiting from a hydroelectric scheme operating outside the farm itself, this rate is reduced to five percent. The differential is to encourage efficient farming.

Elsewhere in the economy, different rates of zakat are levied. The Islamic fiscal system is based on a gold standard, that is, the Islamic currency is readily convertible to gold or silver at a fixed rate which may only be raised or lowered by central bank directives approved by the head of state. Every transaction becomes liable to a one-fortieth zakat tax payable on its value in gold and silver. The tax is assessed at the end of the financial year, and replaces the Western system of "income tax". In addition, zakat is assessed at the same rate on capital gains, including bequests and gifts and return on shares in private corporations, and is also payable on all wealth held in money form including private bank accounts. The third and last principal species of zakat is of particular interest. It falls due on gross profits from the exploitation of natural resources, including mines and oil wells. Covering revenue from all these sources, the zakat rate rises to 20%, discouraging unnecessary waste of non-renewable minerals and energy sources. Renewable sources of energy, such as hydroelectric projects and solar energy are encouraged by being taxed at the substantially lower rate of 5 %.

Zakat Recipients

First among those who receive a share of the zakat are the poor, in particular those who are in danger of losing their lives as a result of simply not finding enough to eat. According to the World Health Organisation, eight million of our fellow men and women die of starvation each year throughout the globe. Aid to these people takes precedence over any other use which might be made of zakat funds. The second area of disbursement is made up of those people within the boundaries of the Islamic state who are not in any immediate danger of starvation but who nevertheless live well below the poverty line. The government is entitled to distribute Zakat funds to such people, especially by providing them with the means to begin a career, for example, in the form of education grants or assistance with buying agriculture equipment.

Thirdly, mention should be made of the expenses incurred unavoidably in the collection and distribution of the zakat itself. It is traditional in the Islamic world that zakat workers are voluntary, but if such labour is not forthcoming, or if it proves necessary to buy documenting equipment, such as computers, then the zakat fund itself may be used to defray expenses. Government officials, including the head of state himself, are not entitled to government funds at all, but must ensure they have sufficient income from other sources before they opt to enter the world of politics, which is a world of service, not of personal gain.

Fourthly, there exists a special facility in the state treasury with regard to what is now in effect an extinct category: slaves. Islam prohibits slavery in the form which is familiar to students of European and American history. But in times of war there nevertheless exists a special mechanism for integrating prisoners of war. Rather than holding enemy troops in camps Islam allows that those who are of good behaviour may be sent for public service in the homes of private citizens. But in time of peace there is no such means of acquiring bonded servants, hence there is no permanent population of non-free people in an Islamic state. This system is called in the Islamic law the "law of indenture." In order to secure their release from their service, or from the prisoner-of-war camps themselves, these bonded servants are entitled to apply for assistance from the zakat fund to compensate the households which they are leaving.

Fifthly, the zakat treasury receives applications for assistance from people in chronic debt. After investigating the request, the treasury is entitled to pay off such debts if it is clear that the debtor is never likely to be in a position to do so himself. Sixthly comes a general category of public services. From the zakat fund, and once the foregoing categories have received their due, the head of treasury may order disbursements upon projects of general benefit, including the provision of infrastructure not furnished by the private sector. The armed forces are likewise provided for from this category. Seventhly, money may be sent overseas as foreign aid over and above the mandatory expenditures mentioned in the first of the eight categories.

Finally, there is a small category, historically of great importance, which provides for travellers who lack the means to return home. A voyager or tourist in a state where Islamic law is applied has a statutory right, should he lose his money (for example) to contact the local administration and request the fare needed to reach his country of origin.

The Benefit of Charity and Sincerity of Intention

As adapted from a saying of the Prophet (pbuh):

There was a man who said to himself "By Allah, I am going to give sadaqah," so he went out that night and gave sadaqah to a man whom he thought looked like a poor man. He was actually a thief going to steal, and he gave him sadaqah. When he woke up he heard people saying 'last night, sadaqah was given to a thief.' When he heard that, he said "Oh Allah, you have praise," the meaning of which according to commentators is that he made a mistake, but his intention was pure, and he said, "O Allah I gave it with a good intention, and You have praise in any state. I gave it to a person who was undeserving of it."

Then again, the next day, he said "I did not give charity," as he felt that he hadn't fulfilled his oath, so he said "I'm still going to do it," and he went out, and gave money to a prostitute. The next morning people were saying "A prostitute was given sadaqah last night." And he said, "O Allah, to You is praise;" he again had made a mistake. So again he felt as if he hadn't given in charity and went out to fulfil his oath. This time he put his money into the hand of a rich man. The next morning again people were talking of the sadaqah saying, 'last night sadaqah was given to a rich man.' So again the man said, "O Allah, to You is praise." Then he saw in a dream, although some say an angel came to him, and he was told "As for your charity to that thief, maybe he will stop stealing because you gave him that." Then it was said, "And as for your charity to that prostitute, maybe she will stop fornicating because of that." And then he said "And as for the rich man, maybe this will cause him to reflect so that he will start to give out from his wealth." (for scholars say that most rich people don't really think about all that Allah has given them and that prevents them from charity.)

The Islamic Scholars say about this hadith that even if you gave charity to the wrong hands, say "O Allah, to You is praise" because if your intention was pure, Allah will make some good come out of it. It might not be from the hands of that person, but it may come later. One of the great scholars, Badruddin Al-Hasani (who was a master of hadith), from the city of Damascus, who died in this age, at every 'Eid, he would go out, and he would give his students charity from his own pocket, and there were places, particularly in the colonialism era, where there were a lot of women that were impoverished and forced into prostitution to support themselves, and he would tell his student to give those prostitutes charity, and he would say to them, "Tell them that Badruddin Al-Hasani asked you to make du'ah (supplication) for him." And those women would weep when they heard that: "Who are we to make du'ah for Badruddin Al-Hasani?" There were people who repented because of that act. (Source: Depending on Allah, Zaytuna Institute Paper)

Thus even if you gave charity to the wrong hands, if your intention was pure, Allah the Most Merciful, will make good come out of it.

Fifth Pillar (Al-Hajj) [Pilgrimage]

Three months after Ramadan comes the season of the great Pilgrimage to Makkah, the birthplace of Islam, where an ever-increasing number of men and women converge each year, from every possible corner of the earth. The origin of the Hajj, the Final Pillar, and a central duty of Islam, dates back to the Prophet Abraham and brings together Muslims of all races and tongues to don two simple white cloths in an impressive display of Islam's disregard for racial or national divisions. Each year nearly several million people make the pilgrimage, making it the largest temporary gathering on the globe. It is an act of recollection and worship, but it is also a symbolic act representing the spirit's return to its homeland-one of the central elements of the Muslim life.

The rites begin and end at the Ka'aba the square 'House' built as Muslims believe, by Abraham and his elder son Ishmael. However, the culminating moment unfolds eight miles away, where Muslims stand and pray near the Mount of Mercy, a desert place where the Prophet (PBUH) used to preach. The pilgrimage is regarded as worship of a lifetime, and in being the Final Pillar of Islam, the seal of consummation, the completion of surrender and the perfection of religion. It was during the Pilgrimage that God sent down His revelation:

"Today I have perfected your religion for you, and completed My grace upon you, and approved Islam as your religion."Qur'an, The Table Spread 5:3

Muslims trace the recorded origins of the divinely prescribed pilgrimage to the Prophet Abraham, or Ibrahim, as he is called in Arabic. According to the Qur'an, it was Abraham who, together with his son Ishmael (Isma'il), built the Ka'bah, "the House of God," the focal point toward which Muslims turn in their worship five times each day. It was Abraham, too - known as Khalil Allah, "the friend of God" - who established the rituals of the hajj, which recall events or practices in his life and that of Hagar (Hajar) and their son Ishmael. In the chapter entitled "The Pilgrimage," the Qur'an speaks of the divine command to perform the hajj and prophesies the permanence of this institution:

"And when We assigned for Abraham the place of the House, saying 'Do not associate Anything with Me, and sanctify My House for those who go around it and for those who stand and bow and prostrate themselves in worship. And proclaim the Pilgrimage among humankind: They will come to you on foot and on every camel made lean by travelling deep, distant ravines" -Qur'an, The Pilgrimage 22:26-27

The Conduct of Hajj

In commemoration of the trials of Abraham and his family in Makkah, which include Abraham's willingness to sacrifice his son in response to God's command, Muslims make a pilgrimage to the sacred city at least once in their lifetime? The Pilgrimage to Makkah is prescribed for all Muslims who can physically and financially perform it. God has prescribed certain rites that a pilgrim should observe properly. If he does not do so, his pilgrimage is not accepted. To perform the pilgrimage means to leave all worldly activities aside and to proceed to meet the Lord, thus as in the case of all other Pillars of Islam, the primary condition is purity of intention (niyyah). The other obligatory rites are:

1. Ihram- Before arriving in the holy city, Muslims enter a state of consecration (dedication) known as ihram, by removing their worldly clothes and donning the humble attire of pilgrims, two seamless white sheets for men, and simple white dresses and scarves for women. The white garments are symbolic of human equality and unity before God, since all the pilgrims are dressed similarly. Money and status no longer are a factor for the pilgrims - the equality of each person in the eyes of God becomes paramount. They are also expected to observe the rules of ihram, which are not to have a sexual relationship, not to kill insects or animals, and not to remove any hair from the body.
2. Tawaf al-qudum- Upon arriving in Makkah, pilgrims performs the initial tawaf, which is a circular, counter-clockwise procession around the Ka'bah. All the while, they state "Labbayka Allahumma Labbayk," which means, "Here I am at your service, O God, Here I am!" The tawaf is meant to awaken each Muslim's consciousness that God is the centre of their reality and the source of all meaning in life, and that each person's higher self-identity derives from being part of the community of Muslim believers, known as the ummah. Pilgrims also perform the sa'i, which is hurrying seven times between the small hills named Safa and Marwah, re-enacting the Biblical and Qur'anic story of Hajar's desperate search for lifegiving water and food.

3. Next, on the first official day of Hajj (8th of Dhul-Hijjah), the two million pilgrims travel a few miles to the plain of Mina and camp there. From Mina, pilgrims travel the following morning to the plain of Arafat where they spend the entire day in earnest supplication and devotion. It is said that when God forgives a sin for one servant at the place-of-standing (the plain of Arafat), He forgives it for everyone there who is guilty of it. It was also on such a day that the Prophet (pbuh) received the revelation from God "Today I have perfected your religion for you, and completed My grace upon you, and approved Islam as your religion."
4. That evening, the pilgrims move and camp at Muzdalifa, which is a site between Mina and Arafat. Muslims stay overnight and offer various prayers there.
5. Then the pilgrims return to Mina on the 10th, and throw seven pebbles at a stone pillar that represents the devil. This symbolises Abraham's throwing stones at Satan when he tried to dissuade Abraham from sacrificing his son. Then the pilgrims sacrifice a sheep, re-enacting the story of Abraham, who, in place of his son, sacrificed a sheep that God had provided as a substitute.
6. Thus the slaughtering of a sheep is another obligation, the meat of which is distributed among family, friends, and the poor and needy in the community.
7. After the sacrifice, the pilgrims return to Makkah to end the formal rites of Hajj by performing a final tawaf and sa'i.
8. They should also drink from the water of ZamZam.
9. And perform two rakahs of Prayer at the place known as Maqam Ibrahim, the place where Abraham and his son stood and prayed after building the Ka'aba.

If the rites (1), (2), (3) and (7) have been performed, then the basic rites are said to have been observed. Even if the other rites are not performed properly, the pilgrimage is said to have been performed. Muslims believe the rites of the Hajj were designed by God and taught through the Prophet Muhammad (PBUH).

The Hajj is designed to develop God consciousness and a sense of spiritual upliftment. It is also believed to be an opportunity to seek forgiveness of sins accumulated throughout life. Prophet Muhammad had said that a person who performs Hajj properly "will return as a newly born baby [free of all sins]." The pilgrimage also enables Muslims from all around the world, of different colours, languages, races, and ethnicities, to come together in a spirit of universal brotherhood and sisterhood to worship the One God together.

The Inner Significance of the Hajj

To understand the inner significance of the Hajj ceremonies it is necessary to remember that Makkah is in many respects a town apart from all others. Good actions and bad are more clearly discerned, and the reward or punishment for them is held to be proportionately greater. Within the limits of the city, fighting and all aggressiveness are forbidden. No pilgrim is allowed for any reason to harm a human being or an animal during his sojourn in the city. In the state of ihram, the pilgrim feels that he is ridding himself for a while of all that linked him to his former life, with its desires and enmities, and can now devote his attention wholeheartedly to his Creator.

The circuits around the Ka'bah themselves symbolise the circulation of the heart around the holiness of God. In entering Makkah, and to perform tawaf where the first holy house of God was established, is to circumambulate the house that is a reflection of that Divine House in the Seventh Heaven, above and beyond which stands the glorified Throne of God, around which all the angels and the entire creation are constantly rotating. In the same vein, the running between the two hills of Safa and Marwa in the great hall now built to enclose them, suggest moving between the two aspects of God's mercy, compassion and acceptance. The culminating point of the Hajj is the simplest rite of all. Here millions of people stand together in a scene of great beauty, surrounded by mountains on all sides.

As the hours pass, one's thoughts already focussed on God by days of uninterrupted worship, have time to look deeply into one's life. And at the same time another symbolism inherent in the psychology of the Hajj becomes clear. Standing on the Plain of Arafat, we cannot but remember the day on which God will resurrect us together with all mankind, when the time of repentance will be irrevocably past. Now, however, there still remains a path back to the world, for soon we will be going home: an opportunity to set our lives right before we die to await the Day of Judgement. The Hajj ends with the second of the great festivals, the Eid al-Adha, which last three days. Returning to our homes after days of physical exhaustion and spiritual uplift we are radically transfigured. The overpowering sense of contrition and repentance, which we bring back with us, is visible.

The Distinction between Faith and Spirituality

To many people, Faith and Spirituality are inter-twined together and inseparable, but are they? If we are thinking of devotional prayer to our Creator, then in that case, Faith and Spirituality are merged together and indistinct, BUT there are many different 'Faiths' in this world, and within each and every Faith, there are followers some of whom we can see as being more Spiritual people, and others as less so! Some definitions:

"Faith" means believing, or trusting in what can't be proved!

"Spirituality" means giving service and kindness to others!

When something is a provable fact, like what the weather was yesterday, it does not require any 'faith' to know this is true, but if we say the weather forecast for tomorrow is 'Dry and Sunny' and we believe it, than that is an act of faith! This simple distinction between 'provable fact' and 'faith' is of vital importance to religions, you cannot reason or prove your religion to a un-believer, no matter how knowledgeable or articulate you are, it takes 'Faith' on their part. The Qur'an does describe this so beautifully with the 'veils of light'. Also, faith is what gives us the strength to keep on going, when life gets tough.

'Spirituality', this is more involved to define: There are many 'Doors' to the Spiritual and Spiritual experience, these include being within certain building built for the praise of The Creator, like Mosques (Masjid), Churches and Temples. Wearing certain clothes or dress reserved for religious practise, or Meditation can be a door to the Spiritual, so can being in awe of the view from the top of a mountain, religious pilgrimage or certain sorts of music can also bring us to the door of the Spiritual, there are many doors but none of them are the Spiritual in themselves, these are only doorways. When we come to a doorway to the Spirit, if we then listen, or feel with our heart to what the Spiritual dimension is saying, it is always the same: Compassion, Peace, Harmony, Fairness, Love for our Creator, Love for all of the Creation, doing good in this world, having patients over our difficulties – This is the beginning of Spiritual experience, but to go with it further and live this way, we start to want to live our lives by 'Giving service and kindness to others', which is the concise definition I used for "Spirituality" above. This is the way of all of the Prophets, May peace and blessings be upon them, and the way of all the Angels as well.

'Spirituality' therefore, is independent of any particular Religious Faith, and it is also independent of a person's; Gender, Ethnicity, Age, Wealth, Education, Abilities or Disabilities!

It is possible to have the frameworks of Islam, with a

society following all the rules, rituals and practises, but the core empty of Spirituality – 'Spirituality' as I have defined above as 'Giving service and kindness to others'. We can find people of very strong Faith but with very little Spirituality, which is where the trouble starts!

Spirituality is the opposite of Prejudice or Exclusion! Your "level of Spirituality" is all you take with you to the Spirit World from this earth-life!

Everything Comes from Within

Spiritual growth does not come from Religion! As we experience the life of this world, and when we are ready; Then direct from Allah to our Spirit Soul comes what is needed for us to grow spiritually. This is a natural process, and it is equal and fair to all the peoples of the world, regardless of what opportunities or teachings they have had access to. It is independent of 'Religion'.

When we have grown spiritually from within up to a level, then we are able to understand the words of the Qur'an or words of teachers up to that same level, We learn from the inside first, not from the outside!

Then which of the favours of your Lord will you deny? Qur'an 55:13

How can anyone possibly understand the meaning of "favours of your Lord" without first understanding in our heart, something of the wonders of nature?

Forcing someone to study religion has the opposite to the intended effect: neither do pupils understand anything spiritually from their forced teachings, but this also blocks the spiritual food coming direct from Allah ever reaching their hearts. Religious Knowledge is NOT the same as Spiritual Understanding: You can learn all there is to know about flowers, but you will never Become a flower! Does a flower have to learn when to blossom, or does it just be itself, and blossom when it is ready? Likewise, learning all

ABOUT religion is NOT the same as being Spiritual. The religion of Islam has a very valuable and necessary role to build the sort of Just Society that spiritual people want to live in, and raise their children in; 'Religion' supports Family life, which is so vitally important to a healthy society, but 'Religion' is not the same as spiritual understanding. Religious teachings can only VERIFY what we already understand in our heart: we cannot grow spiritually from religious teachings! It is the difference between knowing something and being it. Spiritual growth comes from within, fed directly to our heart by Allah, the Great Spirit.

- Be silent, let Allah reach your heart, feel the 'Love and Light' enter.

The true meaning of 'Dhikr' (Zikr)??

Levels

Religion if applied strictly by those who don't understand much spiritually can end up being very wrong: 'religious knowledge' is not the same as 'spiritual understanding', consider this parallel story:

When we are outside on the street, we have the Highway Code, all the rules that we have evolved for traffic regulation so that we can use the roads in safety and with free flowing of traffic. All road users are included; Lorries, Busses, cars, bicycles, horses, and pedestrians. The rules state who has right of way and at what time they have right of way, like a red traffic light means 'Stop', an orange traffic light means 'about to change', and a green traffic light means 'Go'.

Now if we leave the street and come into the house, into the kitchen for example, then those rules of the street no longer apply and we have a different set of rules. In the kitchen we are now concerned about cleanliness, about storing food so that it doesn't go bad, about preparing food so that it is healthy and tasty. In the kitchen, probably the only red light is on the oven, but this does not mean 'stop'! Rather it means that the oven has not yet reached its full temperature, which is a very different meaning to the traffic light 'red'. In the kitchen, probably the only orange light is on the electric kettle, showing whether it is switched on or not, again a very different meaning to the traffic light orange! Probably the only 'green' light is on the freezer when it at the correct temperature, it does not mean 'go'!

The rules we have for the roads outside are different to the rules we have for the kitchen, the kitchen rules do not supersede the traffic rules, because if we go outside again, we then have to follow the traffic rules again. If from the kitchen, we were then to go upstairs to the bedroom, then an entirely different set of rules apply!! A nice humorous story: but if the same thing was done using 'Shariah' law out of context, like the Highway Code in the kitchen, and if people were being punished or shamed because of something that was spiritually in a different level, then it would no longer be a humorous story! This does happen! If this sounds insulting, or a ridiculous comparison, then read the translation from the Qur'an on the page Words of Solace about Hazrat Musa (Moses).

Interpretation of the Holy Qur'an

Please be aware, that most of the original Commentaries (tafsir) on the Qur'an were not written by free writers! They were living in the time of the Khalifat, but after the time of the first Four 'Rightly Guided Khalifs' - so inevitably they had to tow the State line! "Leaving things out is as much a distortion as putting things in!" Also, it must be noted that many Muslim writings advocate very harsh treatment towards Women and non-Muslims, yet nowhere do we find reference to the Prophet himself behaving like this, He only had Love and Kindness!

Those who listen to the Word, and follow the best (meaning) in it: Those are the ones whom Allah has guided, and those are the ones endued with understanding. QUR'AN 39:18

Mathematical miracles in the Qur'an: Unique amongst Holy Books; in counting letters, words, verses, and the reoccurrence of certain letters, the Arabic Qur'an shows a very complex mathematical matrix pattern based on the number 19. For example, the heading 'Bismillah hir-Rahman nir Raheem' in Arabic consists of 19 letters, the first portion of the Qur'an to be revealed (Sura 96: 1 – 5 Iqra) consists of 19 words, the whole Qur'an contains 114 Suras = 19 x 6. There are many, many more instances; some of the more complex patterns have only become apparent by computer analysis! This is amazing evidence showing that the Arabic Qur'an is indeed complete, unaltered, and of Divine or Spirit origin. Therefore it is not the Qur'an itself that is the problem, but un-spiritual interpretations of its meaning; especially by taking one solitary verse out of context to the whole, and adding a man-made (or devious spirit) agenda to make decrees! (Fatwa)

Also interestingly, in 'Numerology' the number 19 is special because it incorporates both the first digit (1) and the last digit (9) yet reduces down to 1 or Unity! (Adding digits 1 + 9 = 10 then reducing again 1 + 0 = 1)

Over it is Nineteen QUR'AN 74:30

Spirits tell us there are many levels in their world, and when we leave the earth life and enter their world, we go to the spiritual level appropriate for us, as like attracts like. Whereas here on the earth, people of all different levels of Spiritual enlightenment are mixed together, providing opportunities for experience, and opportunities to learn from each other! However, Spiritualists will never tell you what you should believe; you must reach your own understanding, and only accept that which appeals to your reason!

6

The Ocean of Divine Knowledge

This is a small explanation of Imam-Islam, the way the Sufis practice it as they develop more and more clarity and wisdom. Throughout the ages, step by step, Allah sent revelations to mankind through the prophets-through Adam, Noah, Abraham, Ishmael, Moses, David, Jesus, and all the other prophets. One prophet brought ten revelations, another brought seven, and others came with only one, two, or three. As His final and ultimate explanation Allah sent 6,666 revelations to the Last Prophet, Muhammad, who was also the Prophet for the beginning, Nur Muhammad. Those revelations are the verses of the Qur'an, and they include all the revelations sent to earlier prophets. We were provided with these explanations so that we could understand the words, conduct, and qualities of Imam-Islam, and so that we could realize the value of the kalimah, the affirmation of faith.

Allah has given us five kalimahs and ordained five times of prayer each day. These are essential for our peace and contentment. Earth, fire, water, air, and ether are also five in number and are necessary for the life of the body. All creations suffer when their bodies are deprived of water, when they do not have enough air to breathe, or when they feel the fire of hunger. If it is too hot the body needs something cool, if it becomes cold the body must have heat. Only after these needs are satisfied can the body feel peaceful. Similarly, only when we receive a full understanding of Iman-Islam and the kalimah can we feel the inner peace that they offer. God has provided all that we require to meet our inner and outer needs, at every moment, wherever we are. But in order to know exactly what will comfort us and what will quench our thirst, we have to know everything in the world of souls, in this world, and in the hereafter. So that we can understand all this, Almighty God has given us the Qur'an.

The Holy Qur' an is an ocean of divine knowledge. It is so vast that its breadth can never be seen and its depth can never be fathomed. To try to limit it, thinking that we can ever fully comprehend its meaning, is ignorant. That ocean contains everything: heaven, hell, this world, and the eighteen thousand universes. We have been told, "Swim! Immerse yourself in that ocean of divine knowledge." To know the secrets it contains, we must obtain the strength of wisdom to dive deep within it and into the depths of the qualities of God. We must cling to the faith that the kalimah inspires as we repeat its words and swim with the power of the kalimah's radiance.

To cross this vast ocean of divine knowledge, each one of us must become a perfected human being, one who lives his life with wisdom. When such a person swims, he knows. But in our present state we seem to be tied to a flimsy raft, floating on this endless ocean. With certitude we must hold fast to the oar of faith in Allah and His Messenger, knowing that Allah is the upper edge and Muhammad is the lower edge of the blade that cuts through the water and pushes us forward. Then we will be able to cross the ocean and reach the shore. My brothers and sisters, if you can know your own life and understand it, you will find the ocean of divine knowledge within you. You will find the Qur'an within you. You are the Qur'an; you are your own book. If you can study that book and reach the state of fully ripened knowledge, then you will be able to speak of its sweetness and know peace and comfort in your life. To establish and understand this state is Iman-Islam. To learn divine knowledge is Islam. Once we understand this, we will understand why the Prophet said, "Study divine knowledge, even if you have to go unto China."

As we mature step by step, that knowledge will reveal to us the right thing at the right time. This is how we must delve within the Qur' an. We cannot understand the Qur' an through the intellect, nor can we receive its benefits by earning titles or the esteem of the world. These things belong to Satan. To try to see the value of the Qur'an with the mind is useless. The mind cannot grasp divine knowledge. That knowledge can only be understood if we surrender to God and have perfect trust in Him, knowing that He is the One who can do all things. We must study divine knowledge through the clarity of pure wisdom, with a pure soul, and through the pure qualities of inner patience, contentment, trust in God, praise of God, and the acknowledgment that God is most great and can do all things.

God's beautiful qualities, duties, and actions are Islam. He is each quality, He is each duty, He is each action. He performs His duties and actions with His qualities. He is what He does. He acts, He sees, He questions, He gives, He receives. These are the meanings of His ninety-nine names. These powers of Allah can be found in the innermost heart of each and every human being as qualities, actions, and behavior. They are the highest ideals of Islam, and they must be developed and established. Man must invite them into his heart. When these ninety-nine powers of Allah, His three thousand divine attributes, and the qualities of His Messenger begin to resonate within the heart of a man, he will not have any enemies. When his heart is filled with the kalimah, when he greets his brothers with peace, and when his heart sings out in supplication for God's blessings upon the prophets and upon all mankind, he will see all lives as his own life.

When patience, contentment, trust in God, praise of God, and the affirmation that God is great shine forth from within him, his innermost heart will resplend with unity, humility, and harmony. He will have no prejudices or differences. When the constant remembrance of and contemplation on God begins to resonate in his heart, that resonance will give forth millions and millions of explanations that will bring peace to millions of hearts. Such a person will care for his neighbor as himself. He will have the ability to hold everyone in an embrace which makes them all one. He will never see anyone as an enemy, because Allah has no enemy. Allah is each one of His names. Not one of His names has the meaning of attacking or causing pain. It is not God's work to attack others; His work is to correct what comes to Him. If something is wrong, He corrects it with His wisdom.

What Allah does is Islam, and in the same way, one who is in Islam will not attack others. He will correct his own faults, so that his peaceful state will bring peace to others. He will correct his own qualities and teach God's qualities to his mind, so that those sweet qualities can soothe and comfort others. He will elevate his own state to the state of God, so that he can help others to grow. When every heart understands this, when these qualities develop in the heart of one human being and then transfer to the hearts of other human beings, when unity and love catch every heart, every life, and every nation, then true Islam will come into being and catch fire and spread throughout the world. This is the unity that occurs when we trust and follow the words, actions, and qualities of Allah and His Messenger.

Allah has no hostility, and the kalimah brought by His Prophet expresses no hostility. Once we say that kalimah and accept the truth of God with absolute faith, we will see everyone and everything as Islam. Drawing a sword, attacking others, or trying to force them into our beliefs is not Islam. True Islam means controlling ourselves, controlling the anger, jealousy, and vengeance that come from our own minds, and attacking all the thoughts within us that hurt others. That is the war we all must wage. God has no need to wage wars. He is capable of creating or destroying universes within the blink of an eye. If He were to close His eye, nothing would exist; when it opened again, creation would come back to life. Similarly, in the blink of an eye, the darkness within the heart can be dispelled and the light of God's qualities can come back to life.

Islam

Lam is light, the light of the pure soul and pure wisdom. The word Islam describes a place where there is no darkness at all, a place where there are no differences, no disputes over races or religions, a place where there is only light. As we open our eyes and our hearts to that light, to inner patience, and to the wisdom of divine knowledge, all our evil tendencies will be burned away, and all of God's beauty will come into being within us. Of course, if we do not recognize the difference between good and evil, we might burn everything indiscriminately. But if we apply our understanding we will burn away only the bad. Then light will come into being, and we will see the power of God's grace and understand what Islam truly is. One who understands this will gain the wealth of the three worlds. For such a man, this world is heaven, the hereafter is heaven, and even the time of creation, of birth, is heaven. Iman-Islam is the name given to this state when it is established with awareness. But as long as we do not understand this properly and continue to say, "I am great, I am greater than you," we have not reached that level of understanding. Only when we have rid ourselves of all our blemishes will we be able to see God.

Faith in Islam

Iman, the word which in Arabic corresponds to "faith",

means knowledge of a thing coupled with a conviction as to its truth so strong as to incite us to strive our utmost to live up to it. The word does not, in Qur'anic terminology, include beliefs which cannot be translated into action, or are not concerned with action. Consequently, belief in something accepted as verity on the basis of a dogma does not come within the category of religious beliefs in Islam. In fact, dogmatic doctrines have no significance for a Muslim. Faith, however, in the Qur'anic sense of the word, plays a most important part in moulding every human word or action. All our movements are the portraits of such of our concepts as are based upon sure and certain faith. Every item of our routine, however insignificant, is but a motion picture of our belief in the existence or the non-existence of things. Any change in such a belief straightaway produces a change in the routine.

Even a slight movement of our lips, or of any other portion of the body, springs from some belief or other. For instance, we cannot utter a word unless we believe as well in the audibility and articulation of the sound we make as in the ability of our hearer to hear and give to our words the same meanings which they convey to us. Similar belief is always present in our mind concerning everything that emanates from us. This emphasizes the importance of a vigilant and wise choice of faith in every avenue of our existence, since soundness of action follows soundness of belief; and more especially is this so in our religious beliefs, seeing that no other belief approaches them in strength and in influence on the ordering of our life.

Beliefs of Religions Unsupported by Reason

Every religion lays down certain articles of faith as its basic principles, demanding from its adherents an implicit faith therein. These basic principles may or may not appeal to our intelligence, or serve any useful purpose for us in this life, but it is nevertheless claimed for them that they possess unique merits in securing salvation and happiness in the life beyond the grave for those who hold them. As to that life, almost every religion strikes the same note. Faith in tenets diametrically opposed to each other in teaching has by different religions been invested with similar merits that are to accrue to the believer in his life after death. If a faith in the divinity of A and B, for instance, brings salvation to the believer according to one religion, it dooms him to everlasting punishment in the life to come, according to the other. No religion, on the other hand, has any decisively logical support for its assertions. No one as yet has returned from behind the veil to bear witness to the truth of his faith.

Even "seance-phenomena", apart from all considerations of their futility or otherwise, are not reliable evidence that such a thing has occurred. The French spiritualist, for example, accepts the transmigration of the soul as a truth on the strength of phenomenal testimony, while his colleague in England will disbelieve in the doctrine on evidence precisely similar. Under these circumstances I am forced to conclude that a religion's claim for belief in its doctrines should never be heeded, unless those doctrines satisfy our intelligence and have been tested in the crucible of utility as regards our present life.

Harmful Beliefs of Some Religions

A plunge in the dark is a dangerous proceeding, but it is infinitely more dangerous to believe in things that not only have no bearing on our present life but sometimes are actually harmful in their effects on the building of our character. By way of illustration I may refer to doctrines like the Atonement, Predestination, Fatalism and the Transmigration of the Soul. No one can prove any of these by reference to anything in this present life. They may seem plausible to some, but belief in them mainly concerns things as to which we are utterly in the dark. On the other hand, they produce no wholesome effects on this life, nor do they leave any incentive for action. In fact, when taken literally they prompt no action at all.

Belief in Atonement

Fear of punishment is, in most cases, the only deterring influence in crushing evil. The pressure of public opinion and legal penalties are the great discouragers of wrong, and wherever they relax their hold, evil begins to crop up. Thus, for example, prostitution, gambling and drinking have been the curse of Christian nations, chiefly for the above reasons. Public opinion in Christian lands is not strong enough to stop evils, while legislation, on its criminal side, is nearly silent on the subject. The fear of punishment in the life to come acts as a deterrent in this respect in non-Christian races; but this can hardly be so with believers in the Atonement.

If God could not find any other remedy for the cleansing of human sin than that of sending His own sons from time to time to pay its penalty - since Jesus was only the last of the Pagan Christs who came to give their lives for human salvation - then there is no need of any good action on our part. There are very few of us who pursue virtue for its own sake. It is the reward of virtue, especially seen in its efficacy in counterbalancing the effects of sin, that we fulfill the law and lead a good life. But if the same thing is attainable merely by our belief in the Grace of Blood, few would think it worthwhile to bear the hardships and trials of the life of righteousness. Belief in the Atonement obviates the necessity for action. So it was held by Luther. Though the Romish Church attaches importance to good actions also, yet logically Luther is in the right in his conclusions.

Belief in Fatalism and Re-incarnation

Similarly, our belief in Predestination - another Christian verity - Fatalism and the Transmigration of the Soul weakens such impulses as we may have towards action. If everything in the form of pain and pleasure in this life has already been chalked out for us in the past, as the principle of the Transmigration of the Soul teaches, and no effort on our part can alter what is to be, then no moral schemes for avoiding adversity or achieving happiness are of the slightest avail. Similarly, if evil follows a man as the shadow of his actions in a past life, he need not strive to free himself from its hold, since it is unavoidable.

If, for example, he is suffering from fever in consequence of some wrongdoing in his past incarnation under the law of "Karma", no medical skill can cure him. Nay, it obviates any necessity for medical attention and, I may say, for the profession itself. It would put a stop to all advancement in that branch of science, and the same can be presumed in regard to other departments of human activity. I admit that believers in these principles do not generally show apathy towards progress. They are interested in it and sometimes contribute to its advancement, but this only means that they do not faithfully believe in things they hold as articles of faith. Their actions belie their belief.

Universal Belief in a Deity

A word here on the subject of the existence of God will not be out of place. Belief in the Deity has been universally the sine qua non of religion from time immemorial. The worshipping instinct in man has always found its gratification in directing his devotional feelings to some kind of deity. Buddhism is an exception to this rule, since no mention of God is contained in its scriptures. But the passion for worshipping established its supremacy there very speedily. All that is reserved for God in other religions goes to Buddha. All Buddhistic countries teem with his images. Their temple is another house of worship for idols, where the worshippers are seen sitting or standing before the images of Lord Buddha, with the same postures and gesticulations as are adopted elsewhere by the worshippers of God. Buddha is addressed in the same terms and receives the same adoration and homage as are ascribed by other religions to God.

In short, this passion for devotion to some Supreme Being is the dominant feature of man's mind. From a stone to a son of a woman, he has adored various manifestations of nature as his God, and he has been none the worse for it - seeing that he has been able to keep a certain moral order under any system of worship. The worship of idols has at times inspired him with noble and lofty feelings, like those which have been observed in the most worthy of the worshippers of God. Prayers addressed to images made by man's own hands have in their beauty, grandeur and sincerity surpassed even the devotional utterances of the holiest of monotheists while adoring the Most High. The Vishnuvites, for example - a class of Hindu idol worshippers in India - are often strict observers of morality. Their piety sometimes surpasses the righteousness of a virtuous Unitarian.

Belief in One God Should Lead to Virtue

The tenets of Islam, however, supported by culture and progress, have played havoc with old beliefs, and the futility of such old beliefs has at last become exposed. They have lost all the force they once possessed for the moulding of good character. The world at large is on the high road to belief in Unity, and even those who, like the Christians, still evince some sort of polytheistic tendencies, are now almost prepared to apologize for them. Belief in the unity of God in its purest form, when rendered into action in our daily life, would - as I will de scribe later on - merely, without doubt, bring our civilization to its climax; but a lip belief in the oneness of God is in my humble opinion, less meritorious than the different forms which polytheism has adopted in the cases above mentioned. Orthodoxy may take strong exception to my statement, but I would make bold to say that a polytheist who leads a virtuous life earns more merit in the eye of the Lord than a wicked person with all his belief in the unity of God.

I also say that I see no excellence in such a belief if it exerts no influence in beautifying the character. It is useless to sing hymns at the top of our voices if we are not leading, and do not lead, godly lives. God does not stand in need of any adoration from us; and if He does, He is not worthy of the great names with which He is revered. I would go further than that; I would say that if our worship of Him lies only in bringing offerings and sacrifices to His altar, and in the recital of praises and thanks to Him, it is neither creditable to God nor profitable to man. He is only another fetish and the biggest in the world of religion. God should stand above these things. He needs no praise from us. The Qur'an is very explicit on the point. It says that our extolling or praising God does not contribute to His glory, nor does blasphemy retract at all from His grandeur and dignity. Our prayers to Him should consist of such expressions, whether praise or thanksgiving to God or supplications to Him for some favour, as may set us to work out our own power and ability to our best advantage.

The Basic Muslim Prayer

In this respect my choice falls on the prayer that Islam prescribes for a Muslim. It is the opening chapter of the Qur'an:

"(All) praise is due to Allah, the Lord of the worlds. The Beneficent, the Merciful Master of the day of requital. Thee do we serve and Thee do we beseech for help. Guide us on the right path, the path of those upon whom Thou hast bestowed favours, not those upon whom wrath is brought down, nor those who go astray."

It begins with words of praise and thanksgiving, but if both these actions do not go beyond the lips of the worshipper they are of no avail in Islam. The opening words of the Muslim prayer are: al-hamdu li-llahi rabbi-l-'alamin, meaning, "All praises and thanksgiving are for God". The word hamd in Arabic is very rich in meaning. It conveys four ideas. First, the word has an exclusive use. It is reserved for the praise of the Lord. Secondly, it conveys the idea of perfection; the worship per sees in God all the best and most excellent attributes. Thirdly, it expresses a longing desire on the part of the worshipper to possess all such attributes to the extent of his abilities, and hence his prayers for them. Fourthly, it means thanks, that is, for his possession of capacity for cultivating such attributes in himself.

In fact, the action of praise psychologically consists of the said four ingredients. Perfection in beauty, sublimity and goodness on the one side, and our lack of them with desire to own them on the other, move our admiration and praise for the owner of those Excellencies; but we never desire to possess a thing unless we own the ability to do so and hence our gratitude for it. Thus the word hamd on the lips of a Muslim while at prayer is no empty word of compliment that may please the ears of the Deity, but a genuine expression of a genuine desire to mould his life on Divine lines; and to this end the Muslims recite, after the word hamd, four names of God which are the most beautiful among their class. They are: Rabb, Rahman, Rahim and Malik-i-yaum-i-din. Each of them, if followed by us, would make a millennium for the world. Rabb means Creator, Nourisher, Maintainer and Bringer of faculties to perfection. Rahman means All-Beneficent Lord whose blessings go to all, unmerited, and undeserved, and not by way of compensation for any good action but of His own goodness.

Rahim means One who rewards an action manifold. Malik means the owner or the king of judgment, whose sentence of punishment is only for reclamation and is not the fruit of anger on account of man's disobedience. The beauty of these four attributes is that in them God does not observe any distinction of class and creed among men. The God of Islam is the God of all nations, who is impartial in the dispensation of His blessings. I wish the rulers of the earth who hold sway over other races could show so broadminded and liberal an attitude, for then the burden of foreign rule would lose its curse. A Muslim says his prayers five times a day, which reminds him of these four Divine moulds in which he has to cast his daily life. High morality in Islam consists in the reflection of Divine morals - a truth that has recently dawned on the minds of Western theologians. Next, the worshipper speaks of his service to God, and the best religious service. According to Islam, this consists of doing actions in conformity with the requirements of the Divine Names. The Prayer then speaks of things for which a Muslim has to pray to his God. He must not pray for earthly good, but for knowledge - knowledge of the right path that may bring him under the grace and blessings of God, and keep him away from wickedness and error.

Comparison of Deities

I have made a somewhat wide digression from my subject, but it was not without its relevancy when dealing with the worshipping side of our nature. I have said that if the worship of a deity produces no moral effect on our life, it need not be pursued. Similarly, if adoring one deity is equal in its results to the worshipping of another, the choice among them is immaterial. By way of illustration I would take man- worship from among the various forms of polytheism as being the last and most refined. Jesus is the last of those favoured persons who from time to time have been placed on the throne of God by their fellow men. And here I would mention two other persons who besides Jesus still command human allegiance as God. These are Krishna and Ram Chandra - the two Indian deities - who were adored as such a thousand years before the birth of Christianity. Like Jesus, they are Eastern and come of coloured races, but as gods they are superior to him in many respects. They are more historic than the Nazarene. They can claim more genuineness for their life-records, though these were not free from folk-lore.

Their precepts and other utterances are, in general, more majestic, more awe-inspiring, and of greater practical utility than visionary sermons from the Mount. Jesus came of humble parentage and did not possess even a roof for shelter, but if Ram Chandra were a prince and later on a ruler, Krishna ruled the destinies of kings in his time. Jesus had nothing to sacrifice, as far as worldly possessions go, but the Indian gods gave up the best of worldly things in the service of humanity. Jesus was crushed by evil, but Rama-Chandra crushed evil, and Rudhra - another name for Krishna - had been the crusher of evil throughout his life. The actions ascribed to these great men by their narrators are transcendent. They are like shadows of the powers of the Almighty while the Bible is silent in the case of the sacred Carpenter in this respect. Undoubtedly the worshippers of these Indian gods did not exhibit a high standard of morals at certain periods of their history, but it is only fair to point out that such periods corresponded with that period in the history of the world - I compare the Middle Ages in Europe - when every corner of it presented a horizon of moral darkness. Christianity was no exception, but in many ways worse.

However, I look at the subject from a different angle. If we have to seek our God in the incarnate form, I see no special reason for giving precedence to Jesus over others. Our belief in him has not helped mankind any more than the Hindu belief in Krishna and Rama-Chandra. In one respect, Christianity has been woefully at fault. In the matter of culture and civilization Christianity has proved an implacable enemy to human advancement. It crushed science as long as it had the power to do so, and would do the same today if the modern world would suffer it. Only the other day the Bishop of Ripon proposed to give scientific research a holiday for ten years. This was but an echo of the old cry of tyranny and oppression that came from the Church against culture and science in the middle Ages, though it is clothed in the euphemisms of modern refinement.

In short, if belief in the divinity of a man has not helped the human race more than belief in the divinity of stones or elements in the days of ignorance, it is as I have shown before, not worthy of our further attention. Modern progress in the West should not be taken as the fruit of man's faith in the Church dogmas. The West made no progress so long as it was in the iron grip of Christianity. But even our belief in the Supreme Being, or the worship of God, is of no consequence if it does not help in the betterment of our race. Religion has been regarded as a necessary human institution from the days of Adam and Eve. But it should be treated as a back number if our pursuit of it possesses no utility. The whole question depends on the articles of faith upon which a religion insists.

If it asks us to believe in such tenets as have come under discussion in these pages, I think we are none the worse for dispensing with it. But if it invites our faith in doctrines that bring out all that is noble and good in us, and urges us to use all the powers of nature, whether reposed in the human frame or in the rest of the universe, to our best advantage, then religion becomes a most essential human institution. I repeat, God is not in need of human worship, but if our worship of Him inspires us to follow His ways as they are to be observed in the universe, ways that work out the best of civilization on righteous lines, it ought to be part and parcel of our life. I would go to my God fifty times a day in such a prayerful mood, though Islam prescribes but five prayers only.

Need and Importance of Law

The greatest blessing that has come to us from science is our belief in the existence of Law and that only our submission to it can bring us to success and happiness. Law is the order of the time. Every atom of nature and its various combinations, including the human frame, owes its very existence and further development to implicit obedience to Law. From the nebulous stage, up to the human frame, everything is a slave to Law. Religion will be doing the greatest possible service to humanity if it inspires man with a strong belief in Law. Virtue and evil, both in their growth and origin, are commensurate with the strength or weakness of our belief in Law and its forces. Criminality comes to the surface in quarters where Law can be avoided without fear of detection, and it becomes absolutely non-existent if we believe in the inexorableness of its punishments.

If Law is all in all in this way, and our belief in it is the greatest factor in the building of our character and in the achievement of success, it needs our strong belief not only in its Maker, who invests it with full force in its operation, but in many other things connected with Law. Law demands as well the services of its "functionaries", who must keep it always in force, since without them it would be but a dead-letter. Again, Law, or such portion of it as rules human destinies, whether discovered or revealed, should be preserved in such a form as may be of service to all units of humanity. It has not fallen to the lot of all men to make researches in the realms of Law, nor to be inspired by the contemplation of its source. There are but a few chosen persons of the human race who are favoured with this gift, and it is their duty to guide and enlighten their fellow men.

Again, Law does not lose all its force, nor can it compel universal adhesion, unless and until some reward or punishment comes inevitably to its fulfiller or breaker. Lastly, there ought to be set times for such reward and punishment - when the fruits of submission or disobedience to Law should become manifest to all. Thus if Law is the lever of the whole machinery in the universe, and our belief in it works wonders for our progress, we should also, to make it a reality in our eyes, believe in the Maker of the

Law, its functionaries, its record, and the custodians thereof. We must believe, too, in the reward and the punishment ordained by such an administrative system. For illustration, take any human institution that contributes to our civilization and we shall find it revolving on the pivot of the seven principles mentioned later, with Law as one of them. Take the government of any country. No society, even in its most primitive state, can work on healthy lines without some sort of government acting in it as a sovereign political authority. It works through its laws.

It must have machinery to set them in motion. It must reduce its laws to a record - they may be laws unwritten but imprinted on the tablet of the human mind - and entrust them to intermediate officials to convey to the general public. The government also needs a court of law to administrate, etc. If the Law is a thing so important, and I may say the only key to our advancement and perfection, it should be the first duty of religion to inspire in us a strong stimulus for respecting it. I find myself unable to attach any value to a faith which lacks such incentive. I cannot imagine any greater harm to the very fabric of human society than that which accrues to us by reason of our belief in a doctrine that either weakens our sense of responsibility or enervates our energy and divests us of motive for action. A religion that belittles the importance of Law is best forgotten. For this reason I had to give up my belief in the Atonement and other similar doctrines. I could not see, as I remarked before, any necessity for believing even in God, if belief is not attended with the results I have just mentioned.

Law and its rules are the main things in the whole universe. Law demands an unswerving belief in its existence and implicit obedience. It is inexorable in awarding its penalties to its disbelievers and breakers. No other belief can save the transgressor of the Law from its demands in this life; and shall not the same apply to the hereafter? Should not religion, then, inculcate first of all the necessity and importance of our faith in Law? It must speak of other verities also, because belief in the Law and that alone, is of no avail, if unaccompanied by belief in other essential things. Divine worship may be taken as a matter of first importance in religion, but we know nothing of God except through His ways of work in nature. Hence our worship of Him should find its real manifestation in our following His ways in our life. Our prayer or other form of adoration should act as a reminder of that Great Truth.

Divine Law in Islam

The recital of certain sacred words is not an act of worship; true worship consists in submission to His laws. In this respect I can safely say that Islam is the only representative of religion from Above. The word itself literally means submission to laws, and a Muslim is one who obeys the Law. Law, of course, means the Divine Laws, whether discovered by us as laws of nature or revealed to man by God Himself. The Qur'an uses several other words as synonyms of Law - ways of God, His limits and His bounds, His government, His pre-measurement of good and evil, and the Throne He sits upon, etc. These words, in fact, convey different functions and aspects of Law. It comes to prescribe limits; for, since no action in itself is either good or bad, it is its use or application, and the circumstances under which it is used or applied, that makes it good or bad. The Law thus defines the limits under which an action brings good to its doer or doers; and in this respect it becomes a virtue. Any transgression from the prescribed bounds means wrong, wickedness and sin.

I cannot cite a stronger statement on behalf of a revealed religion and its necessity than which I found in the last section of the second chapter of the Qur'an:

"Whatever is in the heavens and whatever is in the earth is God's; and whether you manifest what is in your minds or hide it, God will call you to account according to it; then

He will forgive whom He pleases and chastise whom He pleases, and God has power over all things. The Messenger (Muhammad) believes in what has been revealed to him from his Lord, and (so do) the believers; they all believe in God and His angels and His books and His messengers: We make no difference between any of His messengers; and they say: We hear and obey, our Lord! Thy forgiveness (do we crave), and to Thee is the eventual course. God does not impose upon any soul a duty but to the extent of its ability; for it, is (the benefit of) what it has earned, and against it (the evil of) what it has wrought: our Lord! do not punish us if we forget or make a mistake; our Lord do not lay on us a burden as Thou didst lay on those before us; our Lord do not impose upon us that which we have not the strength to bear; and pardon us and grant us protection and have mercy on us, Thou art our Patron, so help us against the unbelieving people." (The Holy Qur'an, 2:284-6).

First it speaks in clear terms of six things written in bold letters on every page of nature, and their existence is palpable even to a most superficial observer, since the denial of it is attended by immediate unrelenting penalty. These are the things in reality that can rightly be given the name of Truth or Verity. The so-called verities adopted as such by various persuasions are more dogmatic. The verities spoken of in these verses are as follows:

1. The universality of Divine Government - the working of His Law in Heaven and in the Earth.
2. Our unavoidable accountability to God for our every action hidden or manifest.
3. His law of retribution ever in operation, with occasional remission under given conditions.
4. Our ability to submit to His Laws.
5. Laws of action and their results, i.e., we reap what we sow.
6, The Hereafter - the time to bear the fruits of our actions.

It may be immediate, since sometimes we are punished immediately for our wrongs, or it may be in the future - what is popularly styled the Last Day or the Day of Judgment in religious parlance.

No special revelation from God, no elaborate teaching of tutor divine is needed to bring home to us these truths. Everything in nature speaks of them. No one with a grain of wisdom in his head can deny them; which being so, the case for religion and its necessity, as well as the nature of its tenets, is obvious enough. Even an atheist must bow down to these six laws. In fact, they are his creed if we eliminate the words "God" or "His" from the above. He accepts the yoke of Law quite meekly. His only trouble is his inability to believe in the Mind from which Law emanates - a thing of easy proof in the light of modern scientific researches. Even those who take exception to some of the above-mentioned verities, for example the fourth - our ability to obey the law - are compelled to believe in the working of these six laws on the physical plane. Everything in the universe contradicts their dogma.

In this connection I would make a few remarks concerning the fundamental doctrine of Christianity - the doctrine of so-called Original Sin. If sin means our violation of Law, the doctrine falls to the ground. Admittedly we are capable of doing wrong, we violate Law, but this propensity in our nature does not deny our ability to observe it. The whole machinery of a government in human society works on the assumption that the members of such society are capable of obeying the mandates of the government. Without such assumption or belief, the very existence of working of a body like the British Parliament - and in the same category come various other legislative bodies - becomes an anomaly. We believe in the working of the above-quoted six laws in the tangible world, but some of us do not see our way to concede the same belief to them in the life beyond the grave. I need not here repeat what I said before to prove the futility of such a position. Suffice it is to observe that I have keenly studied the laws or commandments of God as given in the Bible, and there is not a single word in them that cannot be fulfilled by man.

Some there may be who evince a certain laxity in observing some of the said commandments, but the human race is not lacking in those who are or who have been true Muslims - obedient to those laws. The first four commandments, as given in Exodus, demand our staunch belief in the unity of God. The rest of the commandments have been observed by a larger portion of humanity, as without their enforcement no human society, even in its most primitive steps of development, can stand, even for a short time. A Moses is needed to enforce those commandments in a newly fledged society for its healthy development. But to return. The said six laws compel our belief. If we wish to live as good citizens under the government of the Lord, and attain true success and happiness, we must look for those laws and sit at the feet of those who are their custodians and teachers. It is in this respect that the quoted verses of the Qur'an speak of the prophets and the Books they bring from God.

The Books come to reveal the Will of the Lord of His ways under which He rules all things in heaven and earth. There is one thing more which is so necessary to infuse in us a spirit strong enough to inspire an implicit obedience to law, and that is our belief in its unfailing and unavoidable working together, with its inexorability in the exaction of its penalties. In this connection, revelations from on High that belong to the various religious persuasions speak of certain sentient beings called Angels. According to Qur'anic teachings they are a body that bring Law and every force in nature into operation and keep them so. This is their function and the object of their existence. They act as a life or soul in everything in the universe. They set the faculties of nature in motion. I do not propose to enter into a long discussion of the subject, but merely to emphasize the fact that if we do need a strong belief in Law and our obedience to it, we can never achieve it unless we believe in the existence of beings like angels. It was in this light that I have named them in these pages the "functionaries" of Law.

We may or may not believe in any religious system, but we must and do believe in these verities. They are part and parcel of our health and happiness; and they ought to be the articles of faith in any religion which claims to have come from God. They are as follows:

Law.
God, as the source of Law.
Angels - functionaries of Law.
The Books - the record of Law.
The prophets - the intermediate persons who receive the first message from the Lord on the subject.
The Hereafter.
The Day of Judgment.

These are the seven verities spoken of in the Qur'anic verses which demand our belief, a belief which is given to them by every person in his mundane affairs. The present is the mother of the future. The after-life is the child of the present life. The former evolves out of the latter. Matter, in its evolutionary course on the physical plane, receives its final perfection in the human frame, but it gives rise to another order - the order of morality, ethics, and spirituality. Life with the progressive element in it leaves the body at our death like the aroma from fruit or a flower. It is like a vapour, but it possesses vast potentialities for creating a great cloud full of healthy rain. But Law, as I said before, rules every step of progress in the course of evolution. It is in obedience to it that success or full development attends the progressive element in its journey. We therefore need a System of Law that may help us to work out our future life on the desirable lines so that we may secure a full measure of bliss in higher regions.

And the code of it must and can only come from the original Intelligence, source of all life and its progress; hence the necessity for a Revealed Religion to disclose the above-mentioned verities, with full details for working them out. Any other system of religion is but a nursery-tale, whose functions it is to feed credulity and gratify the "child" in man. But the child matures one day in intelligence and judgment and begins to see things in the light of reason and culture. It is on this account that religions based on dogma and superstitions are becoming exiled from the lands of culture and advancement.

Before concluding these lines I should like to say a word on the Law of Remission as promulgated in the above-mentioned verses from the Qur'an:

"God does not impose upon any soul a duty but to the extent of its ability; for it, is (the benefit of) what it has earned, and against it (the evil of) what it has wrought: our Lord! do not punish us if we forget or make a mistake; our Lord do not lay on us a burden as Thou didst lay on those before us; our Lord do not impose upon us that which we have not the strength to bear ..."

It is based on Equity and Justice, and satisfies every demand for reason. The sacred Book, after mentioning our ability to abide by Law and then referring to our accountability for our actions, speaks of such mitigating circumstances as may avail to remit the penalty of Law for its breach. They are three in number:

Forgetfulness of Law, as in the case of Adam, according to the Qur'anic version (see 20:115 of the Qur'an).

Unintentional omission.

Inability under particular circumstances to meet the demands of Law.

No one can take exception to the logic and rationality

of the provisions. They bring Divine forgiveness for our wrongs, but we must approach the Master of the Judgment for it in prayerful humility. The Qur'an for this reason has formulated the said three provisions in the form of a prayer.

Modern Islamic Philosophy

There are a number of major trends in modern Islamic philosophy. First, there is the challenge of the West to traditional Islamic philosophical and cultural principles and the desire to establish a form of thought which is distinctive. From the mid-nineteenth century onwards, Islamic philosophers have attempted to redefine Islamic philosophy; some, such as Hasan Hanafi and Ali Mazrui, have sought to give modern Islamic philosophy a global significance and provide an agenda for world unity.

Second, there is a continuing tradition of interest in illuminationist and mystical thought, especially in Iran where the influence of Mulla Sadra and al-Suhrawardi has remained strong. The influence of the latter can be seen in the works of Henry Corbin and Seyyed Hossein Nasr; Mulla Sadra has exercised an influence over figures such as Mahdi Ha'iri Yazdi and the members of Qom School, notably Ayatollah Ruhollah Khomeini. The philosopher Abdul Soroush has introduced a number of concepts from Western philosophy into Iran.

Finally, there have been many thinkers who have adapted and employed philosophical ideas which are originally non-Islamic as part of the normal philosophical process of seeking to understand conceptual problems. This is a particularly active area, with a number of philosophers from many parts of the Islamic world investigating the relevance to Islam of concepts such as Hegelianism and existentialism. At the same time, mystical philosophy continues to exercise an important influence. Modern Islamic philosophy is thus quite diverse, employing a wide variety of techniques and approaches to its subject.

Reactions to the West

There has been a tendency in the Islamic world since the late nineteenth century to explore the issue of the relative decline or decadence of Arabic intellectual thought and science as compared with its Western equivalent. During the Christian medieval period the Islamic world was in its cultural and political ascendancy, and was at the centre of theoretical work in both science and philosophy. However, by the nineteenth century an enormous gap had opened between the Islamic world and the West. A wide variety of explanations for this decline have since been sought.

The realization that this gap existed led to the Nahda (rebirth or renaissance) movement between 1850 and 1914. Beginning in Syria but developed largely in Egypt, the movement sought to incorporate the main achievements of modern European civilization while at the same time reviving classical Islamic culture which predated imperialism and the centuries of decadence. The main problem facing the Nahda thinkers had was how to interpret the Islamic cultural tradition, including philosophy, in an environment dominated by the West. Jamal al-Din al-Afghani and Muhammad 'Abduh both argued that Islam is inherently rational and need not be abandoned in the face of the encroachment of Western forms of scientific and cultural thought.

The Egyptian philosopher Mustafa 'Abd al-Raziq also argued that it is possible to demonstrate the authenticity of traditional Islamic philosophical work and its modern relevance within Islamic society. He posits an inseparable link connecting rationalism and revelation in Islam, and he defends the traditional Islamic sciences as compatible with science and rationality. In this he constitutes what might be thought of as a more conservative position than his predecessor 'Abduh, who was more dubious about the values of some of the Islamic schools of thought, in particular of Sufism. Muhammad 'Abid al-Jabiri suggests that a viable Arab future can only come about through a deconstruction and critique of the reasons for the decline of the Arab world. He criticizes the dichotomy between the Islamicists, who hark back to a Golden Age in the past, and the liberal Westernizers, who praise the principles of the European Renaissance from which colonialism originated.

The solution he offers is the freeing of modern Arabic thought from both the language and the theological limitations of the past. The Arab mind has become very much part and parcel of traditional ways of exploring the world, and is restricted in its potential if it remains too closely wedded to its Islamic heritage. Fu'ad Zakariyya' argued that the Arab world declined due to its inability to historicize the past and its dependence on tradition, while Zaki Najib Mahmud brought out the importance of philosophy in taking us from the known to the unknown, and was critical of the ability of religion to interfere with this movement in thought. Hasan Hanafi presents a form of phenomenology which argues that a new concept of tawhid (divine unity) should be developed which will involve a principle of unity and equality for all people.

Hanafi also throws the charge of decadence back at the West, suggesting that the West is now entering a period of decadence and will require an infusion of ideas and energy from the East. He uses the language of liberation theology, which holds that revelation is adaptable to the language of each age. The original revelation was suited to the time and place of the Prophet and not necessarily of the current world. Modern Muslims should reinterpret revelation in modern language and in accordance with present demands; fossilized conservatism is a misinterpretation of the true dynamic and dialectical spirit of Islam. Fazlur Rahman also contends that Islamic conservatism contradicts the essence of Islam. Islam's aims are economic reform and the establishment of a just social order. According to the Qur'an, he argues, moral and economic decline are related events.

Therefore Islamic societies should turn away from petrified conservatism and educate their children in the new technologies. Islam should not be limited to communities of the faithful, but should seek a prominent place in the new ethical and social world order. Another movement in Islamic political philosophy depicts Muslims not as the antagonists of Western culture, but rather as being in the vanguard of the globalization of peace and social justice. The most popular thinker of this school in the USA is Malcolm X, who began his career as an isolationist minister for the Nation of Islam movement. At first he used Islam to separate African-Americans from white people, but later he preached an internationalized Islam that reaches beyond racial and national differences.

An important African thinker in this tradition is Ali Mazrui, who tries to harmonize several interdependent factors in Islamic theology with current global realities. Mazrui proposes a marriage between the Islamic monotheistic jihad (universal struggle), Islam's anti-racist and humanist agenda, and the need for global economic cooperation; he employs culture as a vehicle for social change through his integration of multiculturalism, the politics of pan-Islamicism and the need for globalism. He takes Islam to be the first Protestant revolution in Christi-anity. Moreover, he suggests that Islam's economic message turns monotheism from isolated spirituality to communitarian humanism - in the form of a Muslim world order among a community of faithful (umma) - through global economic cooperation, social justice and the brotherhood of all.

The essence of a multicultural perspective implies the acknowledgement that cultures project their own biases onto their perceptions of other societies. In a world which demands global economic policy-making and increasing interdependency, Mazrui believes that Muslims should see their religion of 'all is Godism' as a type of globalism. His innovation (ijtihad) interprets the Islamic jihad as an agenda of global peace and justice, thereby transforming what is taken to be a negative image of Islam into a signal for economic unity and world peace.

The Persian Approach to Philosophy

The area of the Islamic world which continued most forcefully the Islamic tradition in philosophy after the decline of Peripateticism is undoubtedly Persia. Interestingly, one of the staunchest advocates of the form of thought which might be called neo-Illuminationism, and which stems from the ishraqi principles of al-Suhrawardi, is Henry Corbin (1903-78), a French philosopher who worked in Iran. Corbin was active in translating and interpreting post-Avicennan Islamic philosophy with an emphasis on shi'ism, ishraqi thought and the mysticism of Ibn al-'Arabi. He posited the existence of a perennial school of philosophical wisdom, which can be detected through the recurrence of archetypal symbols such as the icon of light. Such icons exist in the works of Shihab al-Din al-Suhrawardi in the early twelfth century ad, and have their source in Eastern (ishraqi) traditions such as Zoroastrianism, Hermeticism and Manicheism. (The term ishraq, which signifies 'light', also means 'East' or 'Orient'.)

For Corbin, 'ishraq' designates not only a static spatial direction but a prescriptive invitation for a hermeneutic reorientation, whereby persons scrutinize their spiritual needs and points of return to archetypal origins. Corbin also discusses the role of the imagination, a faculty which exists between the senses and the intellect. While the senses perceive discrete data and the intellect categorizes, imagination is concerned with the world of archetypes ('alam at-mithal). For example, the notion of the perfect person (al-insan al-kamil) is an icon for the psychic centre. This centre signifies peace and the perfection of the self-realization process. Corbin asserts that by means of a series of epistemic states - which include revelation (kashf) and recollection (or archetypal memory) (dhikr) - one may return to the eternal origin. This process describes a cycle, thereby reasserting the Islamic theme of the unity of being (al-wahdat al-wujud).

Corbin's followers, such as Hermann Landolt, William Chittick and Seyyed Hossein Nasr, have developed his ideas in a variety of different ways. The latter is the best known contemporary Islamic philosopher. According to him, people share a spiritual component that cannot be actualized by either descriptive or pragmatic accounts of nature. Nasr's world perspective includes a normative element which integrates people in the same way as earlier religions and cosmologies. In the past, everyone considered their religion to be the true religion; today, however, we are confronted with a plurality of religions. How can a Muslim attain a workable relation with the sacred in such an environment? Nasr employs Sufism to refer to the archetypal dimensions common to all religions; it is through the realm of mysticism that different forms of spirituality meet. The contemporary world creates the need for followers of different creeds and cultures to communicate.

Islam must coexist with the Western world, but this does not imply an Islamic surrender to all the practices of Western society. Nasr's views on Western scientific progress show his dissatisfaction with many Western perspectives. Citing the ecological disasters of overpopulation and pollution, Nasr criticizes the value of Western technological advances. According to him, the fault lies in the mistaken meta-scientific presupposition that an innate nature exists which is disconnected from humanity and can be investigated separately and controlled. Moreover, the increasingly pervasive quantitative perspective supplied by units of measurement - like that by which the size of a building might be described - is an incomplete outlook because it does not articulate the qualitative effects of what it describes on the surrounding environment. By contrast, Nasr holds that Islamic and Eastern perspectives on science and technology are integrative and harmonious. They stress unity in their studies of nature, thereby acknowledging the long-term ecological significance of development.

Unless religious and spiritual values are embedded in a technological agenda, ecological disasters as well as a general lack of a sense of meaning in life are inevitable. Western science and its technological consequences are of ecological import to modern civilization. Consequently, neither science nor technology can consider itself irrelevant to environmental ethics. Philosophy along Neoplatonic lines should be pursued, since only this form of analysis does justice to the spiritual wholeness of humanity. The main emphasis in recent Persian philosophy has been on the thought of Mulla Sadra and al-Suhrawardi. Islamic philosophy has moved from the madrasa (traditional school) system and became an important part of the university curriculum. One of the most interesting thinkers is Mahdi Ha'iri Yazdi, whose work on knowledge by presence ('ilm al-huduri) provides an example of the fruitful combination of ideas from Western analytical philosophy and the ishraqi tradition in order to elucidate metaphysical and epistemological problems.

Recent Shi'ite theologians, as students of the work of Mulla Sadra, were versed in the dialectics of time and change. 'Ali Shari'ati, another student of Corbin, is an important social thinker whose work advocates a social process of Islamization. He rejects both the Peripatetic philosophers and the mystical thinkers, claiming that the existential being of each person contains a determination formed through mutual trust and compassion between them and God as their essence. This presumption is the ground for each person's being and the very core of each subject's potential for therapeutic unity (tawhid); its purpose is justice in both the providential and the social contexts. Islamization is achieved through an existential empathy and a phenomenological assimilation of exemplary people - such as the Imam Hossein (the Prophet's grandson) or Fatima (his daughter and the wife of Imam 'Ali) - into archetypal memory.

The martyrdom of 'Ali or Hossein is a paradigmatic message, not for sorrow but for the assimilation of their characters into the self. Further, Shari'ati depicts history as a dialectical process which does not exclude economic and material realities, Islam as a practical religion or people as potential agents of justice. He replaces the Platonic theory of epistemic recollection with a theory of normative archetypal recollection. One may gain normative knowledge through the archetypal recollection of a religion's most exemplary mythical figures. Religion provides social ideals, and yet it demands not a withdrawal to a secret realm but a social revolution in the everyday world. A creative commentary on Mulla Sadra was produced by Ruhollah Khomeini, who argues that people are primarily social as well as private citizens. Thus religious teachings relate not only to the personal morality of individuals but also to their social responsibilities and political actions.

In practice, these ideas imply a theocracy that does not distinguish between politics and religion. Bringing such a dominion into existence, he claims, requires an internal revolution from the masses directed against the existing ruling class, but this revolution must be guided by the directives of the religious authorities. He modifies Islamic theology with the notion of the religious jurist-ruler's guardianship (velayat-e-faqih), whose role is to guide the community of faithful in their universal struggle (jihad). This jihad is not essentially military, but is largely educational and seeks the expansion of monotheistic (that is, Islamic) ethics. Khomeini was a member of the School of Qom, based on the college in that city, which also produced Muhammad Hossein Tabataba'i, Murtaza Mutahheri and Muhammad Taqi Misbah Yazdi, all of whom have directed their influential thought at confronting the challenge to Islamic philosophy coming from the West. It should not be thought that this is an essentially reactionary strategy, however; Misbah has encouraged many of his students to study in the West and to take seriously scientific and logical thought as practised in the West.

Also, although much of Misbah's work has been on Mulla Sadra, he has been far from uncritical of the latter. In particular, he criticizes the notion of prime matter, which Mulla Sadra identifies as the pure potentiality for existents. He questions the principle that a potentiality for existents exists prior to existents themselves; after all, there is nothing but existents. Misbah argues further that many relations are not truly essences. For example, in the mind-dependent realm, we may ascribe 'below' as a relation between a table and book, but this subject-directed ascription does not imply that below is an essence in the actual world. An interesting and quite recent controversy in Persian philosophy has been that between Abdul Soroush on the one hand, and the philosophers of the school of Qom, as well as those influenced by the Corbin school, on the other. Soroush introduced a number of concepts from Western philosophy into Iran, in particular the leading ideas of Popper, Moore, Berlin and Wittgenstein.

This led him to suggest that we should use a notion like that of collective reason to understand and interpret religious ideas. Collective reason is the best way of dealing with theoretical and practical problems, and is preferable to relying solely on solutions attainable through the efforts of the jurisprudents and religious authorities. Not surprisingly, this aroused the ire of the school of Qom philosophers, and their representative Sadiq Larijani engaged Soroush in a debate which largely dealt with the correct interpretation of thinkers such as Popper, Watkins and Stalnaker, and in particular Hempel's paradoxes of confirmation. Soroush was also attacked by the Corbin circle whose basic philosophical approach relies very much on Heidegger along with traditional Islamic philosophy, and who were quite out of sympathy with the analytical nature of Soroush's books. This controversy is interesting in that it brings out the fact that philosophers in Iran are generally familiar now not only with traditional forms of Islamic philosophy but also with the current philosophical ideas of the West. Modern philosophers do not entirely reject Western views, but neither are they completely taken over by the West; they are prepared to examine Western views with a critical sympathy.

Modern Trends

A very vibrant area in Islamic philosophy is the history of philosophy, in particular the Greek tradition in Islamic philosophy. There exists both in the West and in the Islamic world a large number of scholars who have developed accounts of this close relationship and who continue to edit, translate and work on important texts in order to get some idea of the nature of the philosophical material which was produced in the early centuries of Islam. In addition, many philosophers in the Islamic world have adapted Western philosophy so as to make sense of the philosophical problems in which they are interested. C.A. Qadir in Pakistan developed an account of Islamic philosophy which he thought was in line with logical positivism, while 'Abd al-Rahman Badawi applied existentialism to Arab society. Zaki Najib Mahmud followed William James in presenting a pragmatic account of philosophy.

Some thinkers applied particular techniques in the Islamic tradition to philosophy, so that 'Ali Sami al-Nashshar for example based his work on Ash'arite theology, while Muhammad 'Aziz Lahbabi (1954) used Hegelianism to develop a theory of being which is quite unusual within the context of Islamic ontology. Hichem Djait (1986) combines Hegelianism with existentialism. He argues that only dialectical epistemology can be used to understand the modern situation of the Arab world, and that the apparent opposites of decadence/renaissance, Arab/non-Arab, orthodox/heterodox, tradition/modernity needs to be transcended if we are to understand the present nature of Islamic culture. Abdallah Laroui (1976) and Muhammad Arkoun (1985) both stress the contrast between Islam and modernity, and the former advocates the adoption of Westernization as the appropriate strategy for the Islamic world.

In his approach to the Qur'an, Arkoun uses the semiotic ideas current in modern French literature to argue that Islam has always been changing and developing, so that there is no point in referring to a particular constant orthodoxy. While many of these thinkers are hostile to mysticism and its Islamic form, Sufism, there can be little doubt that the latter represents a very potent framework for a good deal of present Islamic philosophy. The tradition of Sufism presents both a way of life which avoids many of the rigidities of traditional Islam and also a complex conceptual system which enables the philosopher to develop ideas and arguments which are intellectually satisfying. Modern Islamic philosophy employs a wide variety of different techniques and approaches to the subject.

7

Islamic Philosophy and the Modern Islamic Thought

From the perspective of Islam, a 'worldview' is not merely the mind's view of the physical world and of man's historical, social, political and cultural involvement in it as reflected, for example, in the current Arabic expression of the idea formulated in the phrase nazrat al-islam li al-kawn. It is incorrect to refer to the worldview of Islam as a na"rat al- islam li al-kawn. This is because, unlike what is conveyed by na"rat, the worldview of Islam is not based upon philosophical speculation formulated mainly from observation of the data of sensible experience, of what is visible to the eye; nor is it restricted to kawn, which is the world of sensible experience, the world of created things. If such expressions are now in use in Arabic in contemporary Muslim thought, it only demonstrates that we are already being unduly influenced by the modern, secular Western scientific conception of the world that is restricted to the world of sense and sensible experience.

Islam does not concede to the dichotomy of the sacred and the profane; the worldview of Islam encompasses both al-dunyâ and al-âkhirah, in which the dunyâ-aspect must be related in a profound and inseparable way to the âkhirah-aspect, and in which the âkhirah-aspect has ultimate and final significance. The dunyâ-aspect is seen as a preparation for the âkhirah-aspect. Everything in Islam is ultimately focused on the âkhirah-aspect without thereby implying any attitude of neglect or being unmindful of the dunyâ-aspect. Reality is not what is often 'defined' in modern Arabic dictionaries as wâqi c îyyah, whose use, particularly in its grammatical form wâqi c îy, is now in vogue. Reality is %aqîqah, which significantly is now seldom used due to the Syed al-Attas preoccupation with wâqi c îyyah which only points to factual occurrences. A factual occurrence is only one aspect in many of %aqîqah, whose ambit encompasses all of reality.

Moreover, a factual occurrence may be an actualization of something false; whereas reality is the actualization always of something true. What is meant by 'worldview', according to the perspective of Islam, is then the vision of reality and truth that appears before our mind's eye revealing what existence is all about; for it is the world of existence in its totality that Islam is projecting. The Islamic vision of reality and truth, which is a metaphysical survey of the visible as well as the invisible worlds including the perspective of life as a whole, is not a worldview that is formed merely by the gathering together of various cultural objects, values and phenomena into artificial coherence. Nor is it one that is formed gradually through a historical and developmental process of philosophical speculation and scientific discovery, which must of necessity be left vague and open-ended for future change and alteration in line with paradigms that change in correspondence with changing circumstances.

It is not a worldview that undergoes a dialectical process of transformation repeated through the ages, from thesis to antithesis then synthesis, with elements of each of these stages in the process being assimilated into the other, such as a worldview based upon a system of thought that was originally god centered, then gradually became god world centered, and is now world centered and perhaps shifting again to form a new thesis in the dialectical process. Such a worldview changes in line with ideological ages characterized by a predominance of the influence of particular and opposing systems of thought advocating different interpretations of worldview and value systems like that which have occurred and will continue to occur in the history of the cultural, religious and intellectual tradition of the West. There have not been in the history of the cultural, religious and intellectual tradition of Islam distinct ages characterized by a preponderance of a system of thought based upon materialism or idealism, supported by attendant methodological approaches and positions like empiricism, rationalism, realism, nominalism, pragmatism, positivism, logical positivism, criticism, oscillating between centuries and emerging one after another right down to our time.

The representatives of Islamic thought—theologians, philosophers, metaphysicians—have all and individually applied various methods in their investigations without preponderating on any one particular method. They combined in their investigations, and at the same time in their persons, the empirical and the rational, the deductive and the inductive methods and affirmed no dichotomy between the subjective 2 and the objective, so that they all affected what I would call the taw%îd method of knowledge. Nor have there been in Islam historical periods that can be characterized as 'classical', then 'medieval', then 'modern' and now purportedly shifting again to 'post-modern'; nor critical events between the medieval and the modern experienced as a 'renaissance' and an 'enlightenment'. Proponents of shifts in systems of thought involving changes in the fundamental elements of the worldview and value system may say that all forms of cultures must experience such shifts; otherwise in the process of interaction with changing circumstances they exhaust themselves and become uncreative and petrified.

But this is true only in the experience and consciousness

of civilizations whose systems of thought and value have been derived from cultural and philosophical elements aided by the science of their times. Islam is not a form of culture, and its system of thought projecting its vision of reality and truth and the system of value derived from it are not merely derived from cultural and philosophical elements aided by science, but one whose original source is Revelation, confirmed by religion, affirmed by intellectual and intuitive principles. Islam ascribes to itself the truth of being a truly revealed religion, perfected from the very beginning, requiring no historical explanation and evaluation in terms of the place it occupied and the role it played within a process of development. All the essentials of the religion: the name, the faith and practice, the rituals, the creed and system of belief were given by Revelation and interpreted and demonstrated by the Prophet in his words and model actions, not from cultural tradition which necessarily must flow in the stream of historicism. The religion of Islam was conscious of its own identity from the time of its revelation.

When it appeared on the stage of world history Islam was already 'mature', needing no process of 'growing up' to maturity. Revealed religion can only be that which knows itself from the very beginning; and that self-knowledge comes from the Revelation itself, not from history. The so-called 'development' in the religious traditions of mankind cannot be applied to Islam, for what is assumed to be a developmental process is in the case of Islam only a process of interpretation and elaboration which must of necessity occur in alternating generations of believers of different nations, and which refer back to the unchanging Source. As such the worldview of Islam is characterized by an authenticity and a finality that points to what is ultimate, and it projects a view of reality and truth that encompasses existence and life altogether in total perspective whose fundamental elements are permanently established.

These are, to mention the most salient ones, the nature

of God; of Revelation (i.e., the Qur'ân); of His creation; of man and the psychology of the human soul; of knowledge; of religion; of freedom; of values and virtues; of happiness—all of which, together with the key terms and concepts that they unfold, have profound bearing upon our ideas about change, development, and progress. I propose here in this Introduction to give a gist only of some of these fundamental elements of the worldview of Islam.

A comprehensive statement of their nature is already set forth in the chapters of this book. It is these fundamental elements of our worldview that we maintain to be permanently established that modernity is challenging, seeing that the shifting systems of thought that have brought modernity forth from the womb of history were fathered by the forces of secularization as a philosophical ideology. But as a matter of fact modernity or post-modernity has itself no coherent vision to offer that could be described as a worldview. If we could strike even a superficial similitude between a worldview and a picture depicted in a jigsaw puzzle, then the jigsaw of modernity is not only far from depicting any coherent picture, but also the very pieces to form such a picture do not fit.

This is not to mention post-modernity, which is already undoing all the pieces. No true worldview can come into focus when a grand scale ontological system to project it is denied, and when there is a separation between truth and reality and between truth and values. These fundamental elements act as integrating principles that place all our systems of meaning and standards of life and values in coherent order as a unified system forming the worldview; and the supreme principle of true reality that is articulated by these fundamental elements is focused on knowledge of the nature of God as revealed in the Qur'ân.

The nature of God as revealed in Islam is derived from Revelation. We do not mean by Revelation the sudden visions great poets and artists claim for themselves; nor the apostolic inspiration of the writers of sacred scripture; nor the illuminative intuition of the sages and people of discernment. We mean by it the speech of God concerning Himself, His creation, the relation between them, and the way to salvation communicated to His chosen Prophet and Messenger, not by sound or letter, yet comprising all that He has represented in words, then conveyed by the Prophet to mankind in a linguistic form new in nature yet comprehensible, without confusion with the Prophet's own subjectivity and cognitive imagination.

This Revelation is final, and it not only confirms the truth of preceding revelations in their original forms, but includes their substance, separating the truth from cultural creations and ethnic inventions. Since we affirm the Qur'ân to be the speech of God revealed in a new form of Arabic, the description of His nature therein is therefore the description of Himself by Himself in His own words according to that linguistic form. It follows from this that the Arabic of the Qur'ân, its interpretation in the Tradition, and its authentic and authoritative usage throughout the ages establishes the validity of that language to a degree of eminence in serving to describe reality and truth. In this sense and unlike the situation prevailing in modernist and postmodernist thought, we maintain that it is not the concern of Islam to be unduly involved in the semantics of languages in general that philosophers of language find problematic as to their adequacy to approximate or correspond with true reality.

The conception of the nature of God that is derived from Revelation is also established upon the foundations of reason and intuition, and in some cases upon empirical intuition, as a result of man's experience and consciousness of Him and of His creation. The nature of God understood in Islam is not the same as the conceptions of God understood in the various religious traditions of the world; nor is it the same as the conceptions of God understood in

Greek and Hellenistic philosophical tradition; nor as the conceptions of God understood in Western philosophical or scientific tradition; nor in that of Occidental and Oriental mystical traditions. The apparent similarities that may be found between their various conceptions of God with the nature of God understood in Islam cannot be interpreted as evidence of identity of the One Universal God in their various conceptions of the nature of God; for each and every one of them serves and belongs to a different conceptual system, which necessarily renders the conception as a whole or the super system to be dissimilar with one another.

Nor is there a 'transcendent unity of religions', if by 'unity' is meant 'oneness' or 'sameness'; and if by 'unity' is not meant 'oneness' or 'sameness', then there is plurality or dissimilarity of religions even at the level of transcendence. If it is conceded that there is plurality or dissimilarity at that level, and that by 'unity' is meant 'interconnectedness of parts that constitute a whole', so that the unity is the interconnection of the plurality or dissimilarity of religions as of parts constituting a whole, then it follows that at the level of ordinary existence, in which mankind is subject to the limitations of humanity and the material universe, any one religion is incomplete in itself, is in itself inadequate to realize its purpose, and can only realize its purpose, which is true submission to the One Universal God without associating Him with any partner, rival, or like, at the level of transcendence. But religion is meant to realize its purpose precisely at the level of existence in which mankind is subject to the limitations of humanity and the material universe, and not when mankind is not subject to these limitations as the term 'transcendent' conveys.

If 'transcendent' is meant to refer to an ontological condition not included under any of the ten categories, God is, strictly speaking, not the God of religion (i.e. ilah) in the sense that there could be such a thing as a 'unity' of religions at that level. At that level God is recognized as rabb, not as ilah; and recognizing Him as rabb does not necessarily imply oneness or sameness in the proper acknowledgement of the truth that is recognized, since Iblîs also recognized God as rabb and yet did not properly acknowledge Him. Indeed, all of Adam's progeny have already recognized Him as rabb at that level. But mankind's recognition of Him as such is not true unless followed by proper acknowledgement at the level in which He is known as ilah. And proper acknowledgement at the level in which He is known as ilah consists in not associating Him with any partner, rival, or like, and in submitting to Him in the manner and form approved by Him and shown by His sent Prophets.

If 'transcendent' is meant to refer to a psychological condition at the level of experience and consciousness which 'excels' or 'surpasses' that of the masses among mankind, then the 'unity' that is experienced and made conscious of at the level of transcendence is not of religions, but of religious experience and consciousness, which is arrived at by the relatively few individuals only among mankind. But religion is meant to realize its purpose for the generality of mankind; and mankind as a whole can never be at the level of transcendence for there to be a unity of religions at that level. Then if it is denied that the unity at that level is the interconnection of the plurality or dissimilarity of religions as of parts constituting a whole, rather that every one of the religions at the level of ordinary existence is not a part of a whole, but is a whole in itself—then the 'unity' that is meant is 'oneness' or 'sameness' not really of religions, but of the God of religions at the level of transcendence (i.e. esoteric), implying thereby that at the level of ordinary existence (i.e. exoteric), and despite the plurality and diversity of religions, each religion is adequate and valid in its own limited way, each authentic and conveying limited though equal truth.

The notion of a plurality of truth of equal validity in

the plurality and diversity of religions is perhaps aligned to the statements and general conclusions of modern philosophy and science arising from the discovery of a plurality and diversity of laws governing the universe having equal validity each in its own cosmological system. The trend to align modern scientific discovery concerning the systems of the universe with corresponding statements applied to human society, cultural traditions, and values is one of the characteristic features of modernity. The position of those who advocate the theory of the transcendent unity of religions is based upon the assumption that all religions, or the major religions of mankind, are revealed religions. They assume that the universality and transcendence of esoterism validates their theory, which they 'discovered' after having acquainted themselves with the metaphysics of Islam.

In their understanding of this metaphysics of the transcendent unity of existence, they further assume that the transcendent unity of religions is already implied. There is grave error in all their assumptions, and the phrase 'transcendent unity of religions' is misleading and perhaps meant to be so for motives other than the truth. Their claim to belief in the transcendent unity of religions is something suggested to them inductively by the imagination and is derived from intellectual speculation and not from actual experience. If this is denied, and their claim is derived from the experience of others, then again we say that the sense of 'unity' experienced is not of religions, but of varying degrees of individual religious experience which does not of necessity lead to the assumption that the religions of individuals who experienced such 'unity', have truth of equal validity as revealed religions at the level of ordinary existence.

Moreover, as already pointed out, the God of that experience is recognized as the rabb, not the ilah of revealed religion. And recognizing Him as the rabb does not necessarily mean that acknowledging Him in true submission follows from that recognition, for rebellion, arrogance, and falsehood have their origin in that very realm of transcendence. There is only one revealed religion. It was the religion conveyed by all the earlier Prophets, who were sent to preach the message of the revelation to their own people in accordance with the wisdom and justice of the Divine plan to prepare the peoples of the world for reception of the religion in its ultimate and consummate form as a Universal Religion at the hands of the last Prophet, who was sent to convey the message of the revelation not only to his own people, but to mankind as a whole. The essential message of the revelation was always the same: to recognize and acknowledge and worship the One True and Real God (ilah) alone, without associating Him with any partner, rival, or equal, nor attributing a likeness to Him; and to confirm the truth preached by the earlier Prophets as well as to confirm the final truth brought by the last Prophet as it was confirmed by all the Prophets sent before him.

With the exception of the people of this last Prophet, through whom the revealed religion achieved utmost perfection whose original purity is preserved to this day, most of the peoples to whom the earlier Prophets were sent deliberately renounced the guidance preferring instead cultural creations and ethnic inventions of their own, claiming these as 'religions' in imitation of revealed religion. There is only one genuine revealed religion, and its name is given as Islam, and the people who follow this religion are praised by God as the best among mankind. As for some among the peoples who preferred to follow their own and diverse forms of belief and practice described as 'religions', their realization of the Truth is their rediscovery, by means of guidance and sincerity of heart, of what is already clearly manifest in Islam even at the level of ordinary existence. Only Islam acknowledges and affirms the Unity of God absolutely without having to arrive at the level of transcendence to do so; without confusing such acknowledgement and affirmation with traditional forms of belief and practice described as 'religions'; without confounding such acknowledgement and affirmation with cultural creations and ethnic inventions interpreted in imitation of revealed religion.

Therefore Islam does not admit of any error in the understanding of the Revelation, and in this sense Islam is not merely a form—it is the essence itself of religion (dîn). We do not admit in the case of Islam of a horizontal dividing line separating the exoteric from the esoteric understanding of the Truth in religion. We maintain rather a vertical line of continuity from the exoteric to the esoteric; a vertical line of continuity which we identify as the Straight Path of islam without there being any inconsistency in the three stages of the spiritual ascent such that the Reality or transcendent Truth that is recognized and acknowledged is in our case accessible to many. It is futile to attempt to camouflage error in the religions, in their respective understanding and interpretation of their scriptures which they believe reflect the original revelation, by resorting to the characteristics and peculiarities of different forms of ethnicity and symbolism, and then to explain away the symbolism by means of a contrived and deceptive hermeneutic such that error appears as truth.

Religion consists not only of affirmation of the Unity of God (al-tawahîd), but also of the manner and form in which we verify that affirmation as shown by His last Prophet, who confirmed, perfected and consolidated the manner and form of affirmation and verification of Prophets before him. This manner and form of verification is the manner and form of submission to God. The test of true affirmation of the Unity of God, then, is the form of submission to that God. It is only because the form of submission enacted by the religion that affirms the Unity of God is true to the verification of such affirmation that that particular religion is called Islam. Islam, then, is not merely a verbal noun signifying 'submission'; it is also the name of a particular religion descriptive of true submission, as well as the definition of religion: submission to God.

Now the manner and form of submission enacted in religion is definitely influenced by the conception of God in the religion. It is therefore the conception of God in the religion that is crucial to the correct articulation of the form of true submission; and this conception must be adequate in serving to describe the true nature of God, which can only be derived from Revelation, not from ethnic or cultural tradition, nor from an amalgamation of ethnic and cultural tradition with sacred scripture, nor from philosophical speculation aided by the discoveries of science. The conception of the nature of God in Islam is the consummation of what was revealed to the Prophets according to the Qur'ân. He is one God; living, self-subsistent, eternal and abiding. Existence is His very essence. He is one in essence; no division in His essence, whether in the imagination, in actuality, or in supposition is possible.

He is not a locus of qualities, nor is a thing portioned and divisible into parts, nor is He a thing compounded of constituent elements. His oneness is absolute, with an absoluteness unlike the absoluteness of the natural universal, for while being thus absolute He is yet individuated in a manner of individuation that does not impair the purity of His absoluteness nor the sanctity of His oneness. He is transcendent, with a transcendence that does not make it incompatible for Him to be at once omnipresent, so that He is also immanent, yet not in the sense understood as belonging to any of the paradigms of pantheism. He possesses real and eternal attributes which are qualities and perfections which He ascribes to Himself; they are not other than His essence, and yet they are also distinct from His essence and from one another without their reality and distinctness being separate entities subsisting apart from His essence as a plurality of eternals; rather they coalesce with His essence as an unimaginable unity.

His unity is then the unity of essence, attributes, and acts, for He is living and powerful, knowing, willing, hearing and seeing, and speaking through His attributes of life and power, knowledge, will, hearing and sight, and speech; and the opposite of these are all impossible in Him. He is unlike the Aristotelian First Mover, for He is always in act as a free agent engaged in perpetual creative activity not involving change in Him or transformation and becoming. He is far too exalted for the Platonic and Aristotelian dualism of form and matter to be applied to His creative activity; nor can His creating and His creation be described in terms of the Plotinian metaphysics of emanation. His creating is the bringing forth of ideal realities that preexist in His knowledge into external existence by His power and His will; and these realities are entities that he causes to become manifest in the interior condition of His being.

His creating is a single act repeated in an eternal process, whereas the contents of the process which are His creation are non-eternal, being originated in new yet similar guises in discrete durations of existence for as long as He wills. It is through Revelation, in which God has described Himself, His creative activity and His creation, and not through Greek or Hellenistic philosophical tradition, neither even through philosophy nor through science, that Islam interprets the world together with all its parts in terms of events that occur within a perpetual process of a new creation. This interpretation entails the affirmation of realities and their double nature consisting of complementary opposites; their existential condition of permanence and change; their involvement in a continual process of annihilation and renewal by similar; their absolute beginning in past time and their absolute end in future time. There are limitations to time and space; and both are the result of the creative act that brings the cosmos into existence.

Change is not in the phenomenal things, as that would

imply the persistence of existence in the things making them substrata for change to take place, but at the ontological level of their realities which contain within themselves all their future states. Change is then the successive actualization, by means of the creative act, of potentialities inherent in the realities of things which as they unfold their contents in correspondence with the creative command preserve their identities through time. The dual condition of the realities involving permanence on the one hand and change on the other presupposes a third ontological category in the interior condition of being between external existence and non-existence. This is the realm of ideal realities subsisting as permanently established entities in the consciousness of God, and they are none other than the forms and aspects of the names and attributes of God considered in their aspect of difference from Him.

Islam affirms the possibility of knowledge; that knowledge of the realities of things and their ultimate nature can be established with certainty by means of our external and internal senses and faculties, reason and intuition, and true reports of scientific or religious nature, transmitted by their authentic authorities. Islam has never accepted, nor has ever been affected by ethical and epistemological relativism that made man the measure of all things, nor has it ever created the situation for the rise of skepticism, agnosticism, and subjectivism, all of which in one way or another describe aspects of the secularizing process which have contributed to the birth of modernism and postmodernism. Knowledge is both the arrival of meaning in the soul as well as the soul's arrival at meaning. In this definition we affirm that the soul is not merely a passive recipient like the tabula rasa, but is also an active one in the sense of setting itself in readiness to receive what it wants to receive, and so to consciously strive for the arrival at meaning.

Meaning is arrived at when the proper place of anything in a system is clarified to the understanding. The notion of 'proper place' already implies the existence of 'relation' obtaining between things which altogether describe a system, and it is such relation or network of relations that determines our recognition of the thing's proper place within the system. By 'place' is meant here that which occurs not only in the spatio-temporal order of existence, but also in the imaginal, intelligible, and transcendental orders of existence. Since objects of knowledge from the point of view of human cognition are without limit, and since our external and internal senses and faculties of imagination and cognition all have limited powers and potentials, each created to convey and conserve information concerning that for which it was appointed, reason demands that there is a limit of truth for every object of knowledge, beyond which or falling short of which the truth about the object as it and its potentials should be known becomes false.

Knowledge of this limit of truth in every object of knowledge is either attained by way of common sense if the object is already something obvious to the understanding, or it is achieved through wisdom, either practical or theoretical as the case may be, when the object is something obscure to the understanding. The apparent and obvious meanings of the objects of knowledge have to do with their respective places within the system of relations; and their 'proper' places become apparent to our understanding when the limits of their significance are recognized. This then is the position of truth: that there are limits to the meaning of things in the way they are meant to be known, and their proper places are profoundly bound up with the limits of their significance.

True knowledge is then knowledge that recognizes the limit of truth in its every object. Our real challenge is the problem of the corruption of knowledge. This has come about due to our own state of confusion as well as influences coming from the philosophy, science, and ideology of modern Western culture and civilization. Intellectual confusion emerged as a result of changes and restriction in the meaning of key terms that project the worldview derived from Revelation. The repercussions arising from this intellectual confusion manifest themselves in moral and cultural dislocation, which is symptomatic of the degeneration of religious knowledge, faith, and values. The changes and restrictions in the meanings of such key terms occur due to the spread of secularization as a philosophical program, which holds sway over hearts and minds enmeshed in the crisis of truth and the crisis of identity.

These crises, in turn, have become actualized as a result of a secularized system of education that causes deviations, if not severance, from historical roots that have been firmly established by our wise and illustrious predecessors upon foundations vitalized by religion. One must see that the kind of problem confronting us is of such a profound nature as to embrace all the fundamental elements of our worldview that cannot simply be resolved by legalistic and political means. Law and order can only find their places when recognition of truth as distinguished from falsehood, and real as distinguished from illusory, is affirmed and confirmed by action in acknowledgement of the recognition. This is achieved by means of right knowledge and right method of disseminating it. So let us not dissipate our energies in attempting to find the way out by groping in the labyrinths of legalism, but concentrate them instead by grappling the main problem, which is bound up intimately with the correct understanding and appreciation of religion and the worldview projected by it, because that directly concerns man, his knowledge and purpose in life, his ultimate destiny.

The process of acquisition of knowledge is not called 'education' unless the knowledge that is acquired includes moral purpose that activates in the one who acquires it what I call âdab. Âdab is right action that springs from self-discipline founded upon knowledge whose source is wisdom. For the sake of convenience I shall translate âdab simply as 'right action'. There is an intrinsic connection between meaning and knowledge. I define 'meaning' as the recognition of the place of anything in a system, which occurs when the relation a thing has with others in the system becomes clarified and understood. 'Place' refers to right or proper place in the system; and 'system' here refers to the Qur'ânic conceptual system as formulated into a worldview by tradition and articulated by religion. Knowledge as we have already defined is the arrival of meaning in the soul, and the soul's arrival at meaning, and this is the recognition of the proper places of things in the order of creation, such that it leads to the recognition of the proper place of God in the order of being and existence. But knowledge as such does not become an education unless the recognition of proper places is actualized by acknowledgement—that is, by confirmation and affirmation in the self—of the reality and truth of what is recognized.

Acknowledgement necessitates action that is proper to recognition. Âdab, or right action, consists of such acknowledgement. Education, then, is the absorption of âdab in the self. The actualization of âdab in individual selves composing society as a collective entity reflects the condition of justice; and justice itself is a reflection of wisdom, which is the light that is lit from the lamp of prophecy that enables the recipient to discover the right and proper place for a thing or a being to be. The condition of being in the proper place is what I have called justice; and âdab is that cognitive action by which we actualize the condition of being in the proper place. So âdab in the sense I am defining here, is also a reflection of wisdom; and with respect to society âdab is the just order within it. Âdab, concisely defined, is the spectacle of justice (c adl) as it is reflected by wisdom (%ikmah). In order to explain what I mean by âdab and to appreciate my definition of it, let us consider, for example, one's self.

The human self or soul has two aspects: the one predisposed to praiseworthy acts, intelligent by nature, loyal to its covenant with God; the other inclined to evil deeds, bestial by nature, heedless of its covenant with God. The former we call the rational soul (al-nafs al-nâmiqah), the latter the carnal or animal soul (al-nafs al-%ayawânîyyah). When the rational soul subdues the animal soul and renders it under control, then one has put the animal soul in its proper place and the rational soul also in its proper place. In this way, and in relation to one's self, one is putting one's self in one's proper place. This is âdab toward one's self. Then in relation to one's family and its various members; when one's attitude and behaviour toward one's parents and elders display sincere acts of humility, love, respect, care, charity; this shows one knows one's proper place in relation to them by putting them in their proper places.

This is âdab toward family. And similarly, such attitude and behaviour, when extended to teachers, friends, community, leaders, manifest knowledge of one's proper place in relation to them; and this knowledge entails requisite acts in order to actualize âdab toward them all. Again, when one puts words in their proper places so that their true meanings become intelligible, and sentences and verses in like manner such that prose and poetry become literature, then that is âdab toward language. Further, when one puts trees and stones, mountains, rivers, valleys and lakes, animals and their habitat in their proper places, then that is âdab toward nature and the environment. The same applies to one's home when one arranges furniture and puts things in their proper places therein until harmony is achieved—all such activity is âdab towards home and furniture.

And we cite also putting colours, shapes, and sounds in their proper places producing pleasing effects— that is âdab toward art and music. Knowledge too, and its many branches and disciplines, some of which have more important bearing upon our life and destiny than others; if one grades them according to various levels and priorities and classifies the various sciences in relation to their priorities putting each one of them in its proper place, then that is âdab toward knowledge. It should already become clear that my interpretation of the meaning of âdab reveals that âdab implies knowledge; it is knowledge derived from wisdom (%ikmah); it manifests the purpose of seeking knowledge; it is also internal and external activity of the soul that springs from ethical and moral values and virtues; its fount of origin is not philosophy nor science, but revealed truth that flows from religion. From the above definitions of some of the major key concepts in Islam, which all converge upon the concept of knowledge, it becomes clear that their meanings are closely interrelated, in particular their meanings which all focus upon the notion of 'proper place' which points to a certain 'order' in the system and one's relation to that order.

The order is in the form of hierarchy which pervades the created order of being and existence, both external existence and mental existence. The hierarchy I mean, when applied to the human order, is not to be misunderstood as the kind of hierarchy created by man and articulated into a social structure such as a system of caste, or a graded priestly organization, or any kind of social stratification according to class. It is not something to be organized into a social structure; it is rather something to be organized in the mind and actualized in the attitude and the behaviour. The organization in the mind is not formulated by the human criteria of power, wealth, and lineage, but by the Qur'ânic criteria of knowledge, intelligence, and virtue. When the mind recognizes the reality that knowledge and being are ordered according to their various levels and degrees, and when the attitude and the behaviour acknowledges by action what the mind recognizes, then this conformity of the acknowledgement with the recognition, by which the self assumes its proper place in coincidence with the act of acknowledgement, is none other than âdab. But when the mind displaces the levels and degrees of knowledge and being, disrupting the order in the legitimate hierarchy, then this is due to the corruption of knowledge.

Such corruption is reflected in the confusion of justice, so that the notion of 'proper places' no longer applies in the mind or externally, and the disintegration of âdab takes place. The disintegration of âdab, which is the effect of the corruption of knowledge, creates the situation whereby false leaders in all spheres of life emerge; for it not only implies the corruption of knowledge, but it also means the loss of the capacity and ability to recognize and acknowledge true leaders. Because of the intellectual anarchy that characterizes this situation, the common people become determiners of intellectual decisions and are raised to the level of authority on matters of knowledge.

Authentic definitions become undone, and in their stead we are left with platitudes and vague slogans disguised as profound concepts. The inability to define; to identify and isolate problems, and hence to provide for right solutions; the creation of pseudo-problems; the reduction of problems to mere political, socio-economic and legal factors become evident.

It is not surprising if such a situation provides a fertile breeding ground for the emergence of deviationists and extremists of many kinds who make ignorance their capital. Language reflects ontology.

Introducing key concepts foreign to a language involves not merely the translating of words, but more profoundly the translating of symbolic forms belonging to the super system of a foreign worldview not compatible with the worldview projected by the language into which such concepts are introduced.

Those responsible for introducing them and advocating their currency are the scholars, academics, journalists, critics, politicians and amateurs not firmly grounded upon knowledge of the essentials of religion and its vision of reality and truth. One of the main causes for the emergence of intellectual confusion and anarchy is the changes and restrictions which they have effected in the meanings of key terms that project the worldview of Islam which is derived from Revelation.

The major factor that influenced their thinking is undoubtedly the introduction of the concept secular and its implications into our language and our universe of discourse, which Muslims as a whole have yet to perceive from its proper perspective.

The early latinized Western Church monopolized learning and coined the term 'secular' (saeculum) to refer to people who are unable to read and write, who are therefore not learned in the arts and sciences, especially in law and medicine, who are then generally called the 'laity': the nonprofessional, not expert. Due to the preoccupation of such people with mundane matters, the term also conveys a general meaning of 'being concerned with the affairs of the world'; of being 'not sacred', 'not monastic', 'not ecclesiastical'; of being something 'temporal', something 'profane'. Hence we find this term being translated by Christian Arabs into Christian.

This translation of the term and its various grammatical forms, in the sense understood by the Western Christian Church and its Christian Arab translators, has been allowed to gain currency in contemporary mainstream Islamic Arabic, despite the clear fact that it has no relevance whatsoever to Islam and to the Muslim ummah. There is no equivalent in Islam to the concept secular, especially when there is no equivalent to 'church' or 'clergy', and when Islam does not concede that there is a dichotomy of the sacred and the profane which naturally brings about a demeaning of the profane world. If the nearest equivalent were to be found in Islam to the concept secular, then it would be that which is connoted by the Qur'ânic concept of al-hayat al-dunyâ: 'the worldly life'.

The word dunyâ, derived from danâ, conveys the meaning of something being 'brought near'. This something that is being 'brought near', according to my interpretation, is the world together with all its parts; for it is the world that is being brought near, that is, being brought near to the experience and consciousness of man. Hence the world is called dunyâ. By virtue of the fact that what is being brought near—that is, the world and the life in it—surround us as it were and overwhelm us, they are bound to distract from consciousness of our final destination, which is beyond this world and this life, which is what comes after, that is, al-âkhirah. Since it comes at the end, al-âkhirah is felt as far; and this accentuates the distraction created by what is near. The Holy Qur'ân says that the Hereafter is better than the life of this world; it is more abiding, everlasting. But the Holy Qur'ân does not derogate the world itself; or dissuade from contemplation and reflection and interpretation of it and its wonders; rather it extols the world of creation and urges us to contemplate and reflect upon it and its wonders in order that we might be able to interpret and derive their practical and beneficial purpose. The Holy Qur'ân only warns of the distracting and ephemeral nature of life in the world.

The warning emphasis in the concept of al- hayat al-dunyâ is the life in it, not the world, so that the world and nature are not demeaned as implied in the concept secular. That is why I said that al-hayat al-dunyâ is the nearest equivalent to the concept secular, because in actual fact there is no real equivalent concept in the worldview of Islam projected by the Holy Qur'ân. Moreover, since the world is that which is 'brought near', and since the world and nature are signs or ayât of God, it is the signs of God that are brought near to our experience and consciousness; and it would be blasphemous, to say the least, to derogate the world and nature knowing them in their true character and purpose. It is God's manifestation of His infinite mercy and loving kindness that He caused His signs to be brought near to us, the better for us to understand their intended meanings. There can be no excuse, therefore, for those who, struck by awe of the signs, worship them instead of God to whom they point; or those who, seeking God, yet demean and abjure His signs because they see tempting evil in them and not in themselves; or again those who, denying God, appropriate His signs for their own materialistic ends and change them in pursuit of illusory 'development'.

The world cannot develop as it is already perfect according to its own fimrah; only life in the world can develop. There is a final end to the world just as there is a final end to life in the world. Development of life in the world is that which leads to success in that which comes after it, for there is no meaning to 'development' unless it is aligned to a final objective. The Latin term saeculum in its original sense relates to the doctrinal formulations of the Western Christian religious tradition. The true meanings couched in it, however, gradually asserted their intentions in the experience and consciousness of Western man extending over a period of more than seven centuries of his intellectual and scientific development until their full implications have now become actualized. Whereas originally the term 'secular', from saeculum, conveyed a spatio-temporal connotation, as can be understood from the way it was used, the order of precedence in the formulation of the dual meaning has now undergone a change emphasizing the temporal rather than the spatial aspect.

The original spatio-temporal connotation is derived historically out of the experience and consciousness born of the fusion of the Graeco-Roman and Judaic traditions in Western Christianity. It is this 'fusion' of the mutually conflicting elements of the Hellenic and Hebrew worldviews which have deliberately been incorporated into Christianity that modern Christian theologians and intellectuals recognize as problematic, in that the former views existence as basically spatial and the latter as basically temporal. The arising confusion of worldviews becomes the root of their epistemological and hence also theological problems. Since the world has only in modern times been more and more understood and recognized by them as historical, the emphasis on the temporal aspect of it has become more meaningful and has conveyed a special significance to them. For this reason they exert themselves in efforts emphasizing what they conceive to be the Hebrew vision of existence, which they think is more congenial with the spirit of 'the times', and denouncing the Hellenic as a grave and basic mistake.

So they now say that the concept secular conveys a markedly dual connotation of time and location; the time referring to the 'now' or 'present' sense of it, and the location to the 'world' or 'worldly' sense of it. Thus saeculum is interpreted to mean basically 'this age' or the 'present time'; and this age or the present time refers to events in this world, and it also then means 'contemporary events'. The emphasis of meaning is set on a particular time or period in the world viewed as a historical process. The concept secular refers to the condition of this world at this particular time or period or age. Already here we discern the germ of meaning that easily develops itself naturally and logically into the existential context of an ever-changing world in which there occurs the relativity of human values. And this natural and logical development of the concept secular is now taking place in contemporary, modern Western civilization, which is propagating it throughout the world. We must see, in view of the fact that secularization is not merely confined to the Western world, that their experience of it and their attitude toward it is most instructive for Muslims.

We must be made aware that secularization, in the way in which it is also happening in the Muslim world, does effect our beliefs and way of life, even if not in the same way it does the beliefs and way of life of Western man; because problems arising out of secularization, though not quite the same as those besetting the West, have certainly caused much confusion in our midst. It is not surprising that these problems are caused due to the introduction of

Western ways of thinking, and judging, and believing emulated by some modernist as well as traditionalist Muslim scholars and intellectuals who have been unduly influenced by the modern West and overawed by its scientific and technological achievements, who by virtue of the fact that they could so readily be thus influenced betray their lack of true understanding and full grasp of both the worldviews of Islam and of the modern West and the essential beliefs and modes of thought that project them.

They have, because of their influential positions in Muslim society, become conscious or unconscious disseminators of unnecessary confusion that is founded upon a crisis of identity. The situation in our midst can indeed be seen as critical when we consider the fact that Muslims are generally unaware of what the secularizing process implies. It is therefore essential that we obtain a clear understanding of it from those who know and are conscious of it, who believe and welcome it, who teach and advocate it to the world. Secularization is defined as "the deliverance of man first from religious then from metaphysical control over his reason and his language" It is the setting free of the world from religious and semi-religious understandings of itself; the dispelling of all closed worldviews, the breaking of all supernatural myths and sacred symbols; the "defatalization" of history; the discovery by man that he has been left with the world on his hands, that he can no longer blame Fortune or the Furies for what he does with it; it is man turning his attention away from the worlds beyond and toward this world and this time. Secularization encompasses not only the political and social aspects of life, but also inevitably the cultural, for it denotes "the disappearance of religious determination of the symbols of cultural integration".

It implies an irreversible historical process in which culture and society are "delivered from tutelage to religious control and closed metaphysical worldviews". It is considered a "liberating development", and the end product of secularization is historical relativism. Hence according to them history is a process of secularization. The integral components in the dimensions of secularization are the "disenchantment of nature", the "desacralization of politics', and the "deconsecration of values". By the disenchantment of nature—a term and concept borrowed from the German sociologist Max Weber 6 —they mean as he means, the "freeing of nature from its religious overtones", which means to deprive nature of spiritual meaning so that man can act upon it as he pleases and make use of it according to his needs and plans, and hence create historical change and 'development'. By the desacralization of politics they mean the "abolition of sacral legitimation of political power and authority", which is the prerequisite of political change and hence also social change allowing for the emergence of the historical process.

By the deconsecration of values they mean the "rendering transient and relative all cultural creations and every value system" which for them include religion and worldviews having ultimate and final significance, so that in this way history, the future, is open to change, and man is free to create the change and immerse himself in the 'evolutionary' process. This attitude toward values demands an awareness on the part of secular man of the relativity of his own views and beliefs; he must live with the realization that the rules and ethical codes of conduct which guide his own life will change with the times and generations. This attitude demands what they call 'maturity'; and hence secularization is also a process of 'evolution' of the consciousness of man from the 'infantile' to the 'mature' states, and is defined as the "removal of juvenile dependence from every level of society"; the process of "maturing and assuming responsibility"; the "removal of religious and metaphysical supports and putting man on his own".

They further say that this recurring change of values is

also the recurrent phenomenon of "conversion" which occurs "at the intersection of the action of history on man and the action of man on history", which they call "responsibility", the acceptance of "adult accountability". Thus as already mentioned, they visualise the contemporary experience of secularization as part of the evolutionary process of human history; as part of the irreversible process of 'coming of age', of 'growing up' to 'maturity' when they will have to 'put away childish things' and learn to have 'the courage to be'. If the full implications of the foregoing brief exposition of the meaning of secularization is understood, it will become obvious that the twentieth century Christian Arabic usage and accepted translation of the term 'secular' as c almâniy merely reflects its meaning as formulated by the latinized Western Christianity of the thirteenth century.

Even though the modern translators vaguely refer to the term 'secular' as meaning also jilîy or qarnîy, yet they were completely unaware of the way in which the concept couched in the term 'secular' has evolved during the last seven centuries in the experience and consciousness of Western man, causing the rise of contemporary problems never encountered before. Their description of secularity as al-ihtimâm bi umur al-dunyâ, or as al-ihtimâm bi al- c alamiyyat is not quite correct, because to be preoccupied with the affairs of the world, or with worldly things, is according to us not necessarily to be opposed to religion; whereas secularity understood in the modern sense is necessarily opposed to religion. Similarly, to secularize is not quite the same as %awwal ila ghara calami ay dunyawi, because to change in accordance with what is good in the pursuit of worldly ends is according to us not necessarily to change in opposition to religion.

Secularization in the modern sense described above, and which is actually happening, is a process which is definitely opposed to religion; it is a philosophical program or an ideology that seeks to destroy the very foundations of religion. C Almâniyyah, then, cannot be a description of 'secularism'; as it seems to me nearer the truth to describe it as wâqi c îyyah in view of its close conceptual connection with the philosophical ideology of positivism. Be that as it may, since the dual connotation of place and time is fundamental to the concept of saeculum, which conveys already the germ of meaning that evolves naturally and logically into its present, contagious fullness; and since the place and the time refer to here and now respectively, it would be more precise to describe 'secularism' literally by some compound word such as hunalâniyyah, from huna and al-ân.

For the 'here-and-nowness' elicited by hunalâniyyah clearly projects a conception of the world and of life in it that rejects other worlds beyond; that repudiates the past except insofar as it confirms the present; that affirms an open future; that altogether denies religion and worldviews having ultimate and final significance. But better still to emulate the method of discerning scholars, savants, and sages among our early predecessors who were very much aware of the paramount importance of language and its profound connection with reason; who were meticulous in the correct usage of language and the pursuit of authentic meaning; who exercised great care not to confuse Islamic terms and concepts with those that do not correspond and cohere with the worldview of Islam; who were not inclined to hasty and negligent arabization of alien terms and concepts opposed to our religion and our vision of reality and truth.

Many of the Greek terms and concepts were transcribed in their original forms so as to render their foreign origin immediately recognizable such that their proper places become known. So it would be better if the term 'secular' were just transcribed into Arabic spelled 'sin ya kaf lam ra', with kasrah to sin; dammah to kaf and fathah to lam. In this way we would know at once that the term and the concept is not Islamic Arabic. To arabize such terms and concepts is to introduce confusion in our minds, because that will give the impression that they are natural to Islam and would encourage Muslims not only to think in those terms and concepts, but to actualize such thought that are alien and opposed to Islam into concrete reality. I strongly believe with sound reason that the arabization and introduction of the ambivalent concept of c almâniyyah into mainstream contemporary Arabic is largely responsible for insinuating into the Muslim mind the dichotomous separation of the sacred and the profane, creating therein the socio-political notion of an unbridgeable gap separating what it considers to be a 'theocratic state' from a 'secular state'.

There is confusion in the Muslim mind in misunderstanding the Muslim 'secular' state by setting it in contrast with the 'theocratic' state. But since Islam does not involve itself in the dichotomy between the sacred and the profane, how then can it set in contrast the theocratic state with the secular state? An Islamic state is neither wholly theocratic nor wholly secular. A Muslim state calling itself or is called by others 'secular', does not necessarily have to divest nature of spiritual meaning; does not necessarily have to deny religious values and virtues in politics and human affairs; does not necessarily have to oppose religious truth and religious education in the way that the philosophical and scientific process which I call 'secularization' necessarily does involve the divesting of spiritual meaning from the world of creation; the denial of religious values and virtues from politics and human affairs; and the relativization of all values and of truth in the human mind and conduct. It is this confusion in the Muslim mind that is causing the emergence in our midst of social and political upheavals and disunity.

Unity has two aspects: the outward, external unity manifested in society as communal and national solidarity; and the inward, internal unity of ideas and mind revealed in intellectual and spiritual coherence that encompasses realms beyond communal and national boundaries. Understanding of our identity as Muslims pertains to the second aspect, which is fundamental to the realization of the first. The coherence of this second aspect depends upon the soundness and integrity of concepts connoted in language, the instrument of reason which influences the reasoning of its users. If the soundness and integrity of concepts in language is confused, then this is due to confusion in 'worldview' caused by the corruption of knowledge. In the languages of Muslim peoples, including Arabic, there is a basic vocabulary consisting of key terms which govern the interpretation of the Islamic vision of reality and truth, and which project the worldview of Islam in correct perspective.

Because the words that comprise this basic vocabulary have their origins in the Holy Qur'ân these words are naturally in Arabic, and are deployed uniformly in all Muslim languages, reflecting the intellectual and spiritual unity of the Muslims throughout the world. The Islamic basic vocabulary is composed of key terms and concepts related to one another meaningfully, and altogether determining the conceptual structure of reality and existence projected by them. The islamization of language, which is a fundamental element in conversion to Islam, is none other than this infusion of the Islamic basic vocabulary into the languages of Muslim peoples. In this way, each language of a Muslim people with every other has in common this Islamic basic vocabulary as its own basic vocabulary; and as such all languages of Muslim peoples indeed belong to the same family of Islamic languages. What I wish to introduce here is the concept of Islamic language—that there is such a thing as Islamic language.

Because language that can be categorized as Islamic does exist by virtue of the common Islamic vocabulary inherent in each of them, the key terms and concepts in the basic vocabulary of each of them ought indeed to convey the same meanings, since they all are involved in the same conceptual and semantic network. If, for example, we find today that the focus word c ilm, which is a major key term in the basic vocabulary of all Islamic languages, conveys different connotations in each member of the family of Islamic languages, then this regrettable fact is not caused by what is vaguely termed as 'social change', but by ignorance and error, which is productive of the confusion that causes social change. To say that restriction of meaning, or alteration of meaning, such that the original intention is no longer conveyed, affecting key terms in the basic vocabulary of Islam, is due to social change, and to acquiesce to such restriction and alteration of meaning as the exponents of modern linguistics teach, is to imply the legitimacy of authority invested in the common people, in society, to effect semantic change.

This kind of teaching, which has in fact been propagated in the name of 'scientific' knowledge, is misleading and dangerous and must not be tolerated, for Islam does not accept 'society' as authoritative in matters of knowledge, or invest it with authority to bring about changes that will lead Muslims astray. Society, insofar as knowledge and the understanding of Islam and its worldview are concerned, has no authority; on the contrary, society is generally ignorant and needs proper education and constant guidance by the learned and the wise within it so as to ensure its salvation. This means that the learned and the wise among Muslims must exercise constant vigilance in detecting erroneous usage in language which impinges upon semantic change in major key concepts in order to prevent the occurrence of general confusion and error in the understanding of Islam and of its vision of reality and truth.

Many major key terms in the Islamic basic vocabulary of the languages of Muslim peoples have now been displaced and made to serve absurdly in alien fields of meaning in a kind of regression towards non-Islamic worldviews; a phenomenon which I call the deislamization of language. Ignorance and confusion, making possible the infusion of alien concepts, have also let loose the forces of narrow national sentiment and ideologization of ethnic and cultura1 traditions. Words conveying meanings which focus upon fundamental truths peculiar to Islam, such as among others, 'knowledge' (c ilm), 'justice' (c adl), right action (âdab), 'education' (ta'dîb), have been tampered with, so that 'knowledge' becomes restricted to 'jurisprudence', or to that which is based only on restricted forms of reason and sense experience; 'justice' to mean unqualified equality, or mere procedure; 'right action' to mean hypocritical etiquette; and 'education' to mean the kind of training leading to ends derived from philosophic and secular rationalism.

If even a few of such focus words were restricted in their meanings, or were made to convey meanings which are not authentic and authoritative—by which I mean whose intentions no longer reflect those understood by authorities among the early Muslims—then this would inevitably create confusion and error in the minds of Muslims and disrupt intellectual and spiritual unity among them. Moreover, it would render sciences once considered praiseworthy to become blameworthy. I am not here suggesting something that may be construed as not allowing language to develop, to unfold itself according to its potential powers of tracing the rich tapestry of life as it unfolds, to evolve with ideas as they evolve, to grasp reality-truth as it manifests itself in the fleeting passage of time. I am only suggesting that the basic vocabulary in the Islamic language can only develop from its roots, and not severed from them, nor can they develop from roots stunted in restriction.

Secular and materialistic value systems have their initial locus in minds, then they are translated into linguistic symbols, and afterwards become manifest in the external world in urban areas whence they spread like a raging contagion to the rural masses. Failure to apply language correctly and to convey correct meaning implies unawareness of proper perspective of the true and real situation, which involves understanding not only the language, but the worldview projected by it. Widespread intellectual secularization due to ignorance of Islam as the true revealed religion, its manifestation as civilization, and its vision of reality and truth as worldview has tended to confuse many of our scholars and intellectuals and their followers into imitating the shifting slogans of modernity, effecting changes and restrictions in the meanings of key terms that reflect our system of values. Meanings reflecting reality and truth whose transparency was known to our experience and consciousness have now begun to become opaque in minds fused with the formulations of modernity.

Fundamental elements of our worldview and the system of values they convey, involving the meanings of 'virtue', 'freedom', and 'happiness', are also affected. Since we maintain that virtue (faîlah) is an activity of the soul, and that man has a dual nature, the animal and the rational, the realization of virtues in the self requires discernment of reality and truth accompanied by action in conformity with that discernment involving subordination of the bodily and appetitive faculties of the animal soul, to the practical and theoretical faculties of the rational soul such that a stable state of soul, commended by intellect and by religion, is attained. This exercise of subordinating the faculties of the animal soul to those of the rational soul requires freedom. The activity that is called 'freedom' is in ikhtîyâr, which is an act, not in %urriyyah, which is a condition.

The act that is meant in ikhtîyâr is that of making a choice, not between many alternatives but between two alternatives: the good or the bad. Because ikhtîyâr is bound in meaning with khayr, meaning 'good', being derived from the same root khâra (khayara), the choice that is meant in ikhtîyâr is the choice of what is good, better, or best between the two alternatives. This point is most important as it is aligned to the philosophical question of freedom. A choice of what is bad of two alternatives is therefore not a choice that can be called ikhtîyâr, in fact it is not a choice, rather it is an act of injustice ("ulm) done to oneself. Freedom is to act as one's real and true nature demands—that is, as one's %aqq and one's fimrah demands—and so only the exercise of that choice which is of what is good can properly be called a 'free choice'.

A choice for the better is therefore an act of freedom, and it is also an act of justice (c adl) done to oneself. It presupposes knowledge of good and evil, of virtues and vices; whereas a choice for the worse is not a choice as it is grounded upon ignorance urged on by the instigation of the soul that inclines toward the blameworthy aspects of the animal powers; it is then also not an exercise of freedom because freedom means precisely being free of domination by the powers of the soul that incites to evil. Ikhtîyâr is the cognitive act of choosing for the better of two alternatives in accordance with virtues that culminate in justice to one and which is, as such, an exercise of freedom. The doing of what is good is accomplished by means of virtues. In Islam all virtues, including those considered as principal virtues such as wisdom, temperance, courage, and justice and their subdivisions, are religious virtues since they are derived from the Qur'ân and from the exemplary life of the Prophet.

The source of these principal virtues and their subdivisions is true faith or imân, which is the verification by deed what tongue and heart affirm as real and true of God's Revelation and His commands and prohibitions. Imân already implies consciousness of God and remembrance of Him that brings about a condition of tranquility in the soul; it is freedom from worry resulting from doubt; freedom from disquietude and from fear that refers to ultimate destiny; it is inward security that comes about when the soul is submissive to God; and being submissive to God is freedom, which causes to arise in the soul the consciousness of peace called islam. These inner activities of the soul imply a prior consciousness in the soul of the truth that comes from divine guidance; and this consciousness is that of certainty of the truth (yaqîn).

From this it is clear that happiness, which is the goal of virtuous activity leading to the state of stability of soul, is not something that relates only to this world; is not something that consists of only feelings and emotions that vary in degree from moment to moment; is not something only psychological and biological, which is shared also by animals. Nor is happiness an end in itself which somehow cannot be experienced consciously as something enduring, something permanent in the course of our worldly existence. The tradition of Western thought takes the position that there are two conceptions of happiness: the ancient who goes back to Aristotle; and the modern which gradually emerged in Western history as a result of the process of secularization. The Aristotelian conception maintains that happiness relates only to this world; that it is an end in itself; and that it is a state that undergoes changes and variations in degrees from moment to moment; or it is something that cannot be consciously experienced from moment to moment and can be judged as having been attained only when one's worldly life, if virtuously lived and attended by good fortune, has come to an end.

The modern conception agrees with the Aristotelian conception that happiness relates only to this world and that it is an end in itself, but whereas for the former the end is considered in terms of a standard for proper conduct, the latter considers it to be terminal psychological states having no relation with moral codes. It is the modern conception of happiness that is acknowledged to be prevalent in the West today. We do not agree with the Aristotelian position that virtue and happiness relate only to this world, and that consequently happiness as a permanent condition experienced consciously in the course of our worldly life is unattainable. We do not restrict our understanding of happiness only to the domain of temporal, secular life, for in accord with our worldview we affirm that the relation of happiness to the hereafter has an intimate and a profound bearing upon its relation to worldly life, and that since in the former case it is a spiritual and permanent condition there is, even in its temporal and secular involvement, an element of happiness that we experience and are conscious of which when once attained is permanent.

As for the modern conception of happiness, it is not much different in essence from the ones known and practiced in ancient times by pagan societies. Happiness (i.e. we mean sa-c-adah) as known in the experience and consciousness of those who are truly submissive to God and follow His guidance is not an end in itself because the highest good in this life is love of God. Enduring happiness in life refers not to the physical entity in man, not to the animal soul and body of man; nor is it a state of mind, or feeling that undergoes terminal states, nor pleasure nor amusement. It has to do with certainty (yaqîn) of the ultimate Truth and fulfillment of action in conformity with that certainty. And certainty is a permanent state of consciousness natural to what is permanent in man and perceived by his spiritual organ of cognition which is the heart (qalb). It is peace and security and tranquility of the heart (tumac ninah); it is knowledge (mac rifah) and knowledge is true faith (imân). It is knowledge of God as He described Himself in genuine Revelation; it also knows one's rightful and hence proper place in the realm of creation and one's proper relationship with the Creator accompanied by requisite action (ibâdah) in conformity with that knowledge such that the condition which results is that of justice (adl).

It is only through such knowledge that love of God can

be attained in earthly life. From this interpretation of the meaning and experience of happiness in Islam we derive conclusion that happiness in this life is not an end in itself; that the end of happiness is love of God; that in worldly life two levels of happiness can be discerned. The first level is psychological, temporal and terminal states which may be described as feelings or emotions, and which is attained when needs and wants are achieved by means of right conduct in accord with the virtues. The second level is spiritual, permanent, consciously experienced, becoming the substratum of worldly life which is affirmed to be probationary, the testing of conduct and virtuous activity being by good fortune or ill. This second level, when attained, occurs concurrently with the first, except that wants are diminished and needs are satisfied. This second level of happiness is a preparation for a third level in the hereafter of which the highest state is the Vision of God.

There is no change in this meaning and experience of happiness in the consciousness of genuine believers throughout the ages. In the foregoing pages I have set forth in bare summary some of the fundamental, permanently established elements, together with the key concepts that they unfold, that act as integrating principles placing all our systems of meaning and standards of life and values in coherent order as a unified super system forming the worldview of Islam. These fundamental elements and the key concepts pertinent to them have profound bearing, we said earlier, upon our ideas about change, development, and progress. Even though diversity and change can and do indeed occur within the ambience of this worldview, such as the diversity in the schools of jurisprudence, theology, philosophy and metaphysics, and in the traditions, cultures and languages; and the change in meeting the tides of changing fortune in the course of history, yet the diversity and the change have never affected the character and role of these fundamental elements themselves, so that what is projected as a worldview by the super system remains intact.

This is so because the diversity and the change have taken their rise within the bounds of cognitive restraint deliberated by a knowing community conscious of its identity, ensuring thereby neither involvement of change nor encroachment of confusion in the key concepts that serve the fundamental elements of the worldview. The worldview resides in the minds of genuine Muslims. The discerning ones among them know that Islam is not an ideal it is a reality; and that whatever may be demanded of them by the challenges of the age in which they live must be met without confusing that worldview with alien elements. They know that the advances in science and technology and their being put to adequate use in everyday life do not necessarily have to involve confusion in their vision of reality and truth. Technology is not the same as science; and acceptance of useful and relevant technology does not necessarily have to involve acceptance also of the implications in the science that gave it birth.

Confusion arises only as a result of inadequate knowledge of Islam and of the worldview projected by it, as well as ignorance of the nature of the confronting intellectual, religious, and ideological challenges, and of the implications inherent in the statements and general conclusions of modern secular philosophy and science. Change, development, and progress, in their true senses ultimately mean for us a conscious and deliberate movement towards genuine Islam at a time when we encounter challenges, as we do now, that seek to encroach on our values and virtues, our modes of conduct, our thought and faith, our way of life. Our present engagement is with the challenges of an alien worldview surreptitiously introduced into Muslim thought and belief by confused modernist Muslim scholars, intellectuals, academics, writers and their followers, as well as by religious deviationists and extremists of many sorts. They have wittingly or unwittingly come under the spell of modern secular Western philosophy and science, its technology and ideology which have disseminated a global contagion of secularization as a philosophical program.

We are not unaware of the fact that not all of Western science and technology are necessarily objectionable to religion; but this does not mean that we have to uncritically accept the scientific and philosophical theories that go along with the science and the technology, and the science and the technology themselves, without first understanding their implications and testing the validity of the values that accompany the theories. Islam possesses within itself the source of its claim to truth and does not need scientific and philosophical theories to justify such a claim. Moreover, it is not the concern of Islam to fear scientific discoveries that could contradict the validity of its truth. We know that no science is free of value; and to accept its presuppositions and general conclusions without being guided by genuine knowledge of our worldview—which entails knowledge also of our history, our thought and civilization, our identity—which will enable us to render correct judgements as to their validity and relevance or otherwise to our life, the change that would result in our way of life would simply be a change congenial to what is alien to our worldview.

And we would neither call such change a 'development' nor a 'progress'. Development consists not in 'activating and making visible and concrete what is latent in biological man' because man is not merely a biological entity: humanity is something much more than rationality and animality. Progress is neither 'becoming' or 'coming-into-being', nor movement towards that which is coming-into-being and never becomes 'being'; for the notion of 'something aimed at', or the 'goal' inherent in the concept of progress can only convey real and true meaning when it refers to that which is understood as something permanently established, as already being. Hence what is already clarified in the mind and permanently established therein and externally, already in the state of being, cannot suffer change, nor be subject to constant slipping from the grasp of achievement, nor constantly receding beyond attainment.

The term 'progress' refers to a definite direction that aligned to a final purpose that is meant to be achieved in worldly life. If the direction sought is still vague, still coming-into-being as it were, and the purpose aligned to it is not final, then how can involvement in it truly mean progress? People who grope in the dark cannot be referred to as progressing, and they who say such people are progressing have merely uttered a lie against the true meaning and purpose of progress. The concepts of 'change', 'development', and 'progress' presuppose situations in which we find ourselves confused by a commixture of the true and the false, of the real and the illusory, and become captive in the ambit of ambiguity. In such ambivalent situations, our positive action in the exercise of freedom to choose for the better, to accept what is good and relevant to our needs, to deliberate correctly in our judgment of needs, all the while maintaining our endeavour to return to the straight path and direct our steps in agreement with it—such endeavour, which entails change, is development; and such return, which consists in development, is progress.

Muslims have faith in only Allah who is One, Omniscient and Omnipotent. He is neither begotten nor does He beget. Muslims believe that only God truly exists. Man and the entire creation exist only because God wills them to exist. God alone is the sole creator of everything that exists, and manifests His glory, power and attributes. Man has been created as a creature with free will so that by his surrender of free will to the divine will he may become worthy of God's fellowship. This faith in God is realized by responding to the message of Allah through His prophet Muhammad.

Muslims have faith in only Allah who is One, Omniscient and Omnipotent. He is neither begotten nor does He beget. Muslims believe that only God truly exists. Man and the entire creation exist only because God wills them to exist. God alone is the sole creator of everything that exists, and manifests His glory, power and attributes. Man has been created as a creature with free will so that by his surrender of free will to the divine will he may become worthy of God's fellowship. This faith in God is realized by responding to the message of Allah through His prophet Muhammad. Allah is the name Muslims use for the supreme and unique God, who created and rules everything.

The heart of faith for all Muslims is obedience to Allah's will.

Allah is eternal, omniscient, and omnipotent.

Allah has always existed and will always exist.

Allah knows everything that can be known.

Allah can do anything that can be done.

Allah has no shape or form.

Allah can't be seen.

Allah can't be heard.

Allah is neither male nor female.

Allah is just.

A believer can approach Allah by praying, and by reciting the Qur'an.

Muslims worship only Allah because only Allah is worthy of worship.

All Muslims believe that God is one alone:

There is only one God.

God has no children, no parents, and no partners.

God was not created by a being.

There are no equal, superior, or lesser Gods.

Muslims worship in a building called a mosque. An alternative word for mosque, from the original Arabic, is masjid, meaning place of prostration. Outside every mosque, or just inside the entrance, is a place where worshippers can remove and leave their shoes. There is also a place where they can carry out the ritual washing required before prayer. The main hall of a mosque is a bare room largely devoid of furniture. There are no pictures or statues. Muslims believe these are blasphemous, since there can be no image of Allah, who is wholly spirit.

Everyone sits on the floor and everyone in the mosque is equal in status. A niche in one of the walls, called a mihrab, shows the direction that the worshippers should face in order to face Mecca. Many mosques have a minaret which is a tall thin tower. A muezzin stands at the top of the tower and calls Muslims to prayer at the five ritual times of the day. Not all mosques in the UK have a minaret. Women can attend the mosque and when they do, they sit separately from the men. This is out of modesty and to prevent any distraction. It is more usual for women to pray at home. As God is transcendent, too high and too holy for human beings, so some intermediaries are necessary to mediate between men and God. Not even the prophet Muhammad could have direct contact with God, though the prophet had a vision of the Heaven in his state of Miraj (620 A.D.).

Islam accepts the existence of angels who serve as intermediaries between God and man. Angels have been created out of light. They have no sex; they do not eat or drink. They have no free will. Their sole function is to sing praises of God and to carry out His command, day and night. They always do the right and so they have not to stand before the judgment bar of God on the Day of Judgment. Some important angels are as follow: Jibrail (Gabriel) is the angel of revelations in relation to Prophet Muhammad, Mikail (Michael) is the champion of faith and a protector of the Jews, Azrael the angel of death who separates the soul from the body of the dead, Israfil who will sound the trumpet on the Day of Judgment.

8

Allah in the Holy Qur'an

"I alone am Allâh. There cannot be, is no other and will never be One for worship but Me." (20:14)

His verses (Ayât) in the Holy Qur'ân have passed the judgement that He is Allâh - Glory be to Him, there is no other Deity but Allâh - He alone possesses this Name, not shared by any other. He is the only Presence that comprehends all presences (al-Wajûd al Jâmi'). All things in the universe come under the sway of this All-Comprehensive Name. Allâh is the mighty name of the Self-Existing and Self-Sufficient Being Who comprises all perfect attributes, Who is free from every weakness and defect, is alone worthy of worship, is without partner or peer and is the source of all Love and Grace. Unlike the word "god" in Arabic, the word Allah is never used for any other object or being. It is a substantive name, neither attributive nor descriptive and is inclusive of all His other names and attributes and has primacy over all other titles. When Moses received his Divine mission he was addressed in the following words:

"Moses! Surely I am, Allâh, the Lord of the worlds" (28:30, 27:9)

In these verses the Lord of the worlds, reveals Moses Who is speaking to him. The word Allâh is accordingly a proper name, whereas the "Lord of all the worlds" (Rabbul-

Alamîn), is His first and foremost title. Allâh is a personal name (Ism al-Dhât) applied to the Supreme Being and distinguished from all other names which are called Asmâ' al-Sifât, or names denoting attributes of God.

In the technical vocabulary of linguistics, the word Allâh is Jâmid, that is, it is not derived from any other word. In the pronunciation of Allâh, the letter 'L' is stressed. The word Allâh is not a construction of al-ilâh as some people think, but a different and an independent word. The first two letters Al in the word Allâh are an integral, inseparable part of the word. They do not denote the definite article Al of Arabic, which is equivalent to the English 'the'. In Arabic, the prefix Al is added before the noun to emphasize the word in the sense of 'most' or 'all', for example al-Rahmân - the Most Gracious. Sîbwaih, the great grammarian, and Khalîl, the great linguistic, say, "Since Al in the beginning of the word Allâh is inseparable from it, so it is a simple substantive, not derived from any other word."

If Al in Allâh were an additional prefix, the common exclamation yâ Allâh, (O Allâh!), would not be permitted according to the rules of Arabic grammar, as the form yâ al-ilâh or yâ al-Rahmân are not permissible in Arabic. Moreover, this supposition would mean that there were different gods - âlihah (plural of ilâh), one of which became gradually known as al-ilâh and was then contracted into Allâh. This supposition is not correct. Allâh has always been the name of the Eternal Being (Hughes: Dictionary of Islam), nor has the word Allâh ever been applied to anyone else but the Divine Being. The pagan Arabs had numerous ilâhs or gods, but none of them was ever called Allâh.

This being the proper name of the Supreme Being has therefore no parallel or equivalent in any other language of the world. The English word 'god' is applied to any religious object of worship. Most probably it is related to 'good' and origins from heathen mythologies. Jehovah, which is the Aramaic or Hebrew expression Ya Howâ, literally means most closely 'O! That' or 'O! Thou' used to address a Deity, the emphasis is on Huwa which is to emphasize an Existence, therefore it can hardly be a proper name. The Hindus give their senior deity the name of Par-Mâtma (the Super Soul), Par-Barham (the Super and the Great), Par-Mishwar (the Great King or Owner), The Parsis give their supreme God the name of Yazdan and Hermes. In the Sikh religion, their great Deity is called Satt which means the Truth.

The use of Jehova in the New Testament by the Witnesses of Jehova is a new invention. In the original Greek version and older versions of the New Testament this name was never used and Jesus never employed the name "Jehova". Although most Christians are unaware of it, the Aramaic speaking Jesus also used the word Allâh (or 'Allaha'). Christians speaking the Semitic languages still use it. In the Greek and Latin writings this was then rendered to theos or deos, the generic words for 'god' in these languages. These words are derived from Dyeus, the name of a heathen god. The French 'dieu' or the English 'deity' are also etymologically based on that word. The names found in other languages for the Supreme Being are either attributive or descriptive and can be used in the plural and or feminine forms (e.g. gods, goddess) whereas the word Allâh cannot be translated and can never be used in plural form nor in any other form nor this word have any root. Allâh says:

"Do you know any other name (which comprises all the Attributes of perfection), and don't you know that there is no one who is called the same." (19:65)

People accept the name of a Deity when it is called in their language, but as soon as the name used by other people is used for their Deity, their is the feeling of prejudice and rejection. The Holy Qur'ân has pointed out this behaviour in the words: And when it is said to them, 'Prostrate to the Most Gracious (Rahmân)', they say, 'What thing is this, the Most Gracious?' People have an individual concept of their Lord, which they ascribe to Him and in which they seek Him. So long as a Deity is presented to them which fits into their fancy and concept, they recognize Him and affirm Him, whereas when the Reality is presented in any other form with another name, they deny Him, flee from Him and treat Him in an improper manner, at the same time thinking they are acting properly and fittingly.

The Holy Qur'ân has not presented a new Deity, but has presented the same Eternal Being Who has always been present in the illuminated human heart, in human conscience (30:8) and in the heavens and the earth, Who is visible in the mirror of the laws of nature and is discernible in the book of nature (30:30). He is the same God who was the God of Abraham, Ismaîl, Isaac, Jacob, Moses, Jesus, Buddha, Krishna, Rama, Confucius and all other prophets known or unknown to us (2:4; 2:132-133,136: 3:84; 40:78; 42:13). He is the Being who combined in Himself all the perfect Attributes and is free from all imperfections and is the very apex of beauty and beneficence.

He proclaims in he Holy Qur'ân:

"I am Allâh, the All-Mighty, the All-Wise" (27:9)

The God of the Holy Qur'ân

"Allâh, there is no other, cannot be and will never be One worthy of worship but He, the Ever Living, Self-Subsisting and All-Sustaining. Slumber overtakes Him not, nor sleeps. Whatsoever is in the heavens and whatsoever is in the earth belongs to Him. Who is there that will intercede with Him, save by His leave? He knows their future and their past; and they encompass nothing of His knowledge (of the things) except of such (things) as He Himself pleases (to tell). His knowledge and sovereignty extends over the heavens and the earth and the care of them both tires Him not. He is the Supreme the Great" (2:255).

"There is nothing like Him (He is beyond all comparison), and He is the All-Hearing, the All-Seeing". (42:11)

"Say, 'Is there anyone of your (associated) partners (with God) who starts the cycle of creation and then continues it?' Say, 'It is Allâh who starts the cycle of creation and then continues it. Wither then are you being deviated away (from this fact)?' Ask, 'Is there any of your (associated) partners (with God) who lead to the truth (through revelation)?' Say, 'It is Allâh alone Who leads to the truth. Is then He who leads to the truth more worthy to be followed or he (assumed to be god or a son of god) that cannot find the way (himself) unless he be guided? What, then, is the matter with you? How do you judge?" (10:34)

He is Allâh, Glory be to Him, and there is no other God but Allâh. This is the only Presence that comprehends all presences (al-Wajûd al Jâmi'), and no worshipper of God worships anything but this Presence (al-Wajûd). There is nothing like Him (He is beyond all comparison), and He is the All-Hearing, the All-Seeing and He has enjoined us to worship none but Him. Whatever is in the heavens and the earth declares the glory of Allâh. And He is the All-Mighty the All-Wise.

The kingdom of the heavens and the earth belongs to Him. He gives life and causes death and He is the Possessor of power to do all that He will. He is (from) the very First (there was nothing before Him), and (He will exist to) the Last (there will be nothing after Him), and when nothing remains He will remain (He being an eternal Being). He is the Supreme Being (subordinate to no one). And (whereas He comprehends everything) He is Incomprehensible. He has full knowledge of every thing. (57:1-3). The physical vision comprehends Him not, but He comprehends all visions, He is the All-Subtle Being (incomprehensible and imperceptible), the All-Aware. (6:103)

He is Incomprehensible, and nothing is like him, therefore the knowledge of Allâh's Reality (His Essence,

Haqîqat al-Dzât), cannot be known through logical proof (Dalîl) or rational considerations (Burhân Aqlî). Revelation is indispensable as a proof of His existence. Nor can any definition or description grasp Him. He is the Originator of the heavens and the earth. 'Prior' to that, He was and nothing was with Him, and He is now, after He has created everything, as He was. Of course, to be precise, the temporal word 'prior' is only well-defined in time and can strictly speaking not refer to anything 'before' the creation of the universe, which includes the creation of time. So in fact, this is just another way of saying He is independent of the heavens and the earth.

He possesses all His Attributes without the need to refer to the worlds He brought into existence, and no new Attribute of Him came into existence. In other words, the way He describes Himself and the names by which He names Himself and by which His creatures call Him now exist independently from the initiation of the creation. When He desired the existence of the universe, He originated the "worlds" from His sacred desire (al-Irâdat al-Muqaddas) in accordance with His knowledge as He calls Himself al-'Alîm- the One Who possesses all and perfect knowledge of everything. He is Rabb al 'âlamîn - the Creator and Nourisher to perfection of all the worlds.'Alamîn translated here as 'all the worlds' has its root in 'alama which means to know. Thus 'Alamîn are the means by which one knows the Creator. Hence 'alamîn signify all forms of creation by which the Creator is known. About the origin of creation we read:

He directed Himself towards the space. Behold! It was (like) a mass of gas (dust), and He said to it (- the space) and to the world, 'Come both of you (in obedience to Me) willingly or unwillingly.' They said, 'We obey you with all our will.' (41:11)

According to Alî Ibn Abî Tâlib and other people of reflection (Ashâb al-Fikr), "Dust" is the first universal reality. Then Allâh manifested Himself in theophany His Light to that "Dust". Within this "Dust" was the entire world in its potentiality and readiness (Salâhiya) and each thing in the "Dust" - living or non living, received from His Light according to its peparedness (Isti'dâd) and potentiality, just as the corners of a room receive light according to their distance from the lamp. He says He is the Light, and then He compares Himself with a Lamp:

Allâh is the Extensive Light of the heavens and the earth. His light can be compared to a (lustrous) pillar on which is a lamp. The lamp is inside a crystal globe. The globe of glass is as if it were a glittering star. It (- the lamp) is lit by (the oil of) a blessed olive tree, which belongs neither to the east nor to the west (rather welds the whole world in its fold). Its oil is likely to glow forth of itself even if no fire has touched it. This (lamp) is a combination of many lights over and over. Allâh guides towards His light whoever desires (to be enlightened). Allâh sets forth excellent parables for the people, and Allâh alone has full knowledge of every thing (24:35).

Within this "Dust" nothing is nearer to the Light in reception than Mohammad followed by his followers.

(This light is now lit) in houses, which Allâh has ordained to be exalted and His name be commemorated in them. Therein (are such as) glorify Him in the mornings and the evenings, Men, whom neither trade nor sale distracts from exalting (the name of) Allâh and from the observance of Prayer and from presenting Zakât (- purifying dues) regularly. They dread the day when the hearts and the eyes will be in a state of agitation and anguish;With the result that Allâh will give them the reward according to their fairest deeds and will (even) give them much more by His grace and bounty. And Allâh does provide without measure to whom He will. (22:36-38)

The cosmos is the sensory realm, and its Ruler is veiled. That is why He describes Himself as being hidden (al-Bâtin) in veils of darknesses (Zulumât) and in veils of light (Nûr). The cosmos cannot perceive Him nor He will ever be unveiled, thus this Present Reality will never be known by an originated thing completely. That is why He says:

"It is not given to a human being that Allâh speaks to him except by direct revelation (Wahî) or from behind a veil or by sending messengers who reveal to the people what He pleases by His command" (42:51)

God's speech is His knowledge, which he imparts to some of His selected servants, who come to know Him through His speech (Kalâm). This is the most definite and absolute knowledge (Ilm al-Yaqîn), which lies beyond the stage of intellect and cannot be attained by reflections and considerations. This knowledge of Him is granted only to prophets (Ambîya), and to His friends (Awliyâ) and to the "people of unveiling" (Ahl al-Kashûf). The originated things have no part in Divine Self-Sufficiency and Independence. His Self-Sufficiency demands that He does not depend on His creation in anyway, therefore He is not in need of any son or a daughter.

The main theme of the Holy Qur'ân, the one that predominates over all other themes is that of Oneness of Being (Wahdat al-Wajûd). This concept of Allâh, which the Holy Qur'ân presents to us is all-embracing, all other concepts are facets of this. He describes Himself in Surah Ikhlâs: "He Allâh is One in His Unique Self. He is the Eternal Refuge in respect to our dependence on Him. He begets none in His identity and relation to us, nor is He begotten, and He has no equal". We on our par part beget and are begotten, for this we depend on Him. So He describes Himself and isolates His Essence in the words "Allâh is One". Indeed Allâh has given us no better description of Him. We know Him through His Attributes and the multiplicity of His Attributes are well known.

The Attributes of The Name Allâh

Allâh manifests Himself to His creation through His

Divine Names and Attributes, and they are many. There are those of His Names that make Him known as the Knower, the Powerful, the Hearing, the Seeing, the Living, the Responder and the Thankful. There are the Names of description like the First, the Last, the Manifest, the Hidden, and there are Names that make known His Works, such as the Creator, the Provider, and the Shaper. There are Names of Incomparability and His Omnipotence. His Attributes are of different ranks (Marâtib). The following paragraphs are an attempt to explain some of His most beautiful Names and Attributes.

Four Basic Attributes of Allâh

All types of perfect and true praise belong to Allâh alone, the Creator and Nourisher to perfection (Rabb) of all the worlds, the Most Gracious (Rahmân), the Ever Merciful (Rahîm), Master (Mâlik) of the Day of Requital. (1:1-4, 2:163)

The Holy Qur'ân begins with the name of Allâh and the name Allâh appears in the very beginning of the opening chapter (al-Fâtihah) of the Holy Qur'ân. This is followed by Rabb; no other attribute of Allâh is mentioned so frequently. Next to Rabb are the attributes Rahmân and Rahîm and finally Mâlik. The name Allâh is found in the Holy Book some 2697 times, the name Rabb occurs 978 times, the name Rahmân and Rahîm 376 times.

Creator, Sustainer, Nourisher

Rabb al âlamîn is the first attribute of Allâh. He is not Abb (Father), rather Rabb of the nations, creations, worlds and all kinds of created beings and things and their classes collectively (- al âlamîn as the Holy Qur'ân says). According to Lisân al-'Arab, Tâj al-Urûs and Mufradât-i-Râghib, the three most authentic lexicons, the Arabic word Rabb has many connotations, as Master, Chief, Determiner, Provider, Sustainer, Rewarder, Perfecter, Ruler, Creator, Maintainer, Reposer of Properties in things of nature, Developer, Framer of Rules and Laws of the Growth of Things, Regulizer, Foster of things in such a manner as to make them attain one condition after another until they reach their goal of perfection and completion, Arranger of different stages through which they have to pass on their way to completion, Author of all existence Who has sole title to it with no one having any share in it. Thus the word Rabb signifies dozens of processes which a thing passes through in the course of creation and evolution before it reaches its final development. These meanings have not been forced on this word Rabb.

All standard lexicons of the Arabic language speak of all of them when they give the meaning of the root Raba. In English the word Rabb is generally translated as Lord, but this word can not at all convey the real significance of the original Arabic word Rabb. The process of creation embodied in the word Rabb covers, of course, with the exception of the Creator Himself, every existing thing whether in the realm of spirit or in the realm of bodies, whether of earthly creation or other celestial objects. As Rabb al âlamîn He has provided all the material means for the physical requirements of all kinds for all creatures collectively and without discrimination, as food, grains, air, water, light and so many other things:

Would you really disbelieve in Him (-the Rabb) who created the earth in two aeons? And do you set up compeers with Him? This is the Lord (- the Rabb) of the worlds. He placed therein (- in the earth) firm mountains rising above (its surface) and showered it with His blessings and placed in it various provisions according to a set measure, (provisions to which) all those who require them have equal rights, (and all this He created) in four aeons. (41:9-10)

All creation bears His signature. He is the Rabb of the world of elements and command, since elements preceded from command and compounds are fashioned: Then He directed Himself towards the space. Behold! It was (like) a mass of gas. And He (- The Lord, Rabb) said to it (- the space) and to the earth, 'Come both of you (in obedience to Me) willingly or unwillingly.' They said, 'We obey you with all our will.'

He commands not only the formation of compounds from elements, but also commands the reversal of process, commanding the formation of elements from compounds.

Do those who disbelieve not see that the heavens and the earth were (once) one mass all closed up, and then We rent them apart. And it is from water that We created all life. Will they not believe? And We have made firm mountains on the earth so that they may be a source of benefit and provision for the people and lest it should quake with them. And We made on it wide pathways that people may find right guidance to reach the goal. And We have made the heaven a roof, well protected, still they turn away paying no heed to its (heavenly) signs. And it is He Who created the night and the day, the sun and the moon. They are all gliding along smoothly in (their respective) orbits. (21:30-33)

Thus the word Rabb al âlamîn conveys not only the idea of creation but also that of regulating, completing and accomplishing, that is of the evolution of things from the crudest state to that of the highest perfection: The word Rabb al âlamîn also signifies the fostering of a thing in such a manner as to make it attain one condition after another until it reaches its goal of perfection and completion. Hence the Rabb is not only the Author of all existence, Who has not only given to the whole creation its means of nourishment, but has also beforehand ordained for each a sphere of capacity and within that sphere provided the means by which it continues to attain gradually its goal of perfection:

We create a human being from an extract of clay; then We reduce him to a drop of sperm (and place him) in a safe depository; then We form the sperm into a clot; then We develop the clot into a lump of flesh; then We fashion bones out of this lump of flesh, then We clothe the bones with flesh, thereafter We evolve him into another being. Therefore blessed be Allâh the Best of Creators. Then as you have passed (these seven stages of physical and spiritual stages) you are heading towards death. Then (after death) you will certainly be raised up to life (for another never ending progress) on the Day of Resurrection.

The Holy Qur'ân in the above verses is drawing our attention to the principle of evolution at work in the creation of all non-living and living things in their sphere. It establishes the working of a grand scheme under the ever vigilant eye of Rabb al âlamîn through hundreds and thousands of years in some cases, in order to bring things to their final perfection. The progressive development of things makes creation all the more marvellous and Allâh becomes all the more deserving of praise and worship. This evolution is prevalent not only in the physical world but also in the spiritual world, and as well as in Revelations (Wahî and Ilhâm) from God. As things grow, develop and change, they do not do so by themselves, they are all undergoing progressive development by stages, so is the case with the spiritual development.

All spiritual life is subjective to Allah's Lordship and He is constantly providing means through revelation (Wahî, Ilhâm) for the spiritual advancement of mankind. This is because Allâh has created human beings for unlimited progress, and beyond every stage of their evolution there is another in a never-ending process as we read:

It is He Who has evolved you from one living entity, then (He has provided for you) a permanent abode (starting after death to the final everlasting abode of paradise) and a temporary lodging (from birth to the grave). Verily We have explained (Our) signs in detail for a people who would understand. (6:98)

Some people deny His Providence and say that whatever they receive is the consequence of their actions.

The believers in Tanâsukh or incarnation and some of the followers of the Hindu religion think, that if some of them had not sinned in a particular fashion and not been born as cows and buffaloes in a previous incarnation there would have been no milk. They also allege that whatever we receive in this life is the fruit of action of some people in their previous incarnation. Such image-worshippers believe their idols to be Divine personification. These people have lost the track, and the very opening verses of the Holy Qur'ân reject such concepts and tell us that all types of perfect and true praise belongs to Allâh alone, the Lord of all the worlds.

The announcement that Allâh is Rabb al âlamîn also clearly opposes those who seek to confine the Providence and grace of God to their own country and people, believing that other communities or peoples of other lands or ages were not created by God or that after creating them, God rejected them or forgot them. They may also believe that all Prophets and Messengers were raised from among the children of Israel and that Allâh was so angry with other peoples that He did not take the least pity on them even when He found them in error or in a state of unawareness, or that Divine revelation and Divine speech always remained restricted within the frontiers of India or Israel. These people do not accept Allâh as Rabb, the Lord of Universal Providence. When He is the Lord of Universal Providence and not only the Lord of Israel or the Lord of Bharat and Arya Varta, why should He attach Himself permanently to a particular people and a particular age? That is partiality and favoritism. The Holy Qur'ân denounces such notions and expounds in diverse ways that Allâh has made provisions for the material welfare of the people of all different lands and He has made provisions for the spiritual sustenance of every people:

There have been no people without a Warner and a Prophet. (35:24)

This is so that no people may have cause to complain

that Allâh was gracious only towards some nation and not towards another, or that particular people were given a book so that they may be guided therewith and others were not, or that He manifested Himself through His words and revelations and signs in a certain age but remained hidden and silent in another age. That is why the Holy Qur'ân says:

(We have sent this revelation) lest you should say, 'The Book has only been revealed to two communities (- the Jews and the Christians) before us, and (as for us) we remained unaware of what those (Books) read.' Or lest you should say, 'Had the Book been revealed to us we would surely have been better guided than they. (6:156-157)

By extending His Providence universally He disposed all such objections and exercised such universal benevolence that no people or age was denied the beneficence of His material and spiritual grace. As Rabb al âlamîn He is the source of all grace and every capacity proceeds from Him, and every thing that exists is sustained by Him. He is the support of every creature. His grace comprehends all people and all epochs.

And indeed We have already sent (Our) Messengers before you. There are some of them whom We have mentioned to you and of them there are some whom We have not mentioned to you. (40:78)

This creates a sense of respect and honour for all the prophets that have appeared among the various nations of the world and by accepting that all as having been sent by Allâh paves the way for the unity among the nations and peace through religion. These words also tell us that Judaism, Christianity, Hinduism, Buddhism, Islam and all such faiths are but different aspects of one and the same religion, which in their original purity conveyed the same message of the Unity of God. Their religion was the submission to the will of One God and to make peace with their Creator and creation:

And We sent no Messenger before you but We revealed

to him, (saying), 'The truth is that there is no other, cannot be and will never be One worthy of worship but I, therefore worship Me (alone).' (21:25)

Therefore we should believe in all those prophets, as this is the foundation of a universal brotherhood. This lays down the sound basis of peace and harmony among the religions of the world. Thus the source of all Divine Scriptures, Bible, Vedas or other similarly claimed Holy Books is the same. Divine revelations or Allah's communion with human beings, men and women, is a necessary factor in the evolution of humanity. This Divine gift is bestowed upon all the nations of the world. He raised His Prophets not only in the Land of Palestine but in all continents. It was from India that Rishîs, Prophets and saints like Buddha, Rama, Krishna and Guru Nanak were chosen and where the Holy Scriptures, the Vedas were revealed in Sanskrit several thousand years ago.

Allâh being Rabb al âlamîn abolishes all individual and racial distinctions and tells that the noblest among us in the sight of Allâh is he who guards against evil, and who is most righteous; and thus opens a door of dialogue among the religions of the world, and establishes a vast brotherhood between all races, tribes and nations. No body is to be deprived of any right on the score of race, language, colour or sex, and no one of us is a believer in Allâh until he not only recognizes the truth of all the previous Prophets but also believes in the Divine origin of their teachings (2:4; 2:136; 3:84). We can understand differences of opinion arising from differences of temperament. They may lead to the existence of several schools of thought, but they cannot affect the real and basic faith, so far as the cardinal principles are concerned in their pure integrity. That is why we are told:

Surely, those who (profess to) believe (in Islam), and those who follow the Jewish faith, the Christians and the Sabians, whosoever (of these truly) believes in Allâh and the Last Day and acts righteously shall have their reward with their Lord, and shall have nothing to fear, nor shall they grieve. (2:62)

Rahmân - the Most Gracious

Rahmân is the second attribute of Allâh. Allâh says:

Call upon Him Allâh or call upon Him al-Rahmân, call upon Him whichever name you like, for all beautiful Names belong to Him. (17:110)

The difference between Rabb and Al-Rahmân is that Rabb is an all-embracing providence by means of which the entire universe came into being and continues to be sustained and nourished whereas the attribute Al-Rahmân, - the Most Gracious, is a special eternal grace which extends only to the living realm without reference to any merit or right of any of them in relation to their respective requirements, and not being a recompense of any action on their part. The special concern of Rabb for the entire living realm has been called al-Rahmân. It is because of this attribute that every thing capable of sensation and consciousness is alive, works, eats, drinks, feels, secures against affliction and has his needs fulfilled.

Rahîm - the Ever Merciful

Rahîm, the Ever Merciful, is the third basic attribute of Allâh. The distinction between Rahîm and Rahmân is that the Rahmân grants of His own accord out of pure grace and beneficence without reference to any deed or request, while Rahîm, on the other hand, means Who causes good results to follow on good deeds, and would not nullify anyone's work and labour. Allâh is Rahmân in the sense that He grants a pure nature to human beings, without the taint of sin, in the finest make and the best proportions with enormous capabilities for an all-round advancement and for the purpose of seeking God, and He is Rahîm in the sense that when he makes use of his faculties He blesses his efforts with goodly results.

The Arabic words Rahmân and Rahîm translated as Most Gracious and Ever Merciful are derived from the same root Rahm signifying love, tenderness, grace, mercy, pity, forgiveness, goodness, all required for exercising beneficence. Both al-Rahmân and al-Rahîm are active participle nouns of different measures denoting extensiveness of significance. An Arabic intensive is more suited to express God's attributes than the superlative degree. It is wrong to think that Rahmân and Rahîm are the repetition of one and the same attribute and they are narrated in the first chapter of the Holy Qur'ân one after another for the sake of emphasis alone (as Allâma Moudûdî explains in his translations and interpretations of the Holy Qur'ân). The fact is that these are two different attributes of Allâh.

Rahmân is in the measure of Fa'lan which conveys the idea of fullness and extensiveness and indicates the greatest preponderance of the quality of mercy which comprehends the entire universe without regard to the effort and asking. It circumscribes the quality of abounding grace inherent in and inseparable from Him. Rahîm is in the measure of Fa'il. This measure denotes the idea of constant repetition and giving of liberal reward again and again to those who ask for it and deserve it. It is on account of this attribute that it is said that he who seeks finds and he who asks is given. It is on account of this grace that Allâh hears the prayers of supplicants when He says:

"Call on Me! I will answer your Prayer" (40:60)

Striving is essential for achieving good results and invoking this grace. For this special benevolence, effort, exertion, hard work, purification of the heart and supplications are necessary conditions. Those who exert in the direction of Allâh and those who do not care cannot be the same. In the Holy Qur'ân there are dozens of verses which remind us of this Attribute of Allâh. The Attribute of al-Rahîm is almost always in association with other

Attributes of Him. His Attribute of being the Most Gracious (al-Rahmân), Oft-Returning (al-Tawwâb), Most Loving (al-Wadûd), the All-Mighty (al-Azîz), the Most Beneficent (al-Barr), the Great Protector (al-Ghafûr), the Ever Loving (al-Raûf) are to be found together with al-Rahîm.

Seek protection of your Lord and turn to Him. Surely, my Lord is Ever Merciful, Most Loving. (11:90)

Take Allâh as your shield, surely Allâh is Oft-Returning with Compassion and Ever Merciful. (49:12)

The attributes of Rahmân and Rahîm rule out the doctrine of Atonement and Transmigration of souls in this very world. According to a saying of the Holy Prophet the attribute of Rahmân generally pertains to this life while the attributes of Rahîm generally pertains to the life to come, (Muhît, Zamakhshari) as this world is mostly the world of actions and the next a world where actions will be particularly rewarded. The attribute of Rahmân provides us with what we need for our deeds in this life, whereas the attribute of Rahîm brings about in the hereafter rewards and blessings after using those resources.

Master of the Day of Requital

Mâlik e Yaum al-Dîn: This is the fourth basic attribute of Allâh. Allâh is called Mâlik e yaum al-dîn - the Master of the Day of Requital. The translation of the word Mâlik is not King, as most English translations have adopted. Mâlik (- Master) and Malik (- king) are two different words from the same root Malak. According to the rules of forming derivations in the Arabic language, the larger the number of letters added to the root word, as the alif in Mâlik the more intensive or more extensive does the meaning become (Muhît, Zamakhshari). Hence a Mâlik or Master is one who possesses the right of ownership over a thing and has the power to deal with it as one likes. It is more than malik or king or ruler (Lane). It shows that the Almighty is not unjust if He forgives His servants, or gives more of their dues, as He is not like a king or a judge who is bound to give his judgment strictly in accordance with the prescribed law, but being Master He can forgive or give more than the due and show love and mercy wherever and in whatever manner He may like. He dominates and rules over every particle of the universe.

To punish every sin is incompatible with the Divine attributes of forgiveness and forbearance. As Mâlik, He has full authority to dispense reward and punishment. It is obvious that no one can be truly called Master unless he has the power to pardon or punish as he may like and determine. He does as He will. There is no room for anyone to find fault with that which He does. The use of the word Mâlik serves a twofold purpose. On one hand it gives courage, hope, and confidence to a person who has in a moment of weakness committed some wrong or sin, not to lose hope as the beneficent Allâh being his Master has the power to forgive or give more. On the other hand it serves as a warning of taking undue advantage of the graciousness and beneficence of Allâh. Both these things are essential for human beings' spiritual progress and advancement.

The Divine Attribute Mâlike yaum al-dîn is a link between the attributes Rabb - the Nourisher to perfection, Rahmân - the Most Gracious and Rahîm - the Ever Merciful. This attribute shows the process of development of great and continuous mercy. The life after is also a creation of the Almighty, so His attributes of Nourishing, Graciousness, and Ever Compassionate Mercy will continue to operate in that life as well, thus effort and action and therefore progress will continue forever. The mentioning of the attributes of fostering and nourishing to perfection, graciousness, and compassionate mercy and love bear a subtle indication that Allah's supreme Lordship is not due to domination by violence or subjugation but to the two forms of compassion, the general form (Rahmanîyyat) and the particular form (Rahîmiyyat). He combines all kinds of glorification in His being and is unique in all His beauties and bounties. He is sublime, perfect, and glorious and subject to no limitation. To Him is due all praise in the beginning and in the end through eternity. All Excellencies belong to Him as a matter of right. No other shares in it.

The word yaum translated as 'Day' also means time, absolutely short or long, day and night (Tâj). This word is used in the terminology of Qur'ân refering to any period of time from a moment (5:28) to fifty thousand years (70:4). Although the process of reckoning is already going on in this life up to some extent, the last and the perfect reckoning will take place on the Day of Requital, the Day of greatest dispensation. There is continuous judgment and requital in this life as well but only in small measure. Award is reward and punishment is in His hands alone. A thief may escape once or twice but he is sure to be caught in the end or to be punished some other day in a different way. He who does evil suffers evil.

The Divine Attribute Mâlik e yaum al-dîn refutes those who do not believe in the Hereafter. The difference between this Divine attribute and Rahîm is that Rahîm opens the path to progress and success through good deeds, supplication and worship, whereby a reward is earned and through the attribute of Rahîm attributes that reward is conferred. Those who do not believe in the Divine attribute of Rahîm are indifferent towards good deeds, as the atheists say there is no reward and no punishment and thus deny the very existence of God and thereby deliberately neglect good actions. Under the attribute of Rahîm and through good actions and prayer one is deemed worthy of grace, but it is through the attribute of Mâlik e yaum al-dîn that the grace is bestowed. Mâlik also indicates that He has not withdrawn Himself from the governance of the universe, committing it to some vicegerent with all authority to award recompense here and Hereafter. He alone is the complete Master and Owner.

In the category of Mâlik e yaum al-dîn it could be asked why Allâh called Himself Master and not Judge? The answer is that the concept of justice does not emerge until after the establishment of right and no one has any right against the Lord. Salvation in the Hereafter is a bounty from Allâh. The Christian concept of vicarious atonement lacks such forbearance, forgiveness and mercy. On the other hand, the contemplation of these four Divine attributes creates in human beings an irresistible longing for seeing his Creator, an intense desire to offer his wholehearted devotion to Him and an irresistible feeling of love. This imperfect, dim, dense, narrow world of limited capacity is not suited to serve as stage for the magnificent manifestation of these attributes. An altogether different realm is needed for its demonstration. Through its mild reflection and forecast we can see in this life of those who 'die in the path of Allâh' before death overtakes them and though they subsist in this world they have their being in the Hereafter, Allâh manifests His light to them in a manner which is not manifested to others except after death. The heart of such a perfect man is a reflection of these four attributes.

The Four Divine Graces

All type of perfect and true praise belongs to Allâh alone, Who is the Creator and Nourisher to perfection of all the worlds. The Most Gracious, the Ever Merciful, Master of the Day of Requital. Him alone do we love and worship with complete and utmost humility, submissiveness, and obedience to receive the impress of His attributes and imbibe them in us and reflect them in our own life, and to Him we implore for help, to lead us on the exact right path till we reach the goal, the path of those on whom He has bestowed His blessings, those who have not incurred His displeasure, and those who have not gone astray. (1:2-7)

The four principle attributes of Allâh are mentioned in the very first chapter and at the very beginning of the Holy Qur'ân: Rabb - Nourisher to Perfection; Al-Rahmân - The Most Gracious; Al-Rahîm - The Ever Merciful; Mâlik e yaum al-dîn - Master of the Day of Requital, and these are expounded in detail in the Holy Qur'ân and its verses flow like a river in exposition of these. These attributes are essential to His being and on them rests the very existence of the universe. They take precedence over everything and comprehend everything and are the source of all other Divine attributes and posts for the throne ('Arsh) on which He has established Himself.

The very first opening chapter of the Holy Qur'ân (al-Fâtihah) also refers to the four Divine Graces which spring from the four basic attributes of God. These four Graces Rubûbîyyat, Rahmâniyyat, Rahîmiyyat and Mâlikîyyat may be called the mother of all Divine Graces which are in operation at all times in universe, and the order in which they are mentioned in al-Fâtihah is their natural order, and they are being manifested in the order mentioned.

They convey us that our Creator and Sustainer and Nourisher to perfection is the Most Gracious, the Ever Merciful, ready to do everything for us without recompense, coming to reward many fold for one good deed and only on rare occasion uses His discretion of punishment, and that only in those cases, where it is necessary for rectification and discipline and not at all for revenge, and that only for a limited period. They convey the idea of love and His All Compassion and create in us an irresistible feeling of love, devotion. Out of this impulse we want to worship Him in complete and utmost humility, submissiveness and obedience and want to receive the impression of His attributes and imbibe and reflect them in our own life.

The First Divine Grace

The first Divine Grace - Rubûbîyyat is the most general grace. This grace perpetually envelopes everything, without distinction of animate or inanimate. Every form of creation, living or non-living, comes into being through it. The coming into being from non-existence and its development from the crudest form to perfection is through the manifestation of this grace. All souls and bodies were manifested and are being manifested through it and all were developed and are developing through it. This grace is the very life of the universe. Were it to be withdrawn for an instant, the universe would come to an end and had it not been for this grace there would have been no creation.

So this attribute of Rubûbîyyat is mentioned before all other attributes of graces, as of all the attributes of grace this has natural priority because it comes into manifestation before the other attributes of grace are manifested. His Rubûbîyyat is in operation all the time. It is not that after having created the world Allâh has withdrawn from its control and that He has committed it to the laws of nature so that He Himself does not intervene in any way. It is not as if like the maker of a machine has no concern with it after he has made it. He exercises this attribute all the time over the whole universe, and at no time is the universe deprived of the benefit of this grace. Even after the creation of the universe the need of that source of grace is as insistent every moment as if He had not yet created anything. As the world depends upon this attribute for its coming into being, it is equally dependent upon it for its continuation and sustenance.

The Second Divine Grace

The operation of the second Grace, His Rahmâniyyat which follows Rubûbîyyat is related only to animate and not to inanimate. We read in The Holy Qur'ân verses like:

"He has taken upon Himself the rule of Mercy" (6:12, 54),

"Your Lord is the Lord of All-Embracing Mercy" (6:146),

"My mercy embraces all things" (7:156),

"Our Lord, You embrace each and every thing in Your mercy" (40:7).

This Mercy is not the consequence of, or reward of any action of ours. It is by the blessing of this Grace that everything lives and eats and has its sustaining needs fulfilled. It is through the operation of this grace that a human being fulfils his requirements of life, the sun for heat, light and energy, the air for breathing and water for drinking. It is by blessing of this grace that all that is needed for spiritual development such as the capacities of rational thinking and speech, embedded love for God and innate drive for worship and the capacity to receive Divine revelation have been provided from the earliest. Every created thing is the object of Rahmâniyyat and Mercy is His Essence and His Grace, but being Merciful is His Attribute. His Mercy embraces everything; it permeates all His objects of creation, and has precedence over all His other attributes.

Every created thing is the object of His Mercy. He is begged for Mercy by everyone by mentioning His other Names and Attributes. As one would say, "O Almighty! Have mercy with me." Or one might say, "O Avenging One! Have mercy on me". This is because the Names of God are referring to His attributes with the various ideas they bear. These attributes can all be appealed to for Mercy. His Pleasure and Wrath exist only by virtue of His Mercy and so is with His Mercifulness. Ibn Arabî says:

"The Mercy of Allâh flows in all created things and courses through His Selves and the Essences. The rank of Mercy is epitome to those who perceive and sublime to those of discursive mind."

It is because of this Rahmâniyyat that He gives respite to the disbelievers. We are told in the Holy Qur'ân if He were to seize people immediately for their wrong committing, no human being would be left on the face of the earth, but He gives them respite till an appointed term (16:61) so that the disobedient may have the favourable combination of circumstances to avail and correct, and chance to repent. He says:

"And do not let those who disbelieve think that the respite We give them is good for them. Surely, We grant them respite (that they may have chance to mend their ways and correct their evil actions) but they do not avail it," (3:178)

In short, through this grace of Rahmâniyyat the human beings and other living beings enjoy the fulfilment of millions of their wants. No one can claim that these are the result of their actions or that they had been engaged in some virtuous pursuit in a previous incarnation or time, in favourable estimate of which God has conferred all these innumerable bounties upon mankind, or because of his demand or request or because of demand or request by somebody else. It is this grace which reveals itself in thousands of ways to elevate the well being of all livings. It is a bounty regardless of merit, claim, or demand on the part of anyone. It is but the upsurge of Divine mercy so that every animate creature may attain his natural goal, and may meet the requirements inherent in his nature and to look after all that are good for him. That the Divine Being possesses this attribute is manifestly established through a study of the law of nature.

No one can dispute the fact that all these objects, like the earth, the sun, the moon, and the elements, that are the mainstay of life, proceeds from this very grace, and that every animal, beast, and human being, believer and disbeliever, good and bad, is getting benefit therefrom. All that is in our bodies owes its origin to His Rahmâniyyat, no body can claim that it is a reward for his action. He provides His bounties out of His sheer grace and not in return for anyone's labour and even long before the birth of His creatures and before the commencement of their deeds and thinking. God's Mercy is universal, and He is begged ever for His Mercy by everyone through His other attributes and names. It is His Mercy (Rahmatî - My Mercy 7:156) which is all encompassing. His Mercy has precedence over His wrath, that is to say that His Mercy is attributed to Him before wrath.

The Third Divine Grace

The third Divine Grace, Rahîmiyyat, follows His Rahmâniyyat. The difference between this and Rahmâniyyat is that in the case of the latter the beneficiary is not under obligation to make himself good or bring his ego out of the coverings of darkness, or to put forward any effort to take advantage of it. In the case of Rahîmiyyat striving and effort and purification of the heart and supplication and attention towards God and every other kind of appropriate effort are needed. He alone receives this grace who seeks it and this grace descends upon those who work for it. Allâh says:

"And those who strive hard in Our cause, We will certainly guide them to the ways that lead to Us" (29:69)

It is out of this grace that our prayers and supplications are accepted:

"And when My servants ask you concerning Me (tell them), I am nearby indeed, I answer the prayer of the supplicant when he prays to Me, so they should respond to My call, and believe in Me (that I possess all these attributes) so that they may proceed in the right way." (2:186).

By virtue of this grace God's name is al-Rahîm, the Ever Merciful. Since the attribute of Rahîmiyyat follows upon the fulfilment of certain conditions it is mentioned after Rahmâniyyat. This Mercy can be acquired by obligations, in a way as the verse 7:156 continues to inform us or by Divine Grace followed by what is said in verse 48:2.

This Qur'ân is sent by the All-Mighty, the Ever Merciful (- Al-Azîz al-Rahîm) (36:5)

The Fourth Divine Grace

The fourth Divine grace - Mâlikîyyat - Master of the Day of Requital is followed by Rahîmiyyat. To bring creation to perfection, the manifestation of Mâlikîyyat is also needed, as submission to the laws brings in the reward which results in the advancement of human beings. Disobedience to the laws must result in punishment and as a result of this retardation in progress. There are ample indications in the nature that the Divine Law of requital is constantly at work and is being manifested every moment. In fact, the punishment of wrong is necessary in the Divine scheme, as is the reward of good. Reward and punishment are different phases of the exercise of the attribute of Rabûbîyyat, for the perfection is still the object, and Hell is nothing but a nursing home, a kind of a hospital till the souls of sinners are completely cleansed of the taint of the disease of sin. Fear of punishment and punishment is the only deterring influence in crushing evil. The pressure of legal penalties is a discourager of wrong and wherever it relaxes its hold, evil begins to crop up.

The fear of punishment in this world and the Hereafter acts as a deterrent in this respect; such can hardly be the case with the belief in the Atonement. If God could not find any other remedy for the cleansing of human sins, then there is no need of any good action on our part. There are few human beings who pursue virtue for its own sake. It is the requital and reward of virtue, especially seen in its efficacy in counterbalancing the effects of sin that they fulfil the law and lead a good life. But if the same thing is attainable merely by a belief in the "Grace of Blood", few would consider it worthwhile to bear the hardships and trials of the life of piety and righteousness. Belief in the Atonement obviates the necessity for good deeds. We must not forget that it is only the awe and fear of Divine Majesty that can safeguard against sin and evil. Once one realizes that God is dispenser of punishment as well and that His punishment is severe (2:165), that awesome consciousness would become a barrier against sins.

The idea of atonement makes a person unbridled and wayward. But compassionate mercy and mastery stimulate both hope and effort. Mâlikîyyat supported by culture and progress has played havoc with the belief in Atonement. Belief in this attribute, when rendered into action in our daily life, would bring our culture and civilization to collapse. It is useless to sing hymns at the top of our voices if we are not leading Godly lives. He does not stand in need of any adoration from us. It is neither creditable to Him nor profitable to us. It is very dangerous to believe in things that not only have no bearing on our life but are actually harmful in their effects on the building of our character. In the matter of culture and civilization such beliefs as Atonement have proved an implacable enemy to human progress. Virtue and vice, both in their growth and origin, are in the right proportion with strength or weakness of our belief in law and its forces.

Crimes come to the surface in quarters where law and order can be avoided without fear of detection and punishment. And law loses all its force and cannot compel universal attachment unless and until some reward or punishment comes to its fulfiller or breaker. We cannot imagine any greater harm to the very fabric of human society than that which comes to us as a natural growth by reason of our belief in a doctrine of Atonement that either weakens our sense of responsibility or causes us to lose our physical or moral strength and divests us of a motive for action. So to bring creation to perfection, the attribute of Mâlik yaum al-dîn, Master of the Day of Requital, is needed. Hence in the very opening chapter of the Holy Qur'ân this basic attribute is mentioned. This sequence is in agreement with the book of nature. Perfect composition in a book of revelation demands that the order followed in the book of nature should also be kept in view in a book of revelation. To reverse the natural order in composition is to reverse the law of nature. For a perfect composition it was also necessary that the order of nature, as if it were its photograph, which is natural, and in fact prior, should be prior in description also.

While describing the attribute the word Mâlik or Master and not the Judge or Administrator of Justice to meet out the requital of good and evil is very significant. The essential difference between a judge and master is that the former is bound to punish the evildoers for each and every evil and crime, while the master can exercise his discretion, and may either punish the evildoer or forgive him and pass over his sins and crimes. It is because of this fact that the Holy Qur'ân says:

"O my servants, who have committed excesses against their own souls, do not despair of the mercy of Allâh (that Allâh is going to punish you at all cost, and cannot forgive your sins). Surely Allâh forgives all sins. Verily He is the Great Protector, the Ever Merciful." (39:53).

Hence the attribute of Mâlik and Master is introduced to link the idea of punishment with that of forgiveness and mercy. In the body of the Qur'ân, Allâh is also mentioned as Al-Ghafûr (91 times), Al-Ghâfir, and Al Ghaffâr with the cognate verb forms (560 times). Hence it will be seen that the Qur'ân gives prominence to the attributes of love and mercy in Allâh to an extent where the parallel is not to be met with in any other book.

On one hand, the Holy Qur'ân stresses the fact that the Divine Law of Requital of deeds is working every moment and thus makes a human being feel the responsibility of what he does, and on the other hand gives prominence to the quality of forgiveness in Divine nature. So the law of requital is not like a rigid law of nature but like the dealing of a most gracious and ever merciful master. It is here that the makers of the modern Christian creed have made their greatest error. Such doctrines were incorporated from paganism. They are contrary to the very teachings of Jesus Christ, who.demands of every person that he should bear his own cross. It is wrong to think that a human being was born with a hereditary stain upon him, and this stain for which he was not personally responsible had to be atoned for, and that God was compelled to make a blood sacrifice of His own innocent son in order to neutralize this mysterious curse. It goes against the justice and mercy of our Creator.

It is a piece of superstition and can no longer receive approval from reason and culture. It was to popularize the Christian faith with the pagan world that the dogma of God incarnate with other mystery tenets in its brain was incorporated into the real and simple faith of Jesus Christ. The borrowed colours, though, remained deep and thick enough for centuries to conceal the real faith and have in the meantime become threadbare and are no longer in demand. The suffering God is no longer an ideal in the estimate of the thinking laity. The crucified deity is thus an old myth, well enough for a child's imagination or for those who are inclined to shift their burden on the shoulders of others. They think that the Son of God is needed to atone for the evil deeds of humanity, since God, being a judge, cannot, and should not, forgive sins without taking revenge unless somebody can be found to provide compensation. This conception of theirs is against both the justice and mercy of God. God is a Master and He is therefore able to forgive.

The Grace of Mâlikîyyat has nothing to do with the autocracy, inexorability, vengeance and cruelty. On the contrary, this Grace along with the graces of Rahmânîyyat and Rahîmîyyat, which are the graces of love and mercy are emphasized in the Holy Qur'ân and in the sayings of the Holy Prophet again and again. Not only does every chapter of the Holy Qur'ân open with the attributes Rahmân and Rahîm, thus showing that the qualities of love and mercy are predominant in Divine nature, but the following text lays a big stress in explicit words on the immeasurable vastness of the Divine Mercy.

We read in the Holy Qur'ân passages like these which were already cited above:

"He has taken upon Himself the rule of mercy" (6:12, 54),

"Your Lord is the Lord of All-Embracing Mercy" (6:146),

"My mercy embraces all things" (7:156),

"Our Lord, You embrace each and every thing in Your mercy" (40:7).

Abû Hurairah told that he heard Allah's Messenger say, "Allâh, Most High, had inscribed a document before bringing the creation into being: 'My Mercy has preceded my anger' and that this is written in His presence above the throne." (Bukhârî)

So great is the Divine mercy and love of Allâh that it encompasses believers and disbelievers alike. The picture of the Divine graces portrayed in the Holy Qur'ân is, first and last, a picture of love and mercy and punishment is to impress that evil is a most hateful thing, which ought to be shunned. The punishment itself, as described, is of a remedial nature and has in it nothing of vengeance or intolerance. His punishment is the treatment of a disease, which a human being has brought upon himself and it is only for a limited time. It is still love and affection, as its object is still to set a person on the path of progress, after healing the disease.

"And We sent (Messengers) towards the communities before you, (because of their rejection) We afflicted them with destitution, calamities, and adversities (to discipline them and) so that they might become humble before us (and to set them again on the path of progress)." (6:42, 7:94).

These four Divine Graces are the prime and fundamental source of all other attributes of Allâh. They form the pivot around which all the other Divine attributes revolve, and the basis of the working of the universe and of the labour between Allâh and human beings.

Our surprise knows no bounds when we think of the Divine economy of words in the selection of these four names for our meditation. Not only do they serve the purpose of theology but they are comprehensive enough to bring with their scope all that is needed to guide us through all conceivable avenues of human activity and perfect civilization. They are our guide in mundane affairs as well as in morals and spiritualism. Whatever branch of life we may enter upon, we find in these attributes the surest of guidance by which we can achieve our aim of life and real progress and greatness.

The Opening Words in the Holy Qur'ân

The Holy Qur'ân begins with the words Al-Hamdo li (A)llâh. In the light of what has been said above these words mean: Every type of true praise, whether relating to external aspects or internal realities, whether relating to inherent Excellencies or as manifested in natural phenomena, is due only to Allâh. No other shares in it. There is no excellence which the wisdom of the wise can imagine or that the mind of a thinker can contemplate, but belongs to Allâh, the Supreme. This praise, which is offered in appreciation of commendable action of One worthy of praise, and lauding One Who has done a favour of His own volition and according to His own choice.

It is the due only of the Being Who is the source of all Grace and Light and exercises beneficences deliberately and not in ignorance or under compulsion or like a robot, mechanical to some extent, efficient but devoid of sensibility, will and volition. All this is formed in Allâh only. He is the true Benefactor and Ever Merciful. If the suspension of His operation for a single moment were to be imagined, the earth and the heavens and all that exists therein would perish instantly. If we tried to count His Excellencies we would not be able to number them, even if we exerted ourselves hard (31:27).

He is known through His glories and Excellencies. Praise is inspired by His qualities, the perfection of beauty (Rabb and Rahmân) and the perfection of beneficence (Rahîm). If a being imbibe in him His Excellencies his heart melts and yearns for Him with fervent devotion and love and worships Him with all his humbleness. He is then drawn closer to that peerless and unique Being. That is why in the very opening chapter (al-Fatihah) of the Holy Qur'ân this charming description and beautiful picture of Allâh has been set forth, Whose Excellencies are the culmination of beauty and beneficence and Who suffers not from any shortcoming or defect. God says:

He has given you of all that you wanted of Him by your natural demand. And if you try to count Allah's bounties you will not be able to number them. Surely a human being is very unjust, very ungrateful. (14:34)

Countless Thy favours O God!

A hundred thousand tongues

Can deliver not the thanks

due to Thee.

Favours upon favours

Has Thou showered

On the handful of dust

Life entire

Is indebted to Thee

Thy universal care

Allâh's Attribute of Love

"And He is the Most Forgiving and the Most Loving" (85:14)

The Qur'ân gives us a long list of Allâh's attributes. If we take a look at them, we will find that a great number of them bear on Allah's love, mercy, grace, concern, affection, friendship and attachment. Majesty (Jalâl) and beauty (Jamâl) are two intrinsic attributes of awe (Haybat), and bewilderment (Hayrat) is the effect of Majesty (Jalâl) and Beauty (Jamâl) on the human being. Many things that are existent become the object of awe. Allâh says that He is Wadûd - Lovely and Loving.

He also is Wallî, a Friend, Companion, and Comrade. In human hearts, Love for Allâh, our Creator, is embedded deep. There is no lover and no beloved except Allâh. This Love is a basic and inborn human instinct. It is a part of human nature and it is part of the human seed. In the words of Rûmî:

> My navel cord was cut
>
> With promise of Thy love
>
> for me
>
> And in my nature didst
>
> Thou sow
>
> the seed of my love
>
> for Thee.

The Holy Prophet said, Allâh loves His servants much more than a mother. It is not that a human being is not acquainted with love. His heart is capable of love of many different kinds - love of parents, love of one's children; love of near relations, love of riches. How is it that the Being to Whom we owe our every thing and to love whom is a guarantee of our welfare in this life and the Hereafter is considered to be inappropriate as an object of love? We can find no peace of mind without His love and without worship. The Holy Qur'ân says,

"I have created the jinn (- fiery natured and haughty) and the ordinary people only that they may worship Me" (51:56)

It would be unworthy of Him that He should have created us for the above purpose and not have provided means and the capacities and capabilities for doing it. The first step towards attaining this goal is strong desire, strong yearning and strong love for the object we worship. Worship without love and adoration is of no meaning. It is for this reason that love of Allâh is part of our natural endowment and an inborn yearning. We have an inborn desire for communion with Him. Worship is not an affliction or an imposition, as He does not have the slightest need for it. He does not depend on us for His praise and glorification. We need to praise and glorify Him for our own sake, to illuminate, purify, get comfort, and peace of mind. Our heart and soul needs the light of worship. The largest measure of worldly success, material wealth, kingly power, personal glory and fame cannot by themselves lead to true happiness and genuine peace of mind. These blessings are vouchsafed only to the soul which is deep in love with God and which has attained communion with Allâh.

Love has its motives, its springs, perfection of beauty and perfection of beneficence, and these are the unique qualities of Allâh. Beauty and beneficence and love are connected naturally and eternally, where there is beauty and beneficence there must be love. And nothing is more beautiful and kind than Allâh. Where there is strong love there is a strong longing to see the loved one. Overpowered with love and affection, Moses was compelled to say:

"Lord! Reveal Yourself to me so that I may look at You (and Your Beauty)". (7:143)

If He were to momentarily unveil Himself and manifest a glimpse of His sublime beauty and glory, all creatures would be stunned prostrate before His overpowering majesty (7:143). But as "the physical vision cannot comprehend Him" (6:103) and He invites us again and again to ponder over the evidences of the perfection of His beauty and perfection of beneficence.

Who is it that created the heavens and the earth, and sends down water for you from the clouds? (It is We.) Then We cause to grow with it orchards full of bloom and loveliness. You had no power to cause their trees to grow. Is there any god with Allâh? (There is none ;) yet there are a people who ascribe (to Him) equals (in all these works) (27:60).

He invites us again and again to ponder over His creation (6:95-99; 10:4; 10:34; 16:6; 50:7; 55:11; 67:3-5). Why this repeated invitation to ponder over His creation? Why the wonderful work of which our Creator is the author is described in the Holy Qur'ân again and again? Why this repeated appeal? Is it not because He wants to kindle the flame of love in our hearts? Knowledge and awareness of perfection is bound to create love of Him. The first thing that moves us to love is beauty. It attracts us. The appreciation of beauty is the part of human nature. It is not possible that there should be beauty and it should not move us. Who has created this beauty? Not self-created, for sure. He Who has created all this beauty, how very beautiful must be He Himself. It does not make good logic that He should be able to create beauty but Himself remain devoid of it.

He Who gives beauty to others, how can He be without it Himself? Who enriches others must be rich Himself. He who has nothing himself, what can he give to others? Surprising, a penniless beggar offering charity. His beauty makes us forget all other beauties. His grace makes us forget those nearest and dearest to us. But for His animating beauty there would have been no beauty anywhere in the world.

The enchantment of beautiful faces comes all from Him; the colour of all flowers too comes from Him. This eternal beauty, even a passing view of it, could inspire verses like the following:

Patent and perverse
Is this Light of lights
The whole world has become
One large mirror
For the willing to see.
Yester night the moon I saw,
Made me lose my peace
For some thing in it resembled
The Beauty of the One
Loved by me.
Its beauty abundant
Has filled my heart
With frenzied joy - therefore
Tell me not of Tartar
or the Turkish beauty.

The waves in the ocean, the sun,
Are witness into Thee.
Each scintillating star is a scene
of radiance
That is Thee.

The beauty of all beauties
of this world,

is Beauty of Thine
The rose, the rose garden,
Receives their colour
From the garden that's Thee.
The heavy-lidded drunken eye
Of every beauty
Reveals only Thee:
The curved lock
On every cheek
Has its hand
Pointing to Thee.

Wave of Thy beauty
Are to be seen
In the effulgence
Of the sun, and every star
Carries a beam
Of Thy flash!
With Thine own hands
Hast Thou sprinkled biting salt
On the wounded souls:
So, naturally, therefore,
On every side, now,
Is raging a tumult
Of the waxing cries of love,
Wrung from the desolate heart
Of the disconsolate lovers!

For those blind
Of eye, thousands of veils
Have come to hang betwixt:
Otherwise, Thine own face,
Thine own approval,
And pleasure, was the final
Aim and object of every
Believer and nonbeliever!

Thy charming looks constitute
A sharp sword, which cuts
Clean through everything—
Cuts clean through every
Other loyalty, and love!

That I be able to meet
Thee, I have mingled
With the dust, hoping, thereby,
To find some remedy, would put
An end to this torture
Of separation
Not even
For a single moment,
Do I find any rest,
Any peace, without Thee:
My life is all the time
Sinking like the heart

Of an ailing person.

Find out quick
What is the meaning
Of these cries, this noise
This tumult, in Thy love?
Turn Thy attention, immediately
Lest the blood of a lovesick
Caught in the violent throes
Of love, should finally come
To lose his life!

The only thing really,
that matters in this world
is Thy love, material life
Is nothing but a pitiful
Groping, in a thick
And baffling darkness!
Thou art, indeed,
My sweetheart,
And this love, alone,
Is the love that is real,
And pure!

So strange, diverse,
In all directions scattered
O beloved Lord!

Is Thy power.
Should we but look—
Around, above, below—
Every time we view
Some aspect of Thee

For Thy sweet sake,
I have scattered the dust,
that is me, on the winds
That blow; This is the way
I have lived my life,
Right from the moment
I came to know this
Is the indispensable
Condition of all genuine
Cases of loyalty
And love!

It is possible that on account of his own insensitive mind a person may not feel the impact of beauty when in its presence - the same as animals would remain unmoved by it. Likewise, his own lack of spiritual insight may not permit him to discern in earthly beauty a pointer to the Divine beauty, Who is the eternal, everlasting and the ultimate source of all other beauties - ephemeral and fleeing, though, essentially in character. It is an undeniable truth that beauty and love are connected naturally and eternally. Where there is beauty there must be love, and nothing is more beautiful than Allâh. As Allâh is without body, so the beauty of Allâh is not confined to the physical what we see. Beauty is excellence proper to the person whose beauty is being judged and is in question.

Another thing that moves us to love and inspire the heart spontaneously with admiration and strong liking, inclination and ardour is the perfection of beneficence. If a being contains both these Excellencies - the perfection of beauty and the perfection of beneficence - the heart melts and yearns for him with fervent devotion. Islam aims at impressing these two Excellencies of the Supreme Being upon the seekers after truth. So that we may be drawn to that peerless and Unique Being and worship Him with fervent devotion and yearning.

(Say O Prophet!,) "I ask no reward from you for (my preaching). All that I ask you is to cherish the strongest love to be near (to Him)." (42:23)

A human being, it is true, is bound to love Allâh; does Allâh also love a human being in return? Yes, Allah's love for a human being is clearly proved and promised. He is One Most Approving and One Most Appreciating (64:16). We cannot have the least doubt that He will not respond to our love by His. A storm of love in one's heart but no response to it by Allâh, this is impossible. How can we in return attract His attention? The way to it is told to us in the following verse:

Say (O Prophet!), "Follow me if you love Allâh. (If you do so) Allâh will love you and grant you protection from your sins. Allâh is Great Protector, Ever Merciful." (3:31).

What a transparent, persuasive and eloquent affirmation we have here of Allah's love for human beings. Not the least doubt is left that Allâh loves him who qualifies for His love and fulfil his obligation towards Him (64:16-17).

Allâh's Attributes of Resemblance

Allah's attributes are either tanzîhî, i.e. attributes of transcendence, or tashbîhî, which are the attributes of resemblance. The tanzîhî attributes leads us into what are called tashbîhî or relative attributes. The tanzîhî attributes describe the way in which Allâh is related to the world which is His creation. The tashbîhî attributes are those which are in the very nature of God, as He is One, He exists of Himself, He depends upon nothing, He is self-existent. He is infinite. He is invincible. He cannot be fully comprehended or grasped, He is Akbar (- Big - It does not mean that He is very big, but means that size is irrelevant to Him), He is Azîm (Great), He cannot be measured quantitatively, He is inseparable, He cannot be grasped by the mind of human beings or anyone else.

If the mind can contain it
And the intellect comprehend it
How can it be God.
The God that is infinite
Allâh is infinite, pervasive.

We cannot comprehend Him fully. He is without limits, without dimension. We would be fools to ask for Him to step down from His throne of infinite attributes to become comprehensible for us, or take birth from the womb of a woman. How can a limitless, infinite Being be contained in the mind of a limited being like man or in the belly of a woman? What logic and what an understanding! In the Holy Qur'ân we read about Moses asking to see Allâh. When Allâh showed him a glimpse of His Glory, Moses, unable to stand it, become dazed and senseless (7:143). The narrative points to the fact that the beauty of Allâh is dazzling, we humans cannot stand it.

Howsoever I may try
I can comprehend not
Thy Beauty Divine-
Farther thou art
Than the farthest I could imagine.

Allâh is spoken of in the Holy Qur'ân as seeing, hearing, speaking, being displeased, affectionate, etc.; yet the use of these words must not be taken in any sense as indicating an anthropomorphic or human-like being. Allâh is not a jism or corporal, He hears but not with ears like our ears, He sees but not with eyes like our eyes. We read that His hands are stretched (bast al yad), this means that He is full of bounties. Thus the hands of God spoken in 5:64 express His unlimited power, favour and protection. God's throne does not signify any place, rather a symbol of His power and represents His control of things as a monarch's throne is a symbol of his power to rule. It is taken as indicating might or power and authority. He does not resemble His creatures in form, nor do any of His creatures resemble Him, He is not like anything else or similar (Fiqh Akbar by Imâm Abû Hanîfah). He is beyond all comparison. So transcendent is He and so far above all material conception that a likeness of Him cannot be conceived. He is not only above all material limitations but even above the limitations of metaphor. He is above all material conception. Vision comprehends Him not and He comprehends all vision.

> Understanding and reasoning
> And imagining besides
> May do their utmost
> But beyond, ever beyond,
> Remains the core, the essence,
> of His Being.

Allâh is inscrutable. He cannot be fully comprehended or grasped by the human mind. Our intelligence is fitted for piecemeal learning about the things which we see, touch, taste, and hear. It is not capable to grasp the infinite in any full and final sense. If we had to depend upon our minds alone or are obliged to be content only with the evidence of our senses, we could never reach to Allâh. If we can never entirely understand the spots on the back of a beetle, as one pointed out, how could we ever hope to understand fully the reality of the Creator?

When we think about Allâh we must use our reason and reflect upon our experience. There is no way by which we can escape this kind of limited anthropomorphism that we think about Allâh in human terms and in terms of our human life. If we try to avoid thinking about Allâh in this fashion we will be obliged to think of Him as though He were either a machine or a blind force. But we do not, in reality, speak of 'It' when we mention Allâh, we speak of Him. That means that Allâh is better understood as being personal rather than impersonal. Obviously, He is not a person in just the same sense in which we are persons. That would be quite absurd, for it would negate the infinite nature of Allâh and His inscrutable quality. His personality is far above that of any human being. When we ascribe personality to Allâh, we are saying that He is One (112:1-4). He is free in His nature and not bound by chains of imposed necessity (2:255).

He has a will (3:26) and a purpose (51:56). He can and does enter into communion with that which is not Himself (2:186). He is not like sticks or stones, unconscious force or energy or a half-personalized being. He is a spiritual Being without a physical body (24:35). He is not bound down by the limitation in time and space which besets us with physical bodies.

He is both immea-surable and eternal, beyond measurement by watches, clocks, or calendars. In spite of all this, the whole of the Scriptural record as well as experience of Prophets and Saints testify to the personal relationship which they had with Him. On the other hand, we can know something about Allâh when we make sense of experience to lead us to recognize certain truths about the ultimate reality. The attributes of Allâh are the most valuable clue we have in order to know Allâh.

Some say that this God of the Qur'ân possesses human morals. It was therefore a human being and not God who pictured Him in the Qur'ân. This is not correct; none of His attributes are like human qualities. When a man is angry, he suffers from anger himself and his heart loses its comfort and perceives a burning sensation and his brain is oppressed and he undergoes a change, but God is free from all such changes. His anger and displeasure means that He removes His support from one who does not desist from evil, and according to His eternal law He metes out to him such treatment as a human being metes out to another when he is angry. Metaphorically it is called God's displeasure and anger. In the same way His love is not like the love of a human being, for a human being suffers in love also when he is separated from his beloved. But God is not subject to suffering. His nearness also is not like the nearness of a human being to a beloved one, for when a human being nears to someone, he vacates the space which he had occupied before. His rahmah or mercy or compassion or love, for instance, means the bestowal of good things and not an actual inclining of the His heart (Hujjatullâh al-Bâlighah).

To indicate His love, power, knowledge and other attributes, the same words had to be used as are in ordinary use for human beings, but the conception is not quite the same. In short, every Divine attribute is distinct from human qualities. There is only a verbal resemblance and no more (Chashma M'arifat). The Holy Names mentioned in the Qur'ân cover attributes like generosity, compassion, intellect and others as worked in the nature long before human beings ever came into existence. It was not a human being who fashion the Qur'ânic God by himself, but it was the Almighty Who made the human being after His own image and revealed to him His such characters so that he may follow Him and act as His vicegerent. God Himself appeared as our prototype in the Book. His attributes are to be taken as referring to the ultimate end of those words.

This God of ours possesses numberless blessings, numberless powers, numberless beauties and beneficences. It is not within the power of a human being to comprehend all the attributes and activity of the Divine Being. They are above intellect and imagination. The truth is that as Allâh Himself is unbounded and limitless, His attributes and activities are unbounded and limitless too. While regarding Divine attributes in general Shah Wallîallah writes that their use is only in the sense of the ultimate end of these words. It is beyond and above human power to count and reach the reality of every name, attribute and activity of Allâh. No one can truly recognize Allâh till he understands that there are innumerable activities and names of Allâh which are far beyond and above human power and reason and speculation. His powers are so numerous that human reason cannot encompass them. His attributes are wonderful; they have depth upon depth and are beyond of and outside comprehension. We do not believe in a God Whose powers are limited by our reason and speculation and there is nothing beyond. We believe in Allâh Whose powers and attributes, like His Being, are unlimited, unconfined and unending.

Allâh's Attributes of Transcendance

According to Alî Ibn Abî Tâlib and other people of reflection (Ashâb al-Fikr) "Dust" was the first universal reality. Then Allâh manifested Himself in theophany His Light to that "Dust". He says:

He directed Himself towards the space. Behold! It was (like) a mass of gas (dust), and He said to it (- the space) and to the earth, 'Come both of you (in obedience to Me) willingly or unwillingly together.' They said, 'We obey you with all our will.' (41:11)

Within this "Dust" was the entire universe in its potentiality and readiness (Salâhiya) and each thing in the "Dust" - living or non living, received from His Light according to its peparedness (Isti'dâd) and potentiality, just as the corners of a room receive light according to their distance from the lamp. He says He is the Light (al-Nûr) of Heavens and the earth, and then He compares Himself with a Lamp:

Allâh is the Extensive Light of the heavens and the earth. His light can be compared to a (lustrous) pillar on which is a lamp. The lamp is inside a crystal globe. The globe of glass is as if it were a glittering star. It (- the lamp) is lit by (the oil of) a blessed olive tree, which belongs neither to the east nor to the west (rather welds the whole world in its fold). Its oil is likely to glow forth of itself even if no fire has touched it. This (lamp) is a combination of many lights over and over. Allâh guides towards His Light whoever desires (to be enlightened). Allâh sets forth excellent parables for the people, and Allâh alone has full knowledge of every thing (24:35)

Within this "Dust" nothing is nearer to the Light in reception than Mohammad followed by his followers.

"(This light is now lit) in houses, which Allâh has ordained to be exalted and His name be commemorated in them. Therein (are such as) glorify Him in the mornings and the evenings, Men, whom neither trade nor sale distracts from exalting (the name of) Allâh and from the observance of Prayer and from presenting Zakât (- purifying dues) regularly. They dread the day when the hearts and the eyes will be in a state of agitation and anguish; With the result that Allâh will give them the reward according to their fairest deeds and will (even) give them much more by His grace and bounty. And Allâh does provide without measure to whom He will" (22:36-38)

The cosmos is the sensory realm, and its Ruler is veiled. Therefore He describes Himself as the Hidden (al-Bâtin) in veils of darknesses (Zulumât) and in veils of light (Nûr). The cosmos cannot perceive Him nor He will ever be unveiled, thus the Present Reality will never be known by an originated thing completely. Every light that is visible on the heights or in the valleys, whether in soul or in bodies, whether personal or impersonal, whether apparent or hidden, whether in the mind or outside it, is a bounty of His grace. This Light of the Lord envelopes everything and nothing is deprived of His light. He is the source of all lights and is the ultimate course of all lights and is the fountainhead of all mercies and laws. He is presented by the light of human beings' hearts, by their conscience and organic and inorganic complexity.

Just as His Light (Nûr) was there at the beginning of our universe, it will be there at the end, when He will roll up the heavens:

They have not yet appreciated (the attributes of) Allâh with the importance and appreciation that He deserves. The earth altogether shall be in His grip of power on the Day of Resurrection, and the heavens shall be rolled up in His All-Powerful hand (and will so lie at His absolute disposal). Holy is He. (He is) far above and beyond the things these (polytheists) associate (with Him). (That Day) there shall be a blast on the trumpet and all who are in the heavens and all who are on the earth will fall into a swoon except whom Allâh will like (to spare). Then there will be a blast another time and behold! The people shall stand up awaiting (judgment before their Lord). (21:104)

And (on that Day) the earth shall radiate with the light of her Lord. And the record (of their deeds) will be produced (before them), and the Prophets and the witnesses shall be brought forward; people shall be judged in all fairness and no injustice shall be done to anyone of them. And every soul shall be repaid in full for its deeds; for He (the Almighty Lord) is well-aware of all that they do. (39:67-70)

The "Word and Speech" of Allâh

God's Speech (Kalâm) is His knowledge and His knowledge is the fact that He knows everything. His sublime knowledge is partly shared by His prophets, His

Friends (Awlîyâ) and the people of "unveiling" (Ahl al-Kashûf):

"Allâh spoke to Moses in explicit words at great lenght" (4:164)

The knowledge also refers to the awareness of the prophets of the inner states of those who do not believe in those messages with the prophets convey. Those who know God, come to know Him through His Kalâm. The intellects cannot know Him with their sound reflections. This is the knowledge (Kalâm) that lies beyond the stage of reflection and intellect (warâ' al-Aql). We are told Moses and his comrade met a noble servant of God to whom He had taught knowledge (18:65). So, there is a station beyond reflection where some kind of knowledge is bestowed by Allâh on His servants (cf.: 18:65-82). When we read the narration 18:65-82 we come to the conclusion that there is none more ignorant than the intellect, which never ceases to inquire.

Allâh desires to be known by us. He reveals Himself by His speech (Kalâm) out of His Grace of Mercy (Rahmâniyat) by which our humanity is surrounded. The word of Allâh, (Kalimat-Allâh) that is, the revelation of Allâh, comes to us through His prophets (2:124), His saints, and even directly if we qualify us for this (2:37). Allah's language in revelation is the language of nouns, verbs, adjectives, and adverbs, and He has the language of action (19: 52; 20:11; 20:25; 7:104; 20:46; 31:71). A living being is one who is active, who can speak, whose actions and words make him known to others, Allâh says: He is Living (al-Hayyî), and His speech (Kalâm) is a proof of Him being Living. Some people regard Allâh as dumb, mute, destitute of the power of speech and incapable of revealing any knowledge concerning Himself and divest Him of all attributes that must be inherent in the true and perfect Guide.

They have not enough faith to believe that He has revealed His existence and His Divinity to the world of His volition. On the contrary, they hold that the Supreme Being was hidden like a dead body or a piece of rock in some dark, gloomy, hidden, vague and obscure corner and the wise and sagacious worked hard to seek Him, and having discovered Him and broadcast His Divinity to the word. True knowledge of Allâh depends upon the fact that we should reach the living Allâh Who speaks clearly to His favourites and bestows satisfaction and contentment upon them with His majestic and delicious speech. He speaks to them as one man speaks to another and converses with them as a certainty that is beyond doubt or suspicion (Ilm al-Yaqîn). He listens to them (al-Samî') and responds to them and hearing their supplications He informs them of their acceptance. He proves to them that He is Allâh, their Creator on one hand by His majestic and delicious words and on the other hand by His miraculous works and His powerful and mighty signs. He says:

"It is not given to a human being that Allâh speaks to him except by direct revelation (Wahî) or from behind a veil or by sending messengers (Engels) who reveal to the people what He pleases by His command" (42:51)

The verse 42:51 cited above tells how Allâh speaks to a person, and makes mention of the three ways in which He speaks to His servants and reveals Himself to them. He speaks to them directly without the aid of an intermediary. It is called Wahî, generally translated as meaning 'revelation'. The word Wahî is from waha meaning: to indicate, reveal, suggest, point out, put a thing into the mind, dispatch a messenger, inspire, speak secretly, hasten, and make sign, sign swiftly, suggest with speed, and write. The root has been used in the Holy Qur'ân in its ten forms 78 times. It is the inspired word, which enters the heart.

The second mode of Allah's speaking is that He speaks from behind a veil, as in a vision (Kashaf) carrying a deeper significance, which may or may not be interpreted, or sometimes makes him hear words in a state of wakefulness when he is not seeing the person speaking to him. The third form of revelation is that in which an angel (a medium) is chosen by Allâh to deliver His Message to the person to whom He wishes to speak. In all these cases the recipient of the revelation is granted certain senses. He sees what others do not see and hears words, which others do not hear. It is, with what may be called, the spiritual senses that he hears and sees and feels things, which others do not hear, see, or feel. The highest form of Wahî or revelation is called, in the terminology of Islam, revelation that is recited (Wahî matlûw) as in the case of the Holy Qur'ân.

The Holy Qur'ân was from the beginning to the end delivered in the third form to the Holy Prophet of Islam. It is in its entirety Wahî matlûw or revelation recited in words. The Holy Qur'ân is the word of Allâh; its essence and meanings, its formation and arrangement, its language, its words, sentences and diction are all revealed by Allâh. It is incorrect to say that the essence of the Qur'ân was revealed to the Holy Prophet and since the Holy Prophet's mother tongue was Arabic, he converted the essence of the Holy Qur'ân in appropriate Arabic words and syntax. Whatsoever is contained in this Book, may it be news or history of the past or the good tiding and prophecies of the coming events, or they be varieties of intellect and faith in the Arabic dialect, all of it is from Allâh. If an iota of it be a human interpretation, it cannot be called the word of Allâh.

When we call the Holy Qur'ân the word of God, its significance is much greater, higher and clearer than that which the Christians conceive when they call the Gospels of Matthew, Mark, Luke, and John as words of God. Christians acknowledge that their words are the words of these men but they believe that the inherent meanings of them were conveyed by God to the authors of these books. They provided words for those meanings. It was the Holy Ghost who supposedly aided the writers of the Gospels in their composition. God did not reveal the words or the style of composition. So the words of the New Testament cannot be called as words revealed by God. On the other hand, the Holy Qur'ân is the literal word of Allâh from the beginning to the end. There is no human effort involved in it, by way of thought, endurance, words or action.

It has no human touch in it, directly or indirectly, or human good will, nor is it the outburst of a man's unconscious stream of thought, natural or unnatural. It is not the outcome of his dreams, suppressed thoughts or emotions, or the inspiration of a poet or the frenzied utterances or violent mental agitation of those who are possessed. It is not a book written by Muhammad (peace be upon him), nor is it the outcome of an individual or collective effort of someone. Its source does not lie in the Zind, Awista, Vedas, Torah or the Gospels. In the words of Carlyle, "It is the word of the Almighty, its source is the same, whose depth no one has been able to plumb." In connection with the revelation of the Holy Qur'ân the Holy Prophet's position is only that of the receptacle. In it the Almighty produced its echo. The Prophet's job was simply to convey this revelation in total and in its complete form to the people and to put its teaching in practice in his own life.

It was not the Holy Prophet who was making use of the revelation; it was the revelation and the sender of the revelation that was making use of the Prophet (2:143; 53:3; 36:69; 69:41; 52:30). The Holy Prophet was unable to resist the great force of the Divine revelation. There were no personal views or wishes of the Prophet in it. His function was that of a receiver that catches the sound coming from outside and re-broadcasting it (17:47; 25:8; 25:4; 16:103). There are people who think the Creator is dumb, mute, and without power of speech, and that wahî and ilhâm (-His Revelations) have no real significance. There are others who believe that the door of speech of Allâh, His wahî and ilhâm was opened in the beginning of the world, and God spoke only to three or four saints or rishis in the beginning, and after that He did not ever speak with anyone and His power of communication was gone.

The Holy Qur'ân is for them a living proof, and if they still reject to give up their false notions, the Holy Qur'ân challenges them to produce a book like this, or come forward with a single chapter, or even a single verse like that to be found in it. Like such peoples, Jews are also in error for thinking that God spoke only to the children of Israel and that the rest of the world is devoid of this Divine blessing. It is the Holy Qur'ân that proclaims that Divine revelation is not limited to any particular time, nation or country. On the contrary, every nation and epoch has been the recipient of this Divine boon. His power of speech has not come to an end and Allah's communication with human beings is not a thing of the past. According to Islam, ilhâm and wahî is a universal phenomenon. Every human being is endowed by nature to with the capacity to benefit from it.

We find that every nation, country and every epoch has received its share of Allah's Messages and holy men appointed by Allâh for the people's guidance. There is not a single nation in the world, which has been left without a Messenger (13: 7; 35:24). Similarly, ilhâm and wahî, which are God's greatest gifts, are not the exclusive privilege of men, it is granted equally to women just as it is granted to the prophets of God and other saints (28:7; 66:11-13). Is it not disgraceful to affirm that Allâh speaks to human beings and that no relationship can subsist between a mortal and the Eternal and Ever-Existing Allâh? This is a baseless objection. It is enough to understand that among the natural condition of human beings is the search for a Higher Being for Whom there is an attraction in the heart of every human being and that the Noble, Gracious, and Ever Merciful Allâh has inspired the hearts of human beings with untold eagerness for His own understanding and has drawn them so powerfully to His love, affection and devotion that they have been lost to their own selves.

To propose that in such a condition Allâh would not desire to converse with them would be tantamount to saying that all their love and devotion was in vain and that all their eagerness was only one-sided. Human beings plunging into the limitless ocean of Allah's love and stopping nowhere in that pursuit by perfect human beings is conclusive evidence that human beings' souls have been fashioned for the understanding of Allâh and that true knowledge of Allâh depends upon His speech. So long as Allâh does not affirm His existence by His words, as indeed He has done, the mere observation of His handiworks does not afford satisfaction. The Holy Prophet said: "There is knowledge that has the guise of the hidden (- Maknûn): none knows it but those who have the knowledge of God. When they speak of it, none denies it but those who are deluded about God."

Human beings may live anywhere in the world but their fundamental nature will be the same everywhere. Neither territories of the east nor those of the west can make any basic change in this nature. Neither the colour of skin, nor the variety of language can produce any effect. Nor can the difference of race or tribe in any manner interfere with the uniformity of this nature and human beings came with an immaculate nature. Rather the human being by nature is inclined to love piety and virtue and hates evil and wickedness. He came with wonderful potentialities and with capacities to make unlimited progress, and Allâh has created him in the best make and the best proportions with enormous capabilities for all round advancement through the process of evolution (95:4), and it is in consideration of these capabilities of human beings that Allâh rendered to him His such attributes and has drawn him so powerfully to His love, affection and devotion.

Human beings plunging into the limitless ocean of Allah's love and stopping nowhere in that pursuit by those who guard against evil is conclusive evidence that human beings' souls have been fashioned for the understanding of

Allah's true knowledge which depends upon His speech. Indeed, Allâh is the Being Who has ever called mankind to Himself by announcing:

"I am present, I am nearby indeed. I answer the prayer of the supplicant when he prays to Me, so they should respond to My call, and believe in Me that I possess all these attributes and that they may proceed in the right way" (2:186).

It would be impertinent to think that human beings have laid Allâh under an obligation through his understanding of Him and that if there had been no philosophers and scientists He would have remained unknown. It is also not at all correct to think that all Allah's speaking has been left behind and that there is nothing in the present or in the future. We cannot seal up His words and His speech in any age. The Holy Qur'ân is a living proof of this, and brings about spiritual awakening, and living consciousness, that he whose soul seeks the truth should arise and search for it as the means of obtaining real knowledge through which one can see Allâh and seek the mirror through which one can behold that High Being during the converse with Him.

The door of Allah's blessing of converse is always open. It is open in this age as it was open in the past, in the age of Adam, Indian rishis, Noah, Abraham, Ismail, Isaac, Jacob, Moses, his mother, Aaron, Jesus, his mother Mary and His disciples and Muhammad, and his Companions and Reformers (Mujaddidîn) and so many other men and women of the Ummah. This is Allâh through Whose verbal and factual manifestation a person acquires a living faith and a true relationship is established with Allâh, which removes all personal dirt. Inner darkness is dispelled by the fierce rays of heavenly light and a wonderful change is manifested. The knowledge through Kalâm arises from a disengaged intellect the preparedness of the soul seeks through the attention of the All-Merciful who ignites in His servant the Light of Knowledge (Nur al-Ilm).

The "Throne" of Allâh

The Throne (al-'Arsh) of the All-Merciful (al-Rahmân) is a figure of speech. It is not a material object nor does it signify neither any place nor it is physically created. It is not a thing on which Allâh is imagined as being seated but is a symbol of His power and rule which indicates His might, ability to control, authority, dominion and mastery. In order to express Allâh's state of Holy Supremacy, that is, when His attribute of Holiness covers up His all other attributes, placing Him far beyond every reach, totally hidden, the state is called 'Arsh in the language of the Holy Qur'ân.

The Most Gracious (al-Rahmân) is firmly and flawlessly established on (His) Throne (of Power). (20:5)

When this figurative is used, it means to convey to us that Allâh is far above the understanding of human intelligence which has not the strength to find Him or to comprehend His eternity, His limitlessness, His Holiness. It is this high Divine rank when He says that He is the Most Gracious (al-Rahmân) Who is firmly and flawlessly established on His Throne of Power (20:5) and:

(He is the Lord) of the Throne (of Power), (Lord of) all Glory. (85:15)

Some people adopt God's attribute of transcendence and call Him Nargan or they accept Him as Sargan - having attributes of resemblance. For the declaration of His attributes of resemblance the Holy Qur'ân mentions His seeing eyes, His hearing ears and then to remove the suspicion of resemblance it states that there is nothing like unto Him. For the declaration of attributes of transcendence the Holy Qur'ân mentions His Oneness (Tauhîd) and His Throne (al-'Arsh). He is beyond all comparison, and He is the All-Hearing, the All-Seeing (42:11). Ponder over the verse to understand what Allâh wants us to understand:

It is not so as they think that We do not hear their talks and their private consultation. Indeed, We do (hear)! Not only that, but Our envoys (the "Angels" who remain) by their side are noting down (everything what they say). Say, 'The Most Gracious (al-Rahmân) has no son and I am the foremost to bear witness to this fact. Holy is He, the Lord of the heavens and the earth, and the Lord of the Throne of Power, far above and free from that what they ascribe (to Him).' (43:80-82)

If we insist only on His Attributes of resemblance, we restrict Him. If we insist only on His Attributes of immanence, we limit Him. If we accept both aspects, we are right (43:80-82). We see Him in essences of things both boundless and limited. Allah's countenance is the mirror of both these attributes. His having established Himself firmly and flawlessly signifies the most complete and perfect reflection of these attributes. Each post of the throne extends down to an "angel" who upholds it and executes its affairs and becomes the means of projecting its manifestation. The four graces Rubûbîyyat, Rahmâniyyat, Rahîmiyyat and Mâlikîyyat - are upholding His throne here in the present world. They are in full operation in this life. In the Hereafter, however, these four attributes shall appear again in full display.

Then the operation of each of these attributes will be displayed doubly and thus appear as eight. It is this phenomenon that has been described in the Divine world as, "the eight (divine powers) will on that Day be above them bearing the Throne of Power of your Lord." (69:17). Thus al'-Arsh is the attribute of transcendence of Allâh.

The Attributes of Allâh

"To Allâh alone belong all the fairest and most perfect Names (- Asmâ al Husnâ), so call on Him by those, and leave alone those who deviate from the right way with respect to His attributes and violate their sanctity" (7:180).

The Name Allâh embraces all His beautiful names

(Asmâ al Husnâ). His other Names are His Attributes, which He ascribes to Himself in His Holy Book. Some of the names He ascribes to Him are the All-Knower (al-Alîm), the Hearer (al-Samî), the Well-Aware (al-Khabîr) and the Crator (al-Khâliq). These are the names that make known a description of Him and the names that make known His acts. There are other names such as He is the One (al-Ahad), He is the Self-Sufficient Being (al-Samad), and nothing is His likeness and He stands High above similarity - these are the attributes of incomparability which denote the Essence of God. And then He possess the attributes of transcendence like He is the Light of the Heavens and the earth.

The Supreme Sovereign.

The Holy One.

The Source of Peace; The Most Perfect.

The Preserver of Security; Guardian of Faith.

The Protector; The Guardian.

The All-Mighty, The Glorious, The Illustrious.

Overpowering; The Compensator of losses.

The Majestic; The Possessor of all greatness.

The Creator of the matter and the Soul.

The Maker; Evolver.

The Fashioner; The Bestower of forms.

The Forgiver; The Great Protector.

The Dominant; The Subduer of all.

The Bestower.

The Provider.

The Decider; The Opener.

The All Knowing.

The Constrictor; The Withholder.

The Expander, The Plentiful Giver.

The Abaser.

The Exalter.
The Honorer, He Who increases another's honour.
The Humiliator.
The All-Hearing.
The All Seeing.
The Judge.
The Just.
The Subtle.
The Aware.
The Clement, He Who shows forbearance.
The Magnificent.
The Forgiving.
The Appreciative, The Rewarder.
The Most High, The Most Sublime.
The Great.
The Preserver.
The Sustainer.
The Reckoner; The Giver of what suffices.
The Sublime; The Majestic.
The Generous.
The Watchful.
The Responsive.
The All-Embracing.
The All-Wise.
The Loving, Lovely; All Love.
The Glorious; The Lord of Honour.
The Resurrection.
The Witness.
The Truth; The Real.
The Trustee, The Dispenser of Affairs.
The Strong.
The Firm.

The Patron.

The Praiseworthy.

The Reckoner.

The Originator.

The Restorer to Life.

The Giver of Life.

The Creator of Death.

The Living.

The Eternal; The Self-Subsisting.

The Finder.

The Grand; The Noble.

The One; The Unique.

The Single.

The Supreme Being Who is the Independent and Besought of all and Unique in all His attributes.

The All-Appraiser; The All-Powerful.

The Prevailing; The Most Powerful.

The Expediter; The Advancer.

The Grantor of Respite.

The Very First; There was nothing before Him.

The Last; There will be nothing after Him.

The Manifest; The Supreme Being, subordinate to no one; He Who reveals the properties of things.

The Hidden; The Incomprehensible; He Who knows the hidden properties of all things.

The Protecting Friend, Comrade.

The Sublime, The Most Exalted.

The Source of All Goodness.

The Accepter of Repentance.

The Lord of Retribution.

The Pardoner.

The Compassionate, The Kindly.

The Owner of Sovereignty; Master of Kingdom.
The Lord of Majesty and Splendour.
The Equitable.
The Gatherer.
The Self-Sufficient, The Independent.
The Enricher.
The Preventer; One Who Withholds.
The Distresser.
The Benefactor; The Propitious.
The Light; He Who enlightens others.
The Guide.
The Incomparable; The First Cause.
The Ever Abiding; The Preserver.
The Everlasting.
The Director, The Guide to the Right Path.
The Constant and Steadfast and One Who overlook one's rudeness. Slow to impose punishment.

God has described Himself as being the Manifest (al-Zâhir) and also the Un-manifest (al-Bâtin).

This is because He brought the cosmos into being as unseen and as sensory realm, so that we may perceive the Un-manifest through our unseen and the manifest through our sensory aspect. He has also attributed Himself pleasure and displeasure which express in our selves both as fear and hope. Fear from His displeasure and hope for His pleasure. He has also described Himself as being possessed of beauty (Jamîl) and majesty (Wajha), having created us combining awe of His Majesty and Intimacy of beauty. He calls himself to be the First (al-Awwal) as the One without beginning contradicting any priority in the sense of existence and non-existence, and He, being infinite, calls Himself the Last.

"The Beloved is so sweet, so sweet" they repeat;

I show then the scars where His Stick thrashed me

"The Beloved is terrible, so terrible, a maniac" they complain

I show them my eyes, melting in His tender passion (Rumi)

The knowledge of Him is inferred in knowledge of ourselves. Whenever we ascribe any quality to Him, we are ourselves representative of this quality. Since we know Him through ourselves from ourselves, we attribute to Him all we attribute to ourselves. An exception to this is His Attributes such as of Being Self-Sufficient, His being the First and His being the Last. Absolute and sure knowledge (Ilm al Yaqîn) of Him cannot be arrived at by the intellect, by any rational thought process. This kind of knowledge comes only by Divine Disclosures. His direct Revelation are aid to get to this knowledge. As we are individuals with varying aptitudes and capacities, not all of us qualify to receive His direct Revelations. Therefore such Disclosures reach us through the mouths of His prophets. Through them He describes Himself to us. He has described Himself as Hidden, being behind the veils. So He speaks to us from behind a veil. Therefore the cosmos cannot perceive Him as He perceives Himself, nor He can ever be unveiled.

The subject needs a voluminous literature and the space at our disposal hardly permits us to enter into any details. So we have given here some Names and attributes according to a tradition of the Holy Prophet on the authority of Abû Hurairah. A Muslim sums up his whole religion when he says La ilâha ill Allaha, this is no other cannot be and will never be one deity worthy of worship but Allâh. It should not be forgotten that Allâh's Names do not at all comprehend and complete the list of Allah's attributes. No one can comprehend them in their entirety. He is the only knower of His own person. The utmost that can be said on this point is that at one occasion the Holy Prophet mentioned these as ways by which Allâh manifested Himself to humanity.

This does not mean that the human mind has clothed Allâh with these attributes only. Here, Allâh has been described to be a Being in whom all that is noble, lovely and good is focused. The human beings have been created to take and adopt His attributes. Different writers had mentioned these attributes under different headings from different angles of view. They classified them with regard to their bearing on human affairs in their material, economic, moral and spiritual aspects but the order adopted by the Holy Qur'ân is a highly scientific. A companion of the Holy Prophet, Abull Yaman narrated, he said Shu'aib told us that Abû al-Zinad told us that Aaraj said on the authority of Abû Hurairah that the Messenger of Allâh said: "Allâh has ninety-nine names, one hundred less one. He who has memorized them all and learns, understands, enumerates, becomes conscious of them and succeeds in implanting, making them part and parcel of himself and knows it by heart, and believes in those qualities derived from those names and should be accompanied by good deed, which Allah's names inspire us to do and behave in accordance with their implications will enter Paradise."

This saying of the Holy Prophet does not mean that Allâh has only 99 attributes. There are further names attributable to Allâh even in the Holy Qur'ân as Rabb and infinite others which He has revealed to His choice creations and so many others which may be read in the pages of nature. Some religious scholars have related that Allâh has 3,000 names. There are so many names of the Divine Being that are taken from some attributes or acts ascribed to Him in the Holy Qur'ân. As for instance Al-Rafi', Al-Bâsit, Al-Mûjib, Al-Muhyî, Al-Wâjid, Al-Muqaddim, and Al-Mua'khkhir. The attribute Kalâm (Speaking) of the Divine Being is mentioned frequently in the Holy Qur'ân. Allâh spoke to (Kallama) Moses (9:164, 7:143). He spoke to other Prophets (42:51). This leaves no doubt that speaking is an attribute of Allâh, as the Holy Qur'ân definitely and decidedly states again and again that Allâh has been speaking to His servants.

In fact all the heavenly bodies and earthly elements, indeed every particle in the lower bodies and earthly elements, visible or invisible, indeed every particle in the upper spheres, what is visible and perceptible, all of them are, by virtue of the various properties that are found in them, attributes of Allâh. Each object manifests some attribute of Allâh, His love, His magnificence, His many names emulate through these objects. It is the power of God that manifests itself through them. There is no end to these manifestations so long as the process of creation exists and continues, the entire creation manifests Allah's names. There is a link that cannot be avoided and evaded and is bound to come between what we see, feel, and ourselves. It sheds a flood of light on the attributes of Allâh. It is because of the fact that it is said he who succeeds in knowing, perceiving, learning, recognizing, judging, and becoming aware of his own self, spirit, desires, his attractions and repulsion, his freedom and obedience, his joy or anger, and there is no end to them, will recognize his Lord, as a human being is the vicegerent of Allâh and His attributes are implanted in his self, and which are going to be manifested in all his life in this world and the Hereafter (2:30-31).

That is why a human being could represent Allâh as His khalîfah (2:30) and become worthy of receiving the homage, obeisance, and salutation of the angels and granted him the mastery of this entire creation (2:34).

> The talents of God are within us.
>
> How could this be otherwise
>
> when our soul was
>
> derived from his Breath (Hafiz?)

The proper names of Allâh and His attributes are innumerable. They index the work of nature when a person falls at His threshold with a new spirit and devotion and carries out a change in him, only to win His pleasure. Allâh also makes, so to say, a change for such a one, so that Allâh

Who appears to him is quite a different God from the One known to the average person. As He says, "Every moment He manifests Himself in a new state of glory and wondrous way" (55:29) and His attributes know no limit. The effects of Allah's attributes are called sunnat Allâh or the way of Allâh or the laws of nature:

You will find no change in the law of Allâh, nor will you ever find the law of Allâh shifting from its course (35:43).

Because Allâh along with His perfect attributes is Unlimited and Endless, it would be folly on our part to claim that the effects of those attributes, that is to say, the laws of nature, do not extend beyond our limited experience or intelligence or observation. It is a great mistake that we first regard the law of nature as something which has been completely defined and then we refuse to accept anything new which we encounter. This attitude is not well founded. If all scientists and philosophers were to employ their intellectual capacities till the day of Resurrection in discovering the qualities of a mustard seed, no one would believe that they would comprehend completely Allah's qualities. Thus there is nothing more absurd than to think that the qualities of heavenly and earthly bodies are limited to those which have so far been discovered through our astronomy, physics, and other sciences.

In short, the law of nature means such Divine actions and attributes which were manifested or might be manifested in a natural way, and Allâh is not tired of manifesting His powers, nor has He become disabled from doing so, nor has He gone to sleep, nor has He moved away into a corner, nor has He been overpowered and has under compulsion ceased manifesting His wonders, leaving us only His actions during a few centuries reason, wisdom, philosophy, science, literature and education. We should not confine the body of natural law to the few demonstrated powers of which innumerable details are still to be discovered and we should not insist that the actions of Allâh and His attributes cannot go beyond what we have already observed. How can these things be the final and absolute measures of truth or be the scale for judging the truth which are still awaiting a further explanation of themselves. Certain heavenly and earthly qualities are manifested after millions of years, which appear supernatural, and which are looked upon with doubt and are considered false. This is the basis of the miracles of the Prophets and can solve the problems of those who find difficulties in crisis and signs of Allâh. The Holy Qur'ân has not presented a new and unfamiliar Allâh, but has presented the same God Who is presented by the light of a human being's heart, his conscious and in the heaven and the earth.

It should be repeated that the sacred list of the Most Beautiful Names is in no sense exhaustive. The Holy Qur'ân and the Holy Prophet do not claim to furnish an exhaustive list of them. No one can comprehend in their entirety. He is the only Knower of His own person. He possesses many other attributes that stand far beyond number and imagination and can come within our comprehension.

"If every ocean become ink for (recording) the words and creation of my Lord, surely the oceans would be spent up before the words and creation of my Lord came to an end, even if we brought to add (therewith) as many more (oceans)." (18:109)

These 99 names are such as can be read in the pages of nature and we can perceive them and can come within the scope of our coping and with them we must imbue ourselves. They show us how to inspire ourselves with all that they require. They remind us of those Divine moulds in which we have to cast our daily life, as high morality in Islam consists in the reflection and doing deeds in conformity of these attributes and to a certain extent imitates them. In this sense we have been spoken of as prototypes of Allâh and we have been asked to assume His colours and imbue ourselves with the Divine character (7:180).

In short, it would be wrong to think that ninety-nine are the only names Allâh has. This inadequate expression of His beauty, greatness, majesty, and beneficence and is all that is possible for us earthbound creatures of limited capacity and knowledge and come within our comprehension and the scope of our imitation and which the Holy Prophet told Abû Hurairah at one sitting. Otherwise His wonderful and glorious attributes are numberless and surpass all description and understanding.

Understanding and reasoning
And imagining besides,
May do their utmost,
But beyond, ever beyond,
Remains the core, the essence
of His Being.

To be virtuous is to walk humbly with Allâh, to imbue ourselves with His attributes. Everything that goes against the demands of these attributes is sin; they sum up the whole of Qur'ân injunction. The traces and signs of His attributes in human beings and upon His other creations are at least a reflection, a symbol, a word, a means, a path to understand and reach Him. Of each attribute less than an atom is given to us; it is in order that we know His perfect attributes which He has given us in traces, in signs in and around us. It is so that we know Him and find Him and love Him and be with Him and act as His vicegerent.

And to Allâh alone belong all the fairest and most perfect attributes, so call on Him by these, and leave alone those who deviate from the right way with respect to His attributes (and violate their sanctity) (7:180)

Oneness of Allâh

And know, your God is One God, there is no other, cannot be and will never be one worthy of worship but He, the Most Gracious (- Rahmân), the Ever Merciful (-Rahîm). (2:163)

The cornerstone of all the basic attributes of Allâh is His Tauhîd or Unity. La ilâha ill-Allah - there is no other, cannot be and will never be one worthy of worship but He. It is this confession which when combined with the confession of the prophethood of the Holy Prophet of Islam admits a man or woman into the fold of Islam. The Unity of Allâh implies that Allâh is One in His Person, One in His attributes and One in His works. His Oneness in His Person means that there is neither plurality of gods nor plurality of persons in this Godhead. His Oneness in attributes implies that no other being possesses one or more of the Divine attributes in perfection. His Oneness in works implies that none can do that which Allâh has done and which He may do and no other being has influence over Him. This doctrine of Unity is very beautifully summed up in one of the shortest and earliest chapters of the Holy Qur'ân:

Say, "(The fact is) He is Allâh, the One and Alone in His Being. Allâh is that Supreme Being Who is the Independent and Besought of all and Unique in all His attributes. He begets none and is begotten by no one, and there is none His equal." (112:1-4)

The above sûrah of the Holy Qur'ân is called al-Ikhlâs (- The Purification of the Unity of Allâh). Another name of this sûrah is al-Asas (- the Foundation), this is because the whole foundation of the Faith of Islam lies in the Unity of Godhead. The highest object of any revealed Book should be to furnish us with the correct and sure knowledge of God. This small sûrah fulfils this very purpose. The verses in their four short sentences point out the fundamental errors of many religions and reject outright all forms of polytheism, including the doctrine of trinity, sonship and partnership. The verses of this sûrah illuminate the heart of a human being with the true knowledge of Allâh and His glory and tell him that defective qualities should not be attributed to Him. They tell him that He is Ahad, the One, the Sole, Who has been and will ever be One and Alone, Who has no second to share in His Lordship nor in His Essence or Love, the idea of a second being inconceivable. He is also Samad, that Being Who is One and Alone in the sense that when we think of Him, the very idea that there is any other being or thing is absent from our minds. He is One and Alone in every sense.

He is neither the starting link of any chain not its last link. Nothing is like Him (42:16), nor is He like anything else. Soul and matter are not co-eternal with Him but are His creation.To Him alone obedience is rendered, without Whom no affair is accomplished. He will continue to exist forever, after all creation has ceased to exist, He is above time, for time is also His creation (103:1). He is above conception and conjecture.

His attributes know no bound or limit. He requires the assistance of nobody without Whom He cannot carry on His work. Everything existing or conceivable goes back to Him as its source. Any attempt at depicting Allâh by means of figurative representation or by abstract symbols is wrong. It is also incorrect to describe Him as father or an incarnate according to which a man is likened to Him. Thus every kind of shirk is rejected. This is Allâh as presented by the Holy Qur'ân.

The true Unity of Allâh is to believe in God Who, in His Being, is free from every associate, whether it is an idol or a human being or the sun or moon or river or fire or tree or another human being or one's ego or one's desires or deceit, and to conceive of no one as possessing power in opposition to Him, nor to accept anyone as sustainer, nor to hold anyone as bestowing honour or disgrace, nor to consider anyone as helper, and to confine one's love and one's worship and one's humility and one's hopes and one's awe to anyone other than Him. No Unity can be complete without the following three types of particularization. First, there is the Unity of Being. Secondly, the Unity of attributes, that is to say, that all good attributes and Godhead are confined to His Being, and that all others who offer or sustain or benefactor are only a part of the system set up by His hand. Thirdly, the unity of love, sincerity, devotion, worship and not to consider anyone as an associate of God in the matter of love and worship and prayer. This drive is embedded in human nature.

He it is Who is (the Only) God in all the heavens and (the only) God in the whole of the earth and He alone is the All-Wise, the All-Knowing. And blessed be He to Whom belongs the sovereignty of the heavens and the earth and all that lies between them and He alone has the knowledge of the promised Hour and to Him you shall all be made to return. And all those whom they call upon, apart from Him, have no authority to intercede (with their Lord), but (this right is given to him) who bears witness to the truth and they know him (the Prophet) and his good conduct well. If you were to ask them, 'Who created them.' They will no doubt say, 'Allâh.' Then whither are they being led astray? (43:84-87)

Unity of the Human Race

Never has there been an obstacle to human advancement so great as the idea of the inequality of mankind. So the greatest task to be performed in the socio-religious life of human race is to establish the Unity of God and through this to bring about unity of human race. The Holy Qur'ân announced, "Mankind are a single community" (2:213; 10:19) therefore we should always keep this fact before us as Allâh is the Rabb, the Creator and the Nourisher to perfection of all nations (1:2) and all the nations of the world are, as it were, the children of the same God, and He takes equal care of all, deals with all alike and bring all to their goal of moral and spiritual completion by degrees. His people benefit from His earth, irrespective of their origin, colour or belief, His moon and sun shine for all. His dealings in the spiritual matters are also marked with the same equality. He hearkens to the supplication of everybody, whatever their religion, language, or nationality. He is equally Gracious and Merciful and forgives the sins whenever He likes because He is the Master and King of all nations. He rewards the good deeds of the believers and nonbelievers (2:62) male and female alike. He says:

O mankind! We have created you out of a male and a female, and We have made you tribes and sub-tribes that you may recognize (and do good to) one another. Surely the most honourable of you in the sight of Allâh is he who guards against evil the most. Verily, Allâh is All-Knowing, All-Aware. (49:13)

So the racial and tribal sense of superiority is of later growth, and it is because of this sense that one section of humanity is fond to look down upon another section. This was not the motive of making different tribes and sub-tribes. Islam expresses disapproval of this feeling and points out that all people belong to one brotherhood and also that it is improper to take pride in one's race or parenthood, as it directs one's course to promote arrogance and to undermine the basic and fundamental unity of the human race.

O you who believe! Let no people look down upon another people for the (latter) people may be better than they, nor let women (look down) upon other women, who (- the women who are treated lightly) may be better than the other ones. And find not fault in one another (in order to defame your own people), nor call one another by nicknames. Bad is the reputation of wickedness after the (profession of) belief. (49:11)

Of course, a person should be honoured but only on the basis of righteousness and honest living. Similarly a nation who guards against evil the most and is actively engaged in rendering services to the fellow nations and to the creatures of Allâh becomes honourable in the eyes of

Allâh and in the eyes of the rest of other nations. Thus, if the Holy Qur'ân has described Allâh as the Lord of all the nations, it has also presented its laws as of universal application. According to the Qur'ânic teachings it is immaterial to what race a person belongs and of what nation he is a member, so long as he guards against evil and is a doer of good deeds he will be favoured by Allâh. The Holy Prophet of Islam has elucidated this principle when he said, "Verily the people who are nearest to me are those who guard against evil, no matter of whatever race they are and to whatever country they belong." This is a message that deserves to be called a Gospel for humanity.

The unity of the human race is a natural corollary of the doctrine of the Unity of God. Only the belief in One Lord of the world can bring solace and comfort and cheer up the hearts of all men and women and can prepare a person for a correct form of godliness and for service to the creatures of God. Surely a person who is mindful of Allâh is also mindful of his sympathy for his fellow beings. All the languages and the art of intelligent speech are equally the creation of Allâh through His grace of Rahmânîyyat. The Holy Qur'ân says, "He (- the Rahmân) created the human being and taught him intelligence and the art of distinct speech." (55:3-4). There are thousands of diversities in this universe and yet there is a unity in the midst of these diversities, and that is because the source of all these diversities lies in One All-Powerful Unity. Allâh, the Lord of the worlds and the nations, has created human beings with different complexions and has created different languages for the expression of their respective feelings, yet in spite of all these differences humanity at the bottom is one and the same.

"The creation of heaven and earth, and in the diversity of your tongues and colours are (also some) of His signs. Behold! There are sure signs for the learned people in this (unity of mankind and Oneness of God). " (30:22).

Unity of Religion

He has ordained for you the same course of faith as He enjoined on Noah (to adopt), and which We have revealed to you, and it is that (same faith) which We enjoined on Abraham, Moses, Jesus, so keep the faith and do not differ in it. (He ordains you) to establish obedience (to Allâh) and not to be divided (in sects) therein. (42:13)

The Unity of God should lead to the unity of religion. The recognition of Allâh is tied up with the recognition of all His Prophets. A Prophet is a mirror for beholding of Allâh. It is only through this mirror that the countenance of Allâh may be seen. It is a part of the Unity of Allâh to believe in those who have been appointed as a means of the recognition of Him. Without this belief, faith in the Unity of Allâh cannot be perfected. The Prophets do not precede Him in speech and they only carry out His bidding. Accordingly Judaism, Christianity, Hinduism, Buddhism are but different aspects of one and the same religion, which, in its original purity, is the religion of Islam (-submission to the will of God and to make peace with God and mankind). Noah, Abraham, Moses, Jesus, Krishna, Rama, Buddha or Confucius, all were Prophets of God and were sent for the guidance of their respective people. The Qur'ân repeatedly claims to be in conformation with the truth of all faiths as the Qur'ân defines the true believers:

And who (also) believe in that (Message) which has been revealed to you and in that which had been revealed before you (2:4)

The Qur'ân, therefore, not only recognizes the truth of all the previous Divine Books and Prophets, but also makes it obligatory for Muslims to believe in the Divine origin of their teachings. The Qur'ân requires not only a belief in Divine revelation to the Prophet of Islam, but also belief in Divine revelation to all the Prophets sent to all nations of the world in all times (3:84). This is one of the matters relating to faith (Îmân) and a fundamental principle of Islam. This is also a broad doctrine of the Unity of God which is taught repeatedly in the Qur'ân (3:184; 13:4). In short, Islam is the religion of the Unity of God and the unity and equality of mankind. Lineage, riches and family honours are accidental things; virtue and service of humanity are matters of real merit. Distinction of colour, race and creed are unknown in the ranks of Islam. All mankind is of one family and only Islam can weld the black and the white, east and west, rich and poor, into one fraternal whole.

Association with Allâh

He lets none associate with Him and shares His judgement (18:26)

Let him who hopes to meet his Lord do deeds of righteousness and let him associate no one in the worship of his Lord (18:110)

The Holy Prophet reported these words directly from Allâh the Most High:

"My mysterious robes are Transcendence and Magnificence. Whoever contends with me for one of these will encounter the Fire." (Abu Hurayra)

Oneness of Lord is His Attribute of Transcendence. Therefore Shirk, the associating of anyone or anything with Allâh, whether such association be with respect to the person of Allâh or His attributes or His works or with respect to worship and obedience which are due to Him alone, is the gravest of all evils and sins.

Allâh does not forgive (unless the sinner repents) that a partner be associated with Him, but He forgives everything short of it to whomsoever He wishes. And whoso associates a partner with Allâh has indeed committed a great sin. (4:48)

Allâh does not forgive (unless the sinner repents) that a partner be associated with Him, but He forgives everything short of it to whomsoever He wishes and he who associates a partner with Allâh has strayed a far off straying (4:116)

Whatever they (who associate partners with Allâh) call beside Him are none but lifeless objects. They call none but Satan the rebellious, whom Allâh has deprived of His blessings

Indeed he who associates anything with Allâh falls from a high place, and either the birds snatch him or the wind blow him off to some deep far away place (22:31)

"Associate no partners with Allâh, surely this (act of) associating partners (with Him) is a grievous wrong." (31:13)

Do they associate (with Him as partners) those who create nothing but are themselves created.

And they (the associated gods) will have no power to give them (who associate partners with Allâh) any help, nor can they help themselves (but will themselves perish).And if you (O Polytheists!) invite these (associated gods) for (your) guidance, they will not respond to you. It makes no difference to you whether you call them or you remain silent.

Verily, those whom you call on beside Allâh are (merely helpless maids or) servants like yourselves. (If it is not so then) call on them, they should then make a response to you if you are right. Have these (false gods) feet with which they walk, or have they hands with which they hold, or have they eyes with which they see, or have they ears with which they hear? Say, 'Call upon your associate gods, then contrive you all against me and give me no respite, (yet you will see that I am triumphant because)

'Verily, My Protecting-Friend is Allâh who has revealed this perfect Book and He takes into (His) protection all the righteous. 'And those whom you call upon besides Him have no power to help you, nor can they help themselves.' (7:191-197)

This is not due to a feeling of jealousy on the part of Allâh, which is unthinkable as an attribute of the Divine being. The Islamic formula of Faith - Kalimah - is:

La ilâha ill Allah, Muhammad rasûlullah, i.e.

"There is no other, cannot be, and will never be One worthy of worship but Allâh and Muhammad is his Prophet."

The human being is Allah's vicegerent on earth (2:30), and he is gifted with the power of controlling the rest of the world and is made to rule the world (95:12) and is placed above the whole of creation. He is placed even above the angels and is the object of their obedience (2:34). Does he not degrade himself by taking others as his object of worship and bowing before the very things which he has been created to conquer and rule?

"Shall I seek for you a god other than Allâh? Whereas He has made you excel all created things" (7:140)

There are various forms of shirk or associating of gods with Allâh. This includes the worship of objects as stones, idols, trees, animals, tombs, heavenly bodies, forces of nature, or human beings supposed as gods or semi-gods or God incarnate in the form of human beings. It is also a form of shirk to suppose that other things and beings possess one or more of the attributes as the Divine Being to the same extent, for example to believe that there are three persons in the Godhead, and that the Son, the Holy Ghost are eternal, omnipotent and omniscient like Allâh Himself or that there is a creator of evil along with a creator of good, or that matter and soul are self-existing and co-eternal with Allâh. It is also a form of shirk to take the learned, the monks, the pîrs and khalîfas (self-made religious leaders) for lords besides Allâh.

They have taken their learned men and their monks for lords apart from Allâh, and (similarly they have taken) the Messiah, son of Mary, whilst they were enjoined to worship none but One God. There is no other, cannot be and will never be One worthy of worship but He. Too glorified is He for what they associate (with Him).They seek to put out the light of Allâh with (the breath of) their mouths, but Allâh disdains every other thing save that He will perfect His light; however much the disbelievers may consider (it) hard. (9:31)

It is also a form of shirk to blindly obey such people and pîrs and self-made khalîfahs in what they enjoin and what they forbid and behest, as a slaved mind is incapable of judging what is good and great and is incapable of doing anything good and great (16:75). Besides the forms of shirk mentioned above, there is another form of shirk which the Holy Qur'ân mentions in following verse:

Have you considered (over the plight of) one who has taken his own low desires for his deity? (25:43)

Going after one's low desires and their requirements is apt to become in the long run the object of adoration. We clothe our own low desires in a Divine garb and our profit or loss and fear and hope goad us to place them at the altar of Divinity. The kind of shirk mentioned in the above verse indicate that only the sublime doctrine of Unity gives to the world an ennobling message of progress all around, physical, moral, and spiritual. We are freed and released, not only from the bondage of animate and inanimate objects but also from subservience to the wondrous forces of nature and from the slavery of human beings, but also of our own low desires. A person becomes a blessing for himself, for his family and for his nation to the extent of his acquiring control over his low desires (91:9-10). Thus all the bonds are fettered and we are set on the road of evolution, betterment and development.

The verse 25:43 shows the breadth of the idea of polytheism or shirks. It is thus not simply worship of idols of devotion to material means that is condemned but blindly following one's desires likewise. Intellectually, human beings may have advanced far enough so as not to bow before stones, stars, trees, rivers, fire and forces of nature, but he has not outgrown his worship of false ideas, prejudices and low desires. It is these idols that lie enthroned in the depth of his heart whose worship is to be condemned. In the Holy Qur'ân doctrine of Tauhîd or the Unity of Divine Being has been brought to a perfection.

Or Who is it that created the heavens and the earth, and sends down water for you from the clouds? (It is We.) Then We cause to grow with it orchards full of bloom and loveliness. You had no power to cause their trees to grow. Is there any god with Allâh? (There is none ;) yet there are a people who ascribe (to Him) equals (in all these works, and deviate from the right path).

Or Who is it that made the earth a resting place; and made the rivers flow in it; and raised (on the earth) firm mountains for its advantage; and put a barrier between the two waters? Is there a god with Allâh (as an associate with Him in His works)? Nay, not so, yet most of them do not know (the truth).

Or Who is it that answers the distressed person when he calls on Him, and removes (his) distress? And Who is it that makes you (the) rulers in the land? Is there any other god with Allâh? Little is the heed you take!

Or Who is it that guides you (to the path of salvation) in all kinds of darkness (and vicissitudes) on the land and the sea; and Who is it that sends the winds as heralds of His mercy. Is there any god with Allâh (to do such things)? Highly-Exalted is Allâh above all the things they associate (with Him).

Or Who is it that originates the creation then keeps on repeating and reproducing it, and Who is it that provides for your sustenance (both physical and spiritual) from the heaven and the earth? Is there any other god with Allâh (capable of being a partner with Him in all these works)? Say, 'Bring forward your proof (in support of your polytheistic beliefs) if you are truthful (in what you claim).'

Allâh is Highly Exalted far above the things they associate with Him (7:190, 9:31, 27:63, 28:68, 10:18, 52:42, 59:24)

9

Transmission of the Classics to the West

The introduction of Greek philosophy and science into the culture of the Latin West in the middle Ages was an event that transformed the intellectual life of Western Europe. It consisted of the discovery of many original works, such as those written by Aristotle in the classical period, commentaries by Hellenistic philosophers written in late Antiquity, and commentaries from early Muslim philosophers in the Arab world, or Muslim world, written during the Islamic Golden Age from the ninth to twelfth centuries.

The Dark Ages

As knowledge of Greek declined with the fall of the Roman Empire, so did knowledge of the Greek texts, many of which remain untranslated. The Byzantines, for whom Greek was the dominant language, were either reluctant or unable to investigate the ideas of Plato and Aristotle while warring with Arabs, Turks, and Huns. Thus, for a long time in Europe after the execution of Boethius (one of the last to understand both Latin and Greek philosophy), there was a disregard for Greek ideas. Scribes destroyed old books, cutting the pages from the binding and burning them or rubbing out old, philosophical words in order to create religious books. After a while, only a few monasteries had Greek works, and even fewer of them copied these works (mainly the Irish).

Irish monks had been taught by Greek and Latin missionaries who probably had brought Greek texts with them. However, Irish preservation of these ideas, though valuable, did not introduce nearly as much Greek philosophy and science to the west as did the work of translators of Arabic from 1100 – 1300 CE. Arab logicians had inherited Greek ideas after their invasion of southern portions of the Byzantine Empire. Their translations and commentaries on these ideas worked their way through the Arab west into Spain and Sicily, which became important centers for this transmission of ideas. This work of translation, though largely unplanned and disorganized, constituted one of the greatest transmissions of ideas in history.

Two Periods of Translation

The transfer of Greek works from the Byzantines to the Latin West took place in two main stages. The first occurred in Babylon, when Greek works were translated into Arabic in the 8th and 9th century during Abbasid rule. The second is "the great age of translation" in the 12th and 13th centuries as Europeans conquered formerly Islamic territories in Spain and Sicily. Scholars came from all over Europe to benefit from Arab learning and culture. About the same period, after the Fourth Crusade, scholars such as William of Moerbeke gained access to the original Greek texts that had been preserved in the Byzantine Empire, and translated them directly into Latin.

First period: Greek - Arabic translations

Ummayyads

The first period of transmission during 8th and 9th centuries was preceded by a period of conquest, as Arabs took control of previously Hellenized areas such as Egypt and Syria in the 7th century. At this point they first began to encounter Greek ideas, though from the beginning, many Arabs were hostile to classical learning. Because of this hostility, the religious Caliphs could not support scientific translations. Translators had to seek out wealthy business patrons rather than religious ones. Until Abassid rule in the 8th century, however, there was little work in translation. Most knowledge of Greek during Umayyad rule was gained from those scholars of Greek who remained from the Hellenistic period, rather than through widespread translation and dissemination of texts. A few scholars argue that translation was more widespread than is thought during this period, but theirs remains the minority view.

Abassids

The main period of translation was during Abbasid rule. The Abbasids, who came from the Persian East, were at an advantage in this area when compared to the Umayyads because they had accepted many Greek ideas already. One of the kings of Persia in the 6th century, Noshinvan the Just, had freely invited pagan philosophers fleeing the Byzantines free refuge in his country, thus introducing many Greek ideas into his kingdom. Aided by this knowledge and juxtaposition of beliefs, the Abassids considered it valuable to look at Islam with Greek eyes, and to look at the Greeks with Islamic eyes. Abassid philosophers also pressed the idea that Islam had from the very beginning stressed the gathering of knowledge as important to the religion these new lines of thought allowed the work of amassing and translating Greek ideas to expand as it never before had.

Syrian Translations

The first stage of this process was the translation into Arabic of Greek philosophical and scientific works that had been preserved by Eastern Christians in Mesopatamia, Syria and Egypt. The translators were mostly Nestorian and Jacobite Christians, working in the two hundred years following the Abbasid period. The most important translator of this group was the Syriac-speaking Christian Hunayn Ibn Ishaq (809-873), known to the Latins as Joannitius. The texts were first translated into Syriac, then into Arabic. Despite this process, the translations were generally accurate, aiming for a literal reading rather than elegance. Almost all translators were Nestorian and Syrian Christians.

Greek-speaking Christian missionaries had spread their religion to Persia, Egypt, and Syria long before Arab rule. Thus, many in these areas had kept Aristotle's ideas alive in order to debate philosophy and increase the quality of their medical practices. They now found themselves in an Arabic-speaking world, and saw that they could be valuable as translators of Greek ideas. It was not until later that actual Muslims, rather than Christians, undertook translation on a large scale. The first text to be translated by Syriacs was probably the New Testament. This may have been an unfortunate choice, as many Muslims, eager to point out the evils of Greek philosophy or any philosophy not truly Arab, trumpeted the fact that Greek translators were "infidels."

Oddly enough, the fact that the Greeks themselves were pagan and polytheistic was less of a problem. Most translators didn't know enough of Greek mythology to see Aphrodite, Zeus, and Apollo as anything more than mysterious names. Also, Greek references to "the gods" were often simply translated as "Allah." Overall, religious confusion, Christian or otherwise, did not prevent Abassid rule from lessening anti-Greek sentiment to a point that even clergymen ("Caliphs") were permitted to support translation. In this early period, Hellenistic schools which had survived the Islamic conquest led the charge. Since Islam was born in a Hellenistic world, it was fortunate to have an affinity for the classics from the beginning, and many used Greek philosophies to give added vigor to their religion, beginning what has been called a "Renaissance of Islam."

Baghdad's House of Wisdom

The Abassids moved their capital from Arabia to Baghdad. Here, translation work exploded within the House of Wisdom, a university of sorts created in 830 under Caliph Abdallah-al-Mamun. Al-Mamun had sent emissaries to the Byzantines to gather Greek manuscripts for his new university, making it a center for Greek translation work in the Arab world. At first only practical works, such as those on medicine and technology were sought after, but eventually works on philosophy became popular. Most scholars agree that during this period rhetoric, poetry, histories, and dramas were not translated into Arabic, since they were viewed as serving political ends which were not to be sought after in Arab states. Instead, philosophical and scientific works were almost the entire focus of translation. This has been disputed by a minority of scholars, however, who argue that stories such as Arabian Nights carry clear parallels to Greek literature—evidence that many Arabs were familiar with Greek humanities more than is thought.

Arabic Commentary on Greek Works

Al-Kindi (Alkindus), a famous logician of Baghdad, is now frequently called the first Arab philosopher. His synthesis of Greek philosophy with Islamic beliefs met with much opposition, and at one point he was flogged by those opposed to his ideas. He argued that one could accept the Koran and other sacred texts, and work from that point to determine truth. Whenever he ran into an impasse, he would abandon the Greek ideas in favor of the Islamic faith. He is considered to be largely responsible for pulling the Arab world out of a mystic and theological way of thinking into a more rationalistic mode.

Previous to al-Kindi, for example, on the question of

how the immaterial God of the Koran could sit on a throne in the same book, one theologist had said, "The sitting is known, its modality is unknown. Belief in it is a necessity, and raising questions regarding it is a heresy." Few of al-Kindi's writings have survived, making it difficult to judge his work directly, but it is clear from what exists that he carefully worked to present his ideas in a way acceptable to other Muslims. After Al-Kindi, several philosophers argued more radical views, some of whom even rejected revelation, most notably the Persian logician, Al-Razi or "Rhazes." Considered one of the most original thinkers among the Persian philosophers, he challenged both Islamic and Greek ideas in a rationalist manner and also, where Al-Kindi had focused on Aristotle, Al-Rhazi focused on Plato, introducing his ideas as a contrast.

After Al-Kindi, Al-Farabi (Alpharabius) introduced Neo-Platonism through his knowledge of the Hellenistic culture of Alexandria. Unlike Al-Kindi or Al-Rhazi, Al-Farabi was hesitant to express his own feelings on issues of religion and philosophy, choosing rather to speak only through the words of the various philosophies he came across. Decades after Al-Farabi, Ibn Sina (Avicenna) compiled the ideas of many Mulim philosophers of the previous centuries and established a new school which is known as Avicennism. After this period, Greek philosophy went into a decline in the Islamic world. Theologians such as Al-Ghazali argued that many realms of logic only worked in theory, not in reality. His ideas would later influence Western European religious ideas.

In response to Al-Ghazali's The Incoherence of the Philosophers, the Andalusian philosopher Ibn Rushd (Averroes), the most famous commentator on Aristotle and founder of Averroism, wrote a refutation entitled The Incoherence of the Incoherence. By 1200, when philosophy was again revived in the Islamic world, Al-Kindi and Al-Farabi were no longer remembered, while Ibn Sina's compilation work still was. Ibn Sina, otherwise know as Avicenna, would later heavily influence European philosophical, theological and scientific thought, becoming known as "the most famous scientist of Islam" to many historians.

Reintroduction of Greek Ideas into Europe

While Greek ideas gradually permeated the Islamic world, Muslims conquests extended to the European continent. Sicily and Spain were conquered by the Arabs at around 700 CE, even reaching as far as southern France by about 730. With the aid of Greek and other ideas, Spain in particular quickly became the most heavily populated and thriving area in Europe. One of the rulers of Muslim Spain, Al-Hakam II, made an effort to gather books from all over the Arab world, creating a library which would later become a center for translation into Latin. As books were gathered, so were many Arab scholars who had studied Greek ideas in the east.

For example, Muhammud ibn 'Abdun and 'Abdu'l-Rahman ibn Ismail came to Spain and introduced many ideas about medicine as well as several of the works of Aristotle and Euclid. Ibn Bajjah (known as "Avempace") and Ibn Rushd (known as "Averroes") were among the other famous philosophers of Spain who furthered the expansion of Greek ideas in medicine and philosophy. Prior to Averroes, many Arab philosophers had confused Aristotle with Plotinus, a Hellenized Egyptian who founded Neoplatonism and had mixed Aristotle's ideas with Plato's. Averroes rediscovered the "true" Aristotle by translating key texts reintroducing him to Arab Spain. He also challenged Al-Ghazali's largely anti-Greek philosophies and offered some of the best reconciliation of Islam and philosophy of the time.

Key to his arguments was the idea that although there was only one truth, that truth could be expressed in many ways, including both philosophy and religion. He even used the Qur'an to back up his arguments in favor of Greek philosophy and logic, especially the passage: "It is [Muhammad] who has revealed the Book to you...some of its verses are unambiguous...and the others are ambiguous...only God and those confirmed in knowledge know its interpretation." Averroes argued that "those confirmed in knowledge" were philosophers. The Scholastic philosophers and theologians of the middle ages such as Aquinas later called Averroes "The Commentator," and Michael the Scot translated several of Averroes' works within fifty years of the Arab's death. However, Averroes' reception in Western Europe contrasted with his ultimate rejection by Arabs in Spain. Soon after Averroes, Greek ideas in the Arab world were largely opposed by those who disliked anything not "truly Arab."

Arabic – Latin or Vernacular

While Arabs were busy translating and adding their own ideas to Greek philosophies, the Latin West was still suspicious of pagan ideas. Leaders of the Orthodox Church in the Byzantine Empire also frowned upon philosophy, and the Empire had just gone through a period of plague, famine, and war. Further west, several key figures in European history who came after Boethius had strengthened the overwhelming shift away from Greek ideas. St. Jerome, for example, was hostile to Aristotle, and St. Augustine had little interest in exploring philosophy, only applying logic to theology. For centuries, Greek ideas in Europe were all but non-existent. Only a few monasteries had Greek works, and even fewer of them copied these works.

There was a brief period of revival, when the Irish-influenced monk Alcuin reintroduced some Greek ideas during the Carolingian Renaissance. After Charlemagne's death, however, intellectual life again fell into decline. Excepting a few persons promoting Boethius, such as Gerbert of Aurillac, philosophical thought was relatively quiet in

Europe for about two centuries. By the 12th century, however, scholastic thought was beginning to develop, leading to the rise of universities throughout Europe. These universities gathered what little Greek thought had been preserved over the centuries, including Boethius' commentaries on Aristotle. They also served as places of discussion for new ideas coming from new translations from Arabic throughout Europe.

By the 12th century, European fear of Islam as a military threat had lessened somewhat. Toledo, in Spain, had fallen from Arab hands in 1085, Sicily in 1091, and Jerusalem in 1099. These linguistic borderlands proved fertile ground for translators. These areas had been conquered by both Arab and Latin-speaking peoples over the centuries and contained linguistic abilities from both cultures. Surprisingly, the crusaders contributed very little to the translation efforts. Sicily was in a better state for it, since it had seen rule under Byzantines, Arabs, and Italians, and many were fluent in Greek, Arabic, and Latin. Sicilians, however, were less influenced by Arabs and instead are noted more for their translations directly from Greek to Latin. Spain, on the other hand, was an ideal place for translation from Arabic to Latin because of a combination of rich Latin and Arab cultures living side by side.

Spain and Italy

As early as the 10th century, scholars in Spain had begun to gather translated texts, and in the latter half of that century began transmitting them to the rest of Europe. After the Reconquista of the 12th century, however, Spain opened even further for Christian scholars, who were now able to work in "friendly" religious territory. As these Europeans encountered Islamic philosophy, their previously-held fears turned to admiration, and from Spain came a wealth of Arab knowledge of mathematics and astronomy. Foreigners came to Spain to translate from all over Europe, and Toledo became a center for such travelers, since so many of its citizens wrote daily in both Arabic and Latin-based languages.

Although there was a huge amount of work being accomplished in Spain, there was no central school for translating and no real organized effort, as there had been at times among the Arabs. Translators came from many different backgrounds and translated for many different reasons. For example, non-Christian Jewish scholars participated by translating Arabic works which had already been translated into Hebrew, into Latin and Vulgate languages. Some scholars, however, have suggested that Archbishop Raimundo of Toledo seems to have started an organized movement of support for translations, and many scholars who seem to be associated with him in history may have translated two-by-two, working together.

Whether Raimundo actually started a truly central, organized effort at translation in Spain remains unknown. What is known is that most translations coming out of Spain dealt with either medicine or astronomy. Hugo of Santalla, for example, translated a large selection of Arabic works all dealing with astronomy, as well as tracing the history of astronomic thought through history, underscoring the work of the Greeks, Persians, Hellenists, an Arabians in one large preface to his volume.

By the 13th century, translation had declined in Spain was on the rise in Italy and Sicily, and from there to all of Europe. Adelard of Bath, an Englishman, traveled to Sicily and the Arab world, translating works on astronomy and mathematics, including the first complete translation of Euclid's Elements. Powerful Norman kings gathered men of high knowledge from Italy and other areas into their courts a signs of prestige. Even the Byzantines experienced an Aristotelian revival in the mid 12th century and gathered men from Italy as well.

William of Moerbeke

William of Moerbeke was one of the most prolific and influential translators of Greek philosophical texts in the middle half of the thirteenth century. Very little is known of William's life. He was born probably in 1215 in the village of Moerbeke, now in Belgium, and probably entered the Dominican convent in Leuven as a young man. Most of his surviving work was done during 1259-72. Though William's contribution to the 'recovery' of Aristotle in the thirteenth century was not as significant as is sometimes claimed, his work undoubtedly helped in forming a clearer picture of Greek philosophy, and particularly of Aristotle, than was given by the Arabic versions they had previously relied on, and which had distorted or obscured the relation between Platonic and Aristotelian systems of philosophy.

William's translation of Proclus was also important, demonstrating that the influential book Liber de Causis, was not a genuine work of Aristotle, but derived from Proclus' Elementatio Theologica. According to a tradition originating in the later Middle Ages, William knew Thomas Aquinas and was commissioned by him to make some of the translations. But there is no contemporary record of the friendship or the commissions. If they did meet, it is most likely during the three or four years Aquinas was working at Orvieto, i.e. not before the election of Pope Urban IV in August 1261, who invited Aquinas to serve at the Papal court, and not after 1265, when Aquinas left for Rome. His translation of De motu animalium is cited by Thomas in Summa Contra Gentiles probably completed in 1264.

The Religion of Islam

The first thing that one should know and clearly understand about Islam is what the word "Islam" itself means. The religion of Islam is not named after a person as in the case of Christianity which was named after Jesus Christ, Buddhism after Gotama Buddha, and Confucianism after Confucius and Marxism after Karl Marx. Nor was it named after a tribe like Judaism after the tribe of Judah and Hinduism after the Hindus. Islam is the true religion of "Allah" and as such, its name represents the central principle of Allah's "God's" religion; the total submission to the will of Allah "God".

The Arabic word "Islam" means the submission or surrender of one's will to the only true god worthy of worship "Allah" and anyone who does so is termed a "Muslim", The word also implies "peace" which is the natural consequence of total submission to the will of Allah. Hence, it was not a new religion brought by Prophet Muhammad (PBUH) I in Arabia in the seventh century, but only the true religion of Allah re-expressed in its final form. Islam is the religion which was given to Adam, the first man and the first prophet of Allah, and it was the religion of all the prophets sent by Allah to mankind. The name of God's religion lslam was not decided upon by later generations of man. It was chosen by Allah Himself and clearly mentioned in His final revelation to man. In the final book of divine revelation, the Qur'aan, Allah states the following:

"This day have I perfected your religion for you, completed My favour upon you, and have chosen for you Islam as your religion". (Soorah Al-Maa'idah 5:3)

"If anyone desires a religion other than Islam (submission to Allah (God) never will It be accepted of Him" (Soorah Aal'imraan 3:85)

"Abraham was not a Jew nor Christian; but an upright Muslim." (Soorah Aal'imraan 3:67)

Nowhere in the Bible will you find Allah saying to Prophet Moses' people or their descendants that their religion is Judaism, nor to the followers of Christ that their religion is Christianity. In fact, Christ was not even his name, nor was it Jesus! The name "Christ" comes from the Greek word Christos which means the annointed. That is, Christ is a Greek translation of the Hebrew title "Messiah". The name "Jesus" on the other hand, is a latinized version of the Hebrew name Esau. For simplicity's sake, I will however continue to refer to Prophet Esau (PBUH) as Jesus.

As for his religion, it was what he called his followers to. Like the prophets before him, he called the people to surrender their will to the will of Allah; (which is Islam) and he warned them to stay away from the false gods of human imagination. According to the New Testament, he taught his followers to pray as follows: "Yours will be done on earth as it is in Heaven".

The Message of Islam

Since the total submission of one's will to Allah represents the essence of worship, the basic message of Allah's divine religion, Islam is the worship of Allah alone and the avoidance of worship directed to any person, place or thing other than Allah.Since everything other than Allah, the Creator of all things, is Allah's creation; it may be said that Islam, in essence calls man away from the worship of creation and invites him to worship only its Creator. He is the only one deserving man's worship as it is only by His will that prayers are answered. If man prays to a tree and his prayers are answered, it was not the tree which answered his prayers but Allah who allowed the circumstances prayed for to take place. One might say, "That is obvious," however, to tree-worshippers it might not be. Similarly, prayers to Jesus, Buddha, or Krishna, to Saint Christopher, or Saint Jude or even to Muhammad, are not answered by them but are answered by Allah. Jesus did nottell his followers to worship him but to worship Allah. As the Qur'aan states:

"And behold Allah will say: "O Jesus the son of Mary Did you say to men, Worship me and my mother as gods besides Allah He will say-"Glory to you I could never say what I had no right (to say')" (Soorah Al-Maa'idah- 5:116)

Nor did he worship himself when he worshipped but rather he worshipped Allah. This basic principle is enshrined in the opening chapter of the Qur'aan, known asSoorah Al-Faatihah, verse 4:

"You alone do we worship and from you alone do we seek help".

Elsewhere, in the final book of revelation, the Qur'aan, Allah also said:

"And your Lord says:"Call on Me and I will answer your (prayer)."(Soorsh Mu'min 40:60)

it is worth noting that the basic message of Islam is that Allah and His creation are distinctly different entities. Neither is Allah His creation or a part of it, nor is His creation Him or a part of Him. This might seem obvious, but, man's worship of creation instead of the Creator is to a large degree based on ignorance of this concept. It is the belief that the essence of Allah is everywhere in His creation or that His divine being is or was present in some aspects of His creation, which has provided justification for the worship of creation though such worship maybecalled the worship of Allah through his creation. How ever, the message of Islam as brought by the prophets of Allah is to worship only Allah and to avoid the worship of his creation either directly or indirectly. In the Our'aan Allah clearlystates:

"For We assuredly sent amongst every people a prophet,(with the command) worship meand avoid false gods " (Soorsh Al-Nahl 16:36)

When the idol worshipper is questioned as to why he or she bows down to idols created by men, the invariable reply is that they are not actually worshipping the stone image, but Allah who is present within it. They claim that the stone idol is only a focal point for Allah's essence and is not in itself Allah! One who has accepted the concept of the presence of God's being within His creation in any way will be obliged to accept this argument of idolatry. Whereas, one who understands the basic message of Islam and its implications would never concede to idolatry no matter how it is rationalized.

Those who have claimed divinity for themselves down through the ages have often based their claims on the mistaken belief that Allah is present in man. They merely had to assert that although Allah according to their false beliefs, is in all of us, He is more present in them than in the rest of us. Hence, they claim, we should submit our will to them and worship them as they are either God in person or God concentrated within the person. Similarly, those who have asserted the godhood of others after their passing have found fertile ground among those who accept the false belief of God's presence in man.

One who has grasped the basic message of Islam and its implications could never agree to worship another human being under any circumstances. God's religion in essence is a clear call to the worship of the Creator and the rejection of creation-worship in any form. This is the meaning of the motto of Islam:

"Laa Elaaha Illallaah" (There is no god but Allah)

Its repetition automatically brings one within the fold of Islam and sincere belief in it guarantees one Paradise.

Thus, the final Prophet of Islam is reported to have said, "Any one who says: There is no god but Allah and dies holding that (belief) will enter paradise".(Reported by Abu Dharr and collected by Al-Bukhaaree and Muslim).

It consists in the submission to Allah as one God, yielding to Him by obeying His commandments, and the denial of polytheism and polytheists.

The Message of False Religion

There are so many sects, cults, religions, philosophies, and movements in the world, all of which claim to be the right way or the only true path to Allah. How can one determine which one is correct or if, in fact, all are correct? The method by which the answer can be found is to clear away the superficial differences in the teachings of the various claimants to the ultimate truth, and identify the central object of worship to which they call, directly or indirectly. False religions all have in common one basic concept with regards to Allah. They either claim that all men are gods or that specific men were Allah or that nature is Allah or that Allah is a figment of man's imagination.

Thus, it may be stated that the basic message of false religion is that Allah may be worshipped in the form of His creation. False religion invites man to the worship of creation by calling the creation or some aspect of it God. For example, Prophet Jesus invited his followers to worship Allah but those who claim to be his followers today call people to worship Jesus, claiming that he was Allah! Buddha was a reformer who introduced a number of humanistic principles to the religion of India. He did not claim to be God nor did he suggest to his followers that he be an object of worship. Yet, today most Buddhists who are to be found outside of India have taken him to be God and prostrate to idols made in their perception of his likeness.

By using the principle of identifying the object of worship, false religion becomes very obvious and the contrived nature of their origin clears. As God said in the Qur'aan:

That which you worship besides Him are only names you and your forefathers have invented for which Allah has sent down no authority: The command belongs only to Allah:

He has commanded that you only worship Him; that is the right religion, but most men do not understand ". (Soorah Yoosuf 12:40)

It may be argued that all religions teach good things so why should it matter which one we follow. The reply is that all false religions teach the greatest evil, the worship of creation. Creation-worship is the greatest sin that man can commit because it contradicts the very purpose of his creation. Man was created to worship Allah alone as Allah has explicitly stated in the Our'aan:

"I have only created Jlnns and men, that they may worship me"(Soorah Zaareeyaat 51:56)

Consequently, the worship of creation, which is the essence of idolatry, is the only unforgivable sin. One who dies in this state of idolatry has sealed his fate in the next life. This is not an opinion, but a revealed fact stated by Allah in his final revelation to man:

"Verily Allah will not forgive the joining of partners with Him, but He may forgive (sins) less than that for whom so ever He wishes"(Soorah An- Nisaa 4:48 and 116)

The Universality of Islam

Since the consequences of false religion are so grave, the true religion of Allah must be universally understandable and attainable, not confined to any people, place or time. There can not be conditions like baptism, belief in a man, as a saviour etc., for a believer to enter paradise. Within the central principle of Islam and in its definition, (the surrender of one's will to God) lies the roots of lslam's universality. Whenever man comes to the realization that Allah is one and distinct from His creation, and submits himself to Allah, he becomes a Muslim in body and spirit and is eligible for paradise. Thus, anyone at anytime in the most remote region of the world can become a Muslim, a follower of God's religion, Islam, by merely rejecting the worship of creation and by turning to Allah (God) alone-It should be noted however, that the recognition of and submission to Allah requires that one chooses between right and wrong and such a choice implies accountability.

Man will be held responsible for his choices, and, as such, he should try his utmost to do good and avoid evil. The ultimate good being the worship of Allah alone and the ultimate evil being the worship of His creation along with or instead of Allah. This fact is expressed in the final revelation as follows:

"Verily those who believe, those who follow the Jewish (Scriptures), the Christians and the Sabians any who believe In Allah and the last day, and work righteousness *hall have their reward with their Lord;They will not be overcome by fear nor grief (Soorah Al-Baqarah 2:62).

If only they had stood by the law, the Gospel, and all the revelation that was sent to them from their Lord, they would have enjoyed happiness from every side. There Is from among them a party on the right course; but many of them follow a course that Is evil.". (Soorah Al-.Maa'idah 5:66)

Recognition of Allah

The question which arises here is, "How can all people be expected to believe in Allah given their varying-backgrounds, societies and cultures? For people to be responsible for worshipping Allah they all have to have access to knowledge of Allah. The final revelation teaches that all mankind have the recognition of Allah imprinted on their souls, a part of their very nature with which they are created. In Soorah Al-A'raaf, Verses 172-173; Allah explained that when He created Adam, He caused all of Adam's descendants to come into existence and took a pledge from them saying, Am I not your Lord? To which they all replied, " Yes, we testify to It:'

Allah then explained why He had all of mankind bear witness that He is their creator and only true God worthy of worship. He said, "That was In case you (mankind) should say on the day of Resurrection, "Verily we were unaware of all this." That is to say, we had no idea that You Allah, were our God. No one told us that we were only supposed to worship You alone. Allah went on to explain that it was also In case you should say, "Certainly It was our ancestors who made partners (With Allah) and we are only their descendants; will You then destroy us for what those liars did?" Thus, every child is born with a natural belief in Allah and an inborn inclination to worship Him alone called in Arabic the "Fitrah".

If the child were left alone, he would worship Allah in his own way, but all children are affected by those things around them, seen or unseen.

The Prophet (PBUH) reported that Allah said, "I created my servants in the right religion but devils made them go astray". The Prophet (PBUH) also said, "Each child is born in a state of "Fitrah", then his parents make him a Jew, Christian or a Zoroastrian, the way an animal gives birth to a normal offspring. Have you noticed any that were born mutilated?"

So, just as the child submits to the physical laws which Allah has put in nature, his soul also submits naturally to the fact that Allah is his Lord and Creator. But, his parents try to make him follow their own way and the child is not strong enough in the early stages of his life to resist or oppose the will of his parents. The religion which the child follows at this stage is one of custom and upbringing and Allah does not hold him to account or punish him for this religion. Throughout people's lives from childhood until the time they die, signs are shown to them in all regions of the earth and in their own souls, until it becomes clear that there is only one true God (Allah). If the people are honest with themselves, reject their false gods and seek Allah, the way will be made easy for them but if they continually reject Allah's signs and continue to worship creation, the more difficult it will be for them to escape.

For example, in the South Eastern region of the Amazon jungle in Brazil, South America, a primitive tribe erected a new hut to house their main idol Skwatch, representing the supreme God of all creation. The homage to the God, and while he was in prostration to what he had been taught was his Creator and Sustainer, a mangy old flea-ridden dog walked into the hut, The young man looked up in time to see the dog lift its hind leg and pass urine on the idol. Outraged, the youth chased the dog out of the temple, but when his rage died down he realized that the idol could not be the Lordof the universe. Allah must be elsewhere. he now had a choice to act on his knowledge and seek Allah, or to dishonestly go along with the false beliefs of his tribe. As strange as it may seem, that was a sign from Allah for that young man. It contained within it divine guidance that what he was worshipping was false.

Prophets were sent, as was earlier mentioned, to every nation and tribe to support man's natural belief in Allah and man's inborn inclination to worship Him as well as to reinforce the divine truth in the daily signs revealed by Allah. Although, in most cases, much of the prophets' teachings became distorted, portions remained which point out right and wrong and for example, the ten commandments of the Torah, their confirmation in the Gospels and the existence of laws against murder, stealing and adultery in most societies. Consequently, every soul will be held to account for its belief in Allah and its acceptance of the religion of Islam; the total submission to the will of Allah. We pray to Allah, the exalted, to keep us on the right path to which He has guided us, and to bestow on us a blessing from Him, He is indeed the Most Merciful. Praise and gratitude be to Allah, the Lord of the worlds, and peace and blessings be on prophet Muhammed, his Family, his companions, and those who rightly follow them.

Bibliography

Abbott, Nabia. *Aishah: The Beloved of Mohammad.* London: Al-Saqi, 1998.

Andrae, Tor. *Mohammed: The Man and His Faith.* London: George Allen & Unwin, 1936.

Armstrong, Karen. *Islam: A Short History.* New York: Modern Library, revised ed., 2002.

Asad, Muhammad. *The Message of the Qur'an.* Gibraltar: Dar al-Andalus, 1980.

Asani, Ali, et al. *Celebrating Muhammad: Images of the Prophet in Popular Muslim Poetry.* Columbia, Ashgate/ Variorum, 2000.

Azam Malik, trans.). Houston, TX: The Institute of Islamic Knowledge, 1997.

Baljon, Jon M.S. *Modern Muslim Koran Interpretation (1880-1960).* Leiden: E.J. Brill, 1961.

Barlas, Asma. *"Believing Women" in Islam: Unreading Patriarchal Interpretations of the Qur'an.*

Bell, Richard. *Introduction to the Qur'an.* Edinburgh: Edinburgh University Press, 1963.

Bell, Richard. *The Qur'an Translated,* 2 Vols. Edinburgh: T. & T. Clark, 1960.

Bowker, John. *What Muslims Believe.* Oxford, UK: Onewworld, 1999.

Burton, John. *The Collection of the Quran.* Cambridge, UK: Cambridge University Press, 1977.

Cook, Michael. *Muhammad.* New York: Oxford University Press, 1983.

Cragg, Kenneth. *The Mind of the Quran: Chapters in Reflection.* London: George Allen & Unwin, CT: Yale University Press, 2002.

Dawood, N.J. *The Koran.* Harmondsworth: Penguin, 1956.

Denny, Frederick Mathewson. *An Introduction to Islam.* New York: Macmillan, 1994.

Elias, Jamal J. *Islam.* Upper Saddle River, NJ: Prentice Hall, 1999.

Esack, Farid. *Qur'an, Liberation and Pluralism.* Oxford, England: Oneworld, 1997.

Esack, Farid. *The Qur'an: A Short Introduction.* Oxford, England: Oneworld, 2002.

Gilsenan, Michael. *Recognising Islam: an anthropologist's introduction.* London: Croom Helm, 1982.

Hawting, G.R. et al., eds. *Approaches to the Quran.* London: Routledge, 1993.

Hodgson, Marshall G.S. *The Venture of Islam,* 3 Vols. Chicago, IL: University of Chicago International, 1983.

Izutsu, Toshihiko. *God and Man in the Koran.* Salem, NH: Ayer Co. Publ., 1980.

Jansen, J.J.G. *The Interpretation of the Koran in Modern Egypt.* Leiden: E.J. Brill, 1974.

Kahn, Muhammad Zafrulla. *Muhammad, Seal of the Prophets.* New York: Viking Press, 1981.

Khalifa, Rashad. *Quran, Hadith, and Islam.* Fremont, CA: Universal Unity, 2000.

Lings, Martin. *Muhammad: his life based on the earliest sources.* New York: Inner Traditions London: Oxford University Press, 1955.

McAuliffe, Jane Dammen, ed. *The Encyclopedia of the Qur'an*, Vol. 1. Leiden: E.J. Brill, 2001.

Mir, Mustansir. *Dictionary of Qur'anic Terms and Concepts*. New York: Garland, 1987.

Motzki, Harald, ed. *The Biography of Muhammad: The Issue of the Sources*. Leiden: E.J. Brill, 2000.,

Nasr, Seyyed Hossein. *Ideals and Realities of Islam*. London: Allen & Unwin, 1966.

Nasr, Seyyed Hossein. *Islamic Spirituality I: Foundations*. New York: Crossroad, 1987.

Nasr, Seyyed Hossein. *Islamic Spirituality II: Manifestations*. New York: Crossroad, 1991.

Nasr, Seyyed Hossein. *Muhammad: Man of God*. Chicago, IL: Kazi Publ., 1995.

Nasr, Seyyed Hossein. *The Heart of Islam: Enduring Values for Humanity*. San Francisco, CA: New York Press, 1984.

Newby, Gordon D. *A Concise Encyclopedia of Islam*. Oxford, UK: Oneworld, 2002.

Peters, F.E. *A Reader on Classical Islam*. Princeton, NJ: Princeton University Press, 1994.

Peters, Francis E. *Muhammad and the Origins of Islam*. Albany, NY: State University of New Press, 1961.

Rahman, Fazlur. *Islam*. Chicago, IL: University of Chicago Press, 2nd ed., 1979.

Rahman, Fazlur. *Major Themes of the Qur'an*. Minneapolis, MN: Bibliotheca Islamica, 1980.

Rippin, Andrew, ed. *The Qur'an: Style and Contents*. Aldershot, UK: Ashgate, 2001.

Rippin, Andrew. *Muslims: Their Religious Beliefs and Practices*. London: Routledge, 2nd ed., 2001.

Rippin, Andrew. *The Qur'an and Its Interpretive Tradition*. Aldershot, UK: Ashgate, 2002.

Robinson, Francis. *Atlas of the Islamic World since 1500.* New York: Facts on File, 1982.

Rubin, Uri, ed. *The Life of Muhammad.* Aldershot: Ashgate, 1998.

Ruthven, Malise. *Islam in the World.* New York: Oxford University Press, 2nd ed., 2000.

Schuon, Frithjof. *Islam and the Perennial Philosophy.* London: World of Islam Festival Publ. Co., SCM Press, 1996.

Sells, Michael. *Approaching the Qur'an: The Early Revelations.* Ashland, OR: White Cloud Press, Society, 1996.

Stowasser, Barbara Freyer. *Women in the Qur'an: Traditions and Interpretations.* New York: T. & T. Clark, 1939.

Tayob, Abdulkader. *Islam: A Short Introduction.* Oxford, England: Oneworld, 1999.

The Koran Interpreted. Arthur J. Arberry, trans. New York: Macmillan, 1955.

The Koran. J.M. Rodwell, trans. London: J.M. Dent & Sons, 1909 (reprint ed., 1974).

Wadud-Muhsin, Amina. *Qur'an and Woman: Reading the Sacred Text from a Woman's Perspective.*

Waines, David. *An Introduction to Islam.* Cambridge, UK: Cambridge University Press, 1995.

Watt, William Montgomery. *Muhammad at Mecca.* Oxford, UK: Clarendon Press, 1953.

Watt, William Montgomery. *Muhammad at Medina.* Oxford, UK: Clarendon Press, 1956.

Watt, William Montgomery. *What is Islam?* London: Longman, 1970.

Wild, S., ed. *The Qur'an as Text: Islamic Philosophy, Theology, and Science.* Leiden: E.J. Brill, 1997.

Williams, John Alden, ed. *The Word of Islam.* Austin, TX: University of Texas Press, 1994.

Index

H

I

L

M

N

O

P